Nancy Jane Barnswallowper said, "Damn it, Sheriff, I only shot him a little bit. I know how to handle a gun. You know that. I'd never really hurt anybody."

Fowler gave an involuntary yelp of pain. Garrett's eyebrows went up. "Okay, Nancy, but you did. Hear that chap? You did hurt somebody. This won't go easy for you. Whatever possessed you to shoot him?"

"Well, I was ..." Nancy began, but Lew burst in.

"When we pulled up, that harridan Barnswallowper was hollering her ass off at the poor guy. He was coming toward her in a gesture of surrender, like this ..." Old Lew spread his arms wide and had to stagger to get his balance. "Like this, and she hollered that if he took one more step, she'd shoot him. He kind of waved his hands, you know, like to say 'hold on a minute' and he lifted his foot and she shot him. Right in the other foot. He went down like a lead balloon."

"That's when we called 911," Fourier interjected helpfully.

"It was self defense," Nancy muttered.

"Self defense!" Garrett exclaimed, as a shout came up from the slope below. The EMTs had apparently begun to cut the boot off the injured foot, and Fowler was objecting. "Don't cut that! Hey, wait! Don't cut ... Those boots cost a fortune!"

They cut the boot.

This novel is a work of fiction. None of the characters herein are intended to be portrayals of any real person, living or dead, nor are real events and places portrayed. All are products of the author's imagination and are used simply to tell a good story.

Also By This Author

All the Bad Stuff Comes in Threes

After the End: The Sumbally Fallacy

Baby Skulls and Fowl Odors

Karen Weinant Gallob

Earth Star Publications

Map illustration by Roxanne Carpenter
Cover design by Ann Ulrich Miller

Baby Skulls and
Fowl Odors

Karen Weinant Gallob

Earth Star Publications
www.earthstarpublications.com

FIRST EDITION

November 2014

Copyright © 2014 by Karen Weinant Gallob
All Rights Reserved

Library of Congress Control Number: 2014954060

This book may not be reproduced in whole, or in part, by digital or mechanical, or by any other means, without the express written consent of the author. For information, address Earth Star Publications (www.earthstarpublications.com), e-mail: starbeacon@gmail.com.

ISBN 978-0-944851-38-8

Printed in the United States of America

This book is for Tanya

Courage, Chaos, and the Heart of a Mama Cougar

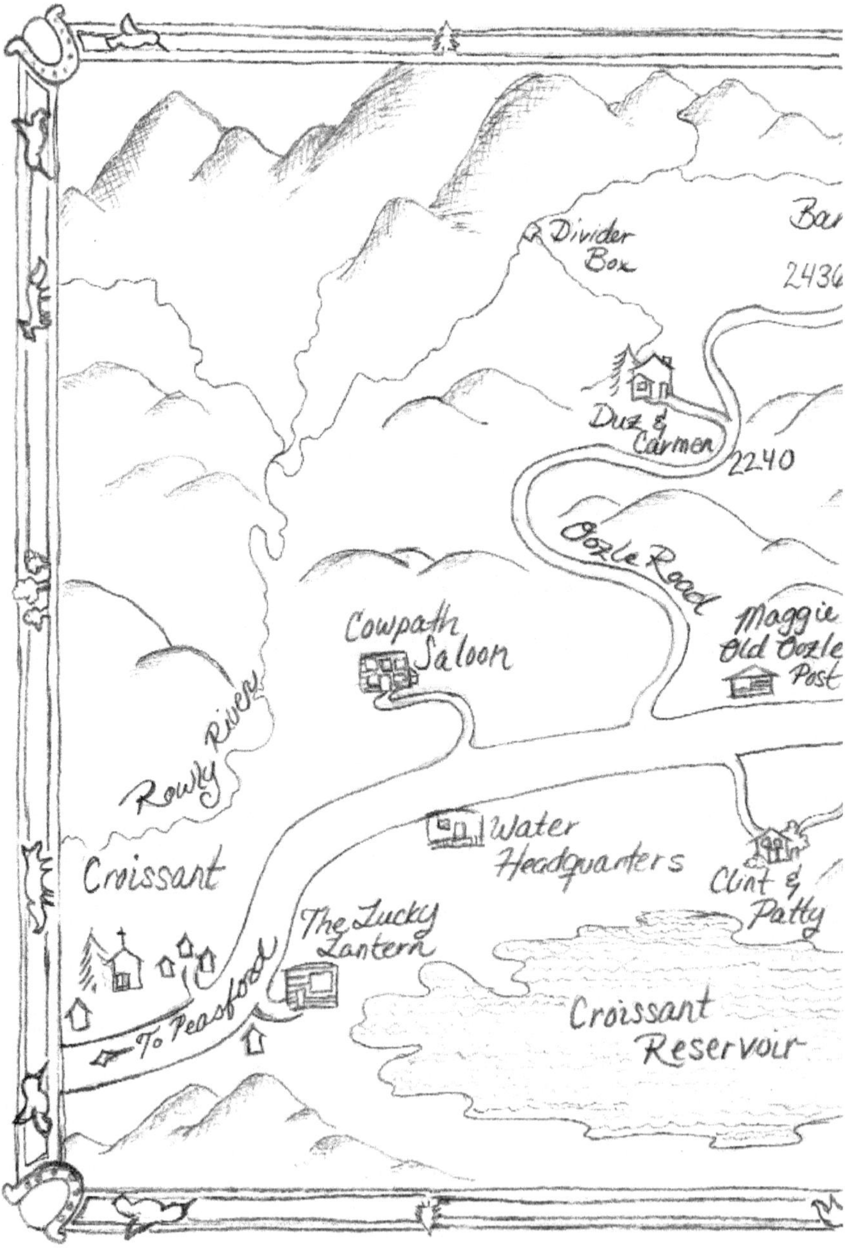

Divider Box
2240
Duz & Carmen
Oozle Road
Cowpath Saloon
Rowly River
Water Headquarters
Clint & Patty
Croissant
The Lucky Lantern
To Peasford
Croissant Reservoir

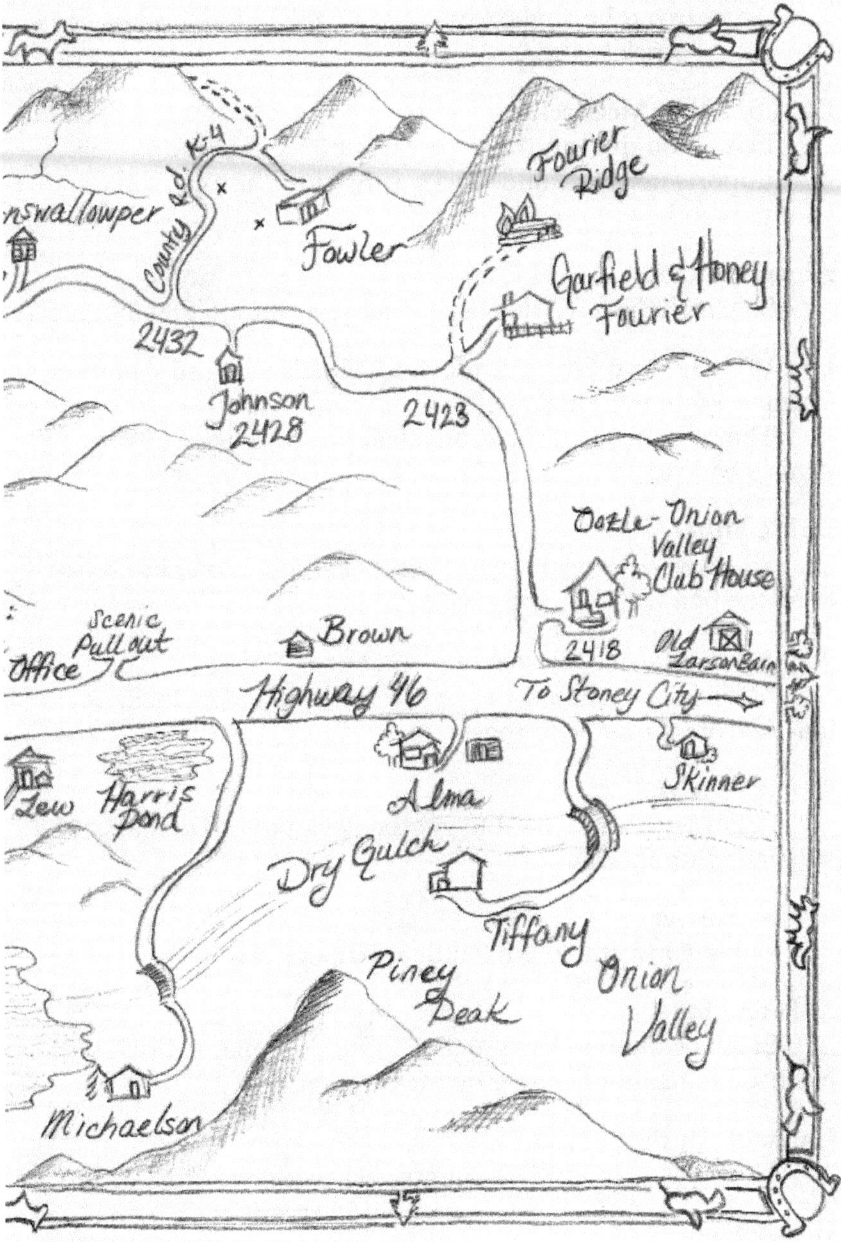
nswallowper
County Rd. K-4
Fowler
Fourier Ridge
Garfield & Honey Fourier
2432
Johnson 2428
2423
Oozle-Onion Valley Club House
Scenic Pull out
Office
Brown
2418
Old Larson Barn
Highway 46
To Stoney City
Lew
Harris Pond
Alma
Skinner
Dry Gulch
Tiffany
Piney Peak
Onion Valley
Michaelson

Cast of Characters

Sheriff Pat Garrett
An ugly old bird who knows you have to break some eggs to make an omelet.

Deputy Leigh McCracken
Even though everything isn't what it's cracked up to be, she supports her boss, and works as hard for him as a hen haulin' wood.

Alma Weinant
She might have been gone, but she just wouldn't fly the coop.

Duz Weinant and Gritty Anderson, Alma's son and daughter; Carmen Weinant, Duz's wife
They'd rather put socks on a banty rooster than get on Alma's bad side.

Hallie Flute
She's dead. She knew that the cock might crow, but it had to be the hen who laid the egg.

Nancy Jane Barnswalloper
Hallie's niece, Tiffany's cousin. Looks like her chickens may be coming home to roost.

Chuck Fowler
A newcomer. He tried to get the flock out of Dodge, but he still ended up in a stew.

Sienna Fowler
Bullied and cranky, this little rotten egg has secrets.

Xi Feng Ling
Sienna's mother, she's a goner. Oh, well, many a rich bird has tried to feather her nest by fowl means.

Garfield Fourier
Does this man love his country? Does a chicken have lips?

Honey Fourier
Garfield's wife, she worries that only birds of a feather can flock together.

Jenny Threewinds
Here is a woman who knows what she wants, but she will have to walk on eggshells to get him.

Brady Xyster
This guy, who can be found at Jenny's, may have put too many eggs in one basket.

Tiffany Gallenas
Nancy Jane's cousin, Hallie's niece. No wonder she wants to wring their necks; she can never tell just where those boys will play chicken next.

Luke and Larry Gallenas
Tiffany's boys. They get caught with egg on their faces.

Xi Gong Ji and Da Xi Gong Ji
They once ruled the roost, but now one is gone, and the fragrance lingers on.

Lew and Lucky Harris
Old-timer Lew is no dumb cluck, and Lucky? Well, I guess that Lucky is dead.

Mac Biedermann
Former owner of Chuck Fowler's place. One day, cock of the walk. Next day, a feather duster.

Lena Larson
Old friend of Hallie and Alma. She's dead, but she surely knew how to hatch an idea.

The Oozle-Onion Valley Community Club, Jilly Brown as president
Many good neighbors. Signing women and cackling hens will drive the devil from his den.

Peaseford school cliques
Including Pewter and Patsy and Cesar and Brandon and of course, Luke, Larry, and that beauteous chick, Ginger.

1

PAT GARRETT WAS FEELING lower than a snake's belly. It wasn't even a year since they'd solved the Reider Biedermann case, but now, when Gritty called, she'd told him Alma was gone. What were her words? "I'm sure you know, Sheriff, that my mother is gone. We'll have to try to understand what happened here without her input."

Gone! Well, she had been up in her nineties, so it was only natural, the way of things. Still, it made him sad. Gone? It seemed like only yesterday that Alma had found Biedermann's body in her old chicken shed, and even with her short term memory loss, she'd been able to help him untangle who'd killed him. He'd miss her.

He wasn't just sad about Alma, though. When they passed the Cowpath Saloon, he thought it looked wrong, not just closed, but empty, somehow. It worried him. Jenny Threewinds worked there, waiting table, playing guitar. He hadn't seen Jenny since the Biedermann case was resolved. He just couldn't get his courage up, even though Jenny had been friendly enough. She probably was just being nice. Unlike his good-looking brother, Lyle, Garrett had a disastrous history with women. He just couldn't imagine what they might see in him, an old guy that, in his own estimation, was uglier than a sack full of assholes. Sure, he'd gone to school with Jenny. She was about his age. But that was different. Unlike him, Jenny was beautiful. And she'd been married once. Some Lakota guy, if he remembered right. And she was a hippie. Or had been.

Passing the desolate Cowpath, Garrett turned to his deputy, Leigh McCracken. "What do you suppose is going on at the Cowpath?"

McCracken didn't answer. She was holding her phone, her face intense, her fingers flying over the keys. Texting! She was really, really bad about that. Garrett didn't text, and he didn't want to, and it irritated him beyond words to be in a room with someone who really wasn't there because they were on with some unknown party, speaking a foreign tongue that he couldn't seem to comprehend. He felt that McCracken had changed. Sure, the bright red hair that boiled down past her ears had pretty much grown back since she'd shaved her head for her disguise as a home boy to help crack the Biedermann case. His other deputy, Red, had clearly been wowed by that transformation. Back then, McCracken had been filled with admiration for every move Garrett made. Now she seemed to just ignore him—and text. Probably texting Red. Garrett knew that they dated now, if that's what you still called it, but he couldn't really add her to his long list of women-who-have-rejected-me. She was just a kid, young enough to be his daughter. Still, watching her text, he felt diminished.

He grunted and repeated, "What do you suppose is going on at the Cowpath?" She looked up from her phone, her own face annoyed.

"I *said*, 'Just a minute. I'm asking Tiffany.'"

Garrett knew she hadn't said that. His hearing wasn't that bad yet. He refrained from challenging her, though, and instead asked, "Who's Tiffany?"

"She's Hallie's ..." McCracken began, but just then her phone gave a snort. Garrett knew that one. It was an incoming text alert. He decided it sounded like a sick pig.

McCracken's eyes shot back and forth over the phone screen, absorbing the incoming message. "Tiffany says that there was a fire there. Not too bad, just a lot of smoke damage, mostly. They closed 'er down for repairs."

Garrett felt a shiver of fear. He swallowed and said, "Could you text her... Could you ask her if anyone was hurt? Was Jenny there?"

McCracken grinned, still pleased to be of service to her boss. Just like in the old days. She poked at the keys. Garrett slowed; they were getting awfully close to Alma's. The texted reply seemed to be taking infinite time, and Garrett slowed more, pretending to look at a herd of deer near the road. Finally,

Baby Skulls and Fowl Odors

the phone snorted.

"Jenny was there, but no one was hurt." McCracken continued to read. "Tiffany says that Jenny was there, but that she should have been out with that new boyfriend she has that has the funny name." McCracken leaned down to the phone and said, "I can't pronounce it. I'll spell it: X-Y-S-T-E-R. If the text came through right. Maybe 'Zyster'? Tiffany says he's a Black guy. lol."

Garrett slumped in his seat, his eyes back on the road, his foot now hard on the accelerator. McCracken dropped the phone in her pocket. "So anyhow," she said, mildly interested in the new speed at which they were traveling, "So anyhow, you asked who Tiffany is. She's Hallie's niece. Remember Hallie Flute, Alma's good friend? Tiffany and her boys have been living in Hallie's house since Hallie died." McCracken sighed, looking at the passing fields. "Poor old thing. I liked Hallie."

Now Garrett slowed the car again and stared at his deputy. Hallie and Alma, both gone? He felt as if he were going to cry.

2

"YOU SEE, SHERIFF, we just thought we should straighten up Mom's things," Gritty said as she wheeled across the room in her chair, leading him and McCracken through the living room, past the now silent TV, and into the back bedroom. Passing Alma's favorite chair, Garrett lowered his head, an unconscious gesture of respect. He wished he hadn't missed the funeral notice; he would have gone.

Carmen, Alma's daughter-in-law, was perched on the bed in the crowded room. She was surrounded by at least a dozen large dolls. She smiled and nodded. Garrett and McCracken positioned themselves in the small space at the foot of the bed. They were both curious, as Gritty had refused to tell them on the phone about why she wanted them to come. She just said it would be easier to show them.

"So, here are the dolls Mom used to make. When she was younger her and Aunt Lena made a lot of them. As you can see." Gritty had stopped her chair near the door to make room for the visitors.

Carmen added, "She always loved dolls, but these are kind of special. They're called the Dells. She made one for every kid and grandkid, and each was given the name of the kid that got it, plus Dell. So it would be like, Nancy Dell, Charlie Dell, Erin & Sara Dell, and so-on."

McCracken frowned and mumbled under her breath, "You brought the sheriff all the way up here for a stolen doll or something?" Garrett wanted to poke her, especially since just then her phone snorted. She resisted the text, and he resisted the poke. Instead, he said politely, "They are very interesting dolls." He was looking them over carefully, trying to get some hint as to why he was here.

Baby Skulls and Fowl Odors

The dolls were all large, as big as a two-year-old child. Most had skin of a pinkish, flesh-colored cloth, a pattern sewn together and stuffed with something to round out chubby little limbs and torsos. The two which were not pink were brown, and wore big Mexican sombreros and very bright serapes. The garb of the rest was also creatively designed; two were in sleeveless tees and shorts, and Garrett could see that the arms and legs had been stuffed, then sewn on, a button joint at elbow and hip. Hands and feet, Mickey-Mouse-like, had thumbs but no fingers or toes. The faces were painted on, not stitched, and they appeared to be a happy group: big-lashed eyes, smiling mouths, and cunning little drawn noses with tiny nostrils. Yarn in a variety of 'dos and colors adorned the heads. Alma had clearly had fun with faces and hair, as well as with their clothes: the pants and chaps and cowboy hats; velvet skirts and dresses ruffled from chest to hem; ribboned bonnets and button shoes; hot-chocolate-seeking cozy flannel pajamas. It was a carnival of color and texture, filling the room with movement and joy. McCracken interrupted Garrett's thought process. "So. Why 'Dell'?"

Carmen shrugged. "Oh, the first kid that got one was just learning to talk, and they kept trying to tell her it was a little Chrissie doll, because Alma had tried to make it look like Chrissie, the hair and all, but she insisted on calling it 'Cwissie Dell.' The name stuck." With a half smile, Carmen looked at Garrett. "But that's not why we called you."

Garrett nodded, patient, and McCracken returned to looking annoyed as Gritty turned her chair toward the panel of plywood behind them that served, in this old ranch house, as a closet door. Sliding it with some effort along its tracks, she opened it a couple of feet and removed another doll, which she slid into her lap.

"What we thought, Sheriff," she said, "Is that we would wash and tidy these dolls up, their clothes and all, and get them back closer to how they were when Alma first made them. We looked them over and decided to start with this one. Her face was badly stained, and we had ideas that it would be easier to remove the dirty face and replace it with a nice clean one. Carmen's an artist; we thought she could draw the face back."

Gritty had the doll crunched into her lap and Garrett couldn't see much about it. He started to step closer, but just then Gritty said, "Look, you've seen the dolls now. How many there are. Let's get the hell out of this stuffy, crowded room and go out back by the yard swing where the light is good. We can show you better there, I think."

They filed out of the room, Gritty holding the doll and rolling ahead. McCracken lagged behind, messing with her phone. Probably checking out the sick pig, Garrett allowed himself to think with a touch of self-satisfaction at his own lame wit, and when she caught up with him and said, "Chief ... " he shook his head at her sternly and mouthed, "Not now. Not now."

Gritty had rolled to a position across from the swing, and to be courteously at her level, everyone else sat on the swing facing her. She set the doll up in clear view. It appeared that Alma had intended to make an "Indian" doll. Her cloth skin was coppery-brown; her yarn hair fell in two long, black, tidy braids; she wore moccasins and a dress, both of which appeared to be from tanned deer hide. The creamy-white dress had fringing at the arms and hem, and both the dress and the moccasins were decorated with elaborate, softly-colored beadwork of turquoise, sunset red, and wheat-stalk yellow. The doll was beautiful, except for her face. Under her wide, brown-eyed gaze was a deep, scarlet smear of what could have been catsup, and her face had been unsewn from the rest of her head along the seam line, then loosely pinned back.

Garrett could hear a car pulling in at the front of the house, and the car door slamming, followed by creaking and bumping noises. He pried his eyes from the doll to glance a question at Carmen, but she said, "Oh, that's just Duz. I'm sure you can't have forgotten Duz, my husband? Alma's son? Tried to kill Biedermann with a shovel? He was supposed to pick me up after getting some irrigation pipe in town, but he's always late—gets tied up with friends and gabbin'." McCracken's phone snorted. Garrett's eyes went back to the doll, where he could see that Gritty was industriously unpinning the scrap of cloth that portrayed the skin of the little face. It fell forward, and both Garrett and McCracken sucked in their breath.

Exposed under the face cloth that the women had intended to repair was what appeared to be the skull of a child. Garrett could restrain himself no longer. He reached forward and took the doll from Gritty as she said, "Sheriff, we have no idea what

Baby Skulls and Fowl Odors

this means! How did that skull get there? Do all those dolls have skulls? We don't want to know, if they do! What were Alma and Lena up to, all those years ago? Or is it ... is it even a real skull? Did they have some source of ... of like a dressmaker's model ... models to give the heads shape? That's just beyond far-fetched! Is it real, Sheriff?"

"Is it real?" Carmen echoed. Garrett was examining the skull, to the extent that he could do so with it embedded as the doll's head. He pressed on the nasal bone, put his finger in the eye socket. To himself, he thought, "I can't say anything; I don't know that much anatomy, but good lord! This looks alarmingly real. Like the real skull of a child." He was speechless.

McCracken had drawn near. She hesitantly extended a finger and lovingly stroked the maxilla. "Oh, Chief," she breathed. "Oh, Chief. This is real, I think. Maybe we need to ... maybe we should get her to the lab."

For once relieved by his deputy's intercession, Garrett carefully pulled the doll to him and stood. "Yes. Yes, I think we must take her," he said. "This must be sorted out." Then, addressing Carmen, he said, "Could I have a little blanket to wrap her in? We will return it."

"Oh, certainly, Sheriff," and she bustled toward the house, Garrett, McCracken, and Gritty tagging behind. They passed through the kitchen, but as they entered the living room, Garrett received the shock of his life. He stopped so abruptly in the door that McCracken collided with his back.

Alma was there. Sitting in her chair!

She was sitting as she always had, her feet up on the foot rest, fluffy hair thin across the noble head, an expression of extreme interest on her animated face. For a weird moment Garrett had a twilight zone flash of her being, somehow, a wax figure of the real Alma, a bizarre Alma Dell, something put in place by this crazy family to ... to what? But she was ... she was obviously real. Alive.

Pushed forward by an exasperated McCracken, whose pathway and view he was blocking, he stepped into the room. Gritty, who had been behind them, had also grown impatient with the blocked door, and, more politely, had rolled through the other kitchen door to go past the living room couch. She was now parked near her mother and eyeing her with an irritated frown. Garrett managed to get out, "But I thought ... but I thought ..."

Gritty sighed. "I know. So did we. We thought that this time when she went to the rehab center she'd stay put long enough to let them do something with those old stiff bones of hers. Stretches and medication or something. She keeps going down there, but she's only gone about two seconds before she turns around and ends up home again. What happened this time, Duz?"

Suddenly Garrett realized that Alma's son, Duz, had been there all along, too, standing by the buffet cabinet. A little like a pup caught peeing on the floor, and addressing himself more to Carmen than to Gritty, he said, "I just stopped by to say 'hi' to her, but she insisted on coming home. You try telling her no."

Alma interjected, "Young Lady (this to Gritty), you know it's no rehab center. It's an old folks' home. Packed with a bunch of old people just waiting to die. They weren't doing me one bit of good. And they won't! What do they expect? I'm 99 years this year, 100 soon." This last she said with great pride.

Carmen shrugged toward her husband and headed for the bedroom to emerge with a small blanket. Trying to collect himself, Garrett managed, "Well, I'm glad to get to see you, Alma," and McCracken grinned a "Me, too."

Alma was pleased. "So what brings you here, Lyle?" Garrett's expression, so recently stunned, turned wry. Same old Alma! She always had confused him with his brother, Lyle—a neat trick, since Lyle was the good-looking one. He opened his mouth to reply, but Carmen stepped forward, holding out the blanket for the doll that Garrett had temporarily forgotten, unconsciously clutching it to the breaking point against his heavy chest.

"He wanted to borrow one of your dolls, Mom. He's heard a lot about how unusual they are and ..." She was folding the doll into the blanket when the Sheriff's radio gave a deafening squawk, drowning out her voice.

"Car 101. Sheriff. Call dispatch immediately." The sheriff grabbed the doll and shoved it toward McCracken, who made a football receiver's grab, plucking it out of thin air. They both headed for the door as Alma said, "Oh, he shouldn't take that one," and the radio crackled again, repeating the call: "Sheriff ...

call dispatch ..."

The rest of Alma's sentence was drowned by the commotion, but she finished anyway. "He shouldn't take that one! I didn't make that one."

3

DISPATCH HAD A SHOOTING at County Road K4, more or less just around the corner. Garrett found himself thinking, "What is this, a Croysant crime wave?" He hadn't been here in nearly a year, and now two calls up this way in one afternoon. Close. He could get to K4 by turning right from Alma's drive, then left on Oozle at the old one-room school, which was now the Oozle-Onion Valley Club House. K4 was a couple miles on up, to the right, about half way around the Oozle road loop. Alma's drive being steep, the cop car struggled with ice and slush from the early spring storm. Garrett muttered under his breath until the studded tires achieved purchase, then he drove with all due haste, as sheriffs are wont to drive.

Beside him, McCracken was cranky. "I kept trying to tell you."

"You kept trying to tell me what?"

"Tiffany texted me. Her and Bags are there, and they need the scene to be secured before they can get in to help the shot guy."

Garrett scowled, confused. "Tiffany? Bags? Scene ... What does your little buddy Tiffany have to do with a crime scene? And what do they want to bag, a body?"

With exaggerated patience, McCracken said, "She's not just 'my little buddy,' as you say. She's Hallie Flute's niece, new here, but a good community member, and a damn good EMT. I guess you don't remember him, but Bags is Jack Bagly. He's been around here for*ever*. Him and Ralph drive the ambulance sometimes as well as EMT. They can't go in until you secure the scene. Nancy still has the gun."

Now Garrett shot her a sharp look. "Oh, no! Not Nancy ... Nancy Jane ..."

Baby Skulls and Fowl Odors

"Yeah. I guess it's Nancy Jane Barnswallowper that shot." Garrett grunted. They were already passing 2423 Oozle. McCracken, her head swiveling as they shot past, said, "Well, there's where the Biedermanns used to live. Till he bit the dust in that shed." She chuckled. "Wonder if anybody lives there now?" Just then they passed an ambulance pulled off in a driveway to the left.

Shooting it a glance but continuing to drive, Garrett commented, "What the hell are they doing down here? Isn't the address 2432, up K4?"

McCracken sighed. "They're staging. You know they can't go up until you secure the scene. They decided to stage there because Frieda Johnson — you remember her? That heavy woman? — anyhow, she had a false lifeline alert, and that's her drive. They were there, anyhow." Just then her phone snorted, and she squinted at the screen. "They're gonna come on up. They figure you'll have it secured in a minute, since it's just Nancy Jane."

Garrett didn't answer. He was still scowling, and the car slewed on the melting ice as he turned right at the 2432 mailbox. Righting it, he tackled the snow-packed incline that was K4 road. "Say, wait a minute. If they stayed down there, how did they know it was Nancy Jane?"

McCracken shrugged. "Tiffany said they drove by once, to be sure they had the right place. When we didn't show up right away, they started wondering if it was at 2423. You know. The numbers are kinda alike."

Now it was Garrett's turn to sigh. "Good grief," he expelled under his breath. They rounded a bend and ahead of them a group of people could be seen along the road just below the entrance to where Mac and Alice Biedermann's tepee had been, before Mac disappeared and Maggie Merimeister took Alice under her wing. The faces of the figures by the road turned downhill toward the approaching sheriff's car and followed its progress as it made its way to a pullout opposite a dark green SUV that had been heading downhill. The ambulance pulled into a slot a little further up the road. To himself, Garrett thought grumpily, "Well, here they are, at the scene, and it still hasn't been secured. Small town protocols."

A cranky looking woman with weather-roughened skin and cropped hair was trying to separate herself from the group, but a snowy-haired old fellow had placed himself in front of her and was dancing up and down, a little jig. "You ain't goin' nowhere, Barnswallowper," he shouted. "You ain't goin' nowhere until you hand over that gun!" He glanced to his side and spoke to what appeared to be empty space. "Help me, Lucky! Help me hold 'er here." The ranch woman gripped the gun more fiercely and glared at him.

Ah, Lucky. Garrett began to feel at home. He remembered Lew Harris, all right, and his wife, Lucky. Lucky was dead, but Lew was in denial. He refused to give her up, so Lucky went with him wherever he went. The first time Garrett and McCracken had met Lucky, it had been quite a shock. They almost sat on her. Once they realized she was there, at least in spirit, they learned to open doors for her, save her a seat in restaurants, and so-on, and things went smoothly with Lew after that.

Garrett was just glad to see that Lew, at least, was alive and not much changed. He unfolded his lanky frame from the car, stopped by the front fender, and said soothingly, "It's okay, Lew. Tell Lucky to relax a minute. You settle down, too, Nancy. You people just give me a second here." Everyone stopped stone still, a game of freeze tag, as Garrett took in the tableau they presented, shoving his hat back and scratching the round bald head he shaved every morning to greet the day. The ugly, puckered scar that ran across his lower cheek, dropped down his neck, and disappeared under his collar began to redden with the brisk cold breeze as he squinted thoughtfully at the group.

Down the hill, a couple of dozen feet off the road, sat some guy that Garrett didn't know, or at least that he didn't think he knew. Maybe he should know him, but he didn't have that kind of memory for faces. The guy was bleeding. Garrett could see the blood in the snow. It seemed to be in the area of the guy's foot, and as near as Garrett could tell, his expression was one of surprised exasperation, maybe impatience. He was half propped against a dead juniper stump, and he kept looking on the ground to the left and right, shouting, "Please give me a hand here. If I had a stick to lean on, I think I could make it up there." Everyone

Baby Skulls and Fowl Odors

ignored him.

Halfway up the hill was Nancy Jane Barnswallowper, holding a .22 rifle, her mouth grim, her face defiant. Coveralls, manure and dirt around the cuffs, a John Deere farmer's cap. Of course.

Now, who else? His gaze roamed past the EMTs, already standing at the rear of the ambulance. Now he remembered the one EMT, Bagly, and the little woman next to him, long brown hair pulled back in a tail, must be the famous Tiffany, McCracken's texting buddy.

So, on to Lew with his dead Lucky, still confronting Nancy, arms crossed and determined, poised to burst into speech, railing and explaining, at the slightest sign of a go-ahead from Garrett. A few feet away stood Lew's son, Clint, sober and quiet eyed, arms also folded as he assessed the scene with as much restraint as Garrett. This was no good. Lew would drown them with words, but Garrett remembered Clint. Clint had good sense, but he never spoke; he probably wouldn't even say "boo" about this fiasco.

Next to Clint was some guy that Garrett was actually certain he had never seen before, decked out in new ranch clothes, a Cabelas coat, all topped off with a camo duckbill. Hell, this was going to be annoying. Garrett hated to see Nancy in trouble; she was a roughneck, but a decent sort. He sighed. May as well get started.

"McCracken, could you please take that gun from Nancy? And could somebody please tell me what happened here?"

Expelling a whoosh of restrained air, Lew launched. "Let me tell you, Sheriff, Barnswallowper here is just a god-damn hot head." Nancy was pushing past him to hand the gun to McCracken. To Garrett's surprise, the stranger in the new clothes also stepped forward, past Lew, and held out his hand. "Sheriff, Garfield Fourier here, just back from finishing an oil line contract in Iraq. My wife, Honey, and I plan to settle here now, just like my ancestors. My family were early pioneers in this area. You probably know Fourier Ridge over there?" He gestured to the south with a proud nod.

Garrett freed his hand from Fourier's hearty grip and said, "So were you here when the shots were fired?"

"Oh, yes, we were, right, Clint?" Fourier shot a glance

toward Clint, who gave an almost imperceptible nod of his head, while Lew, triggered, began again. "You bet we were. We were coming down the hill, minding our own business, in that SUV over there, when we saw ..."

Bagly stepped in, interrupting, his smile restrained. "You know, Sheriff, if you'll officially pronounce this scene secure, Tiff and I would like to get down there to the victim."

Garrett glanced at the man in the muddy snow downslope from them. Now he was bent over, holding his head in his hands. Garrett couldn't say for sure, but the pool of blood by his foot might have increased in size. With a stern look at Nancy, who was standing, legs apart, arms folded, he grunted, "Sure, right. I now pronounce it secure. You two go ahead and help that fellow."

Nancy said, "Damn it, Sheriff, I only shot him a little bit. I know how to handle a gun. You know that. I'd never really hurt anybody."

The EMTs began working to remove the victim's boot, and he gave an involuntary yelp of pain. Garrett's eyebrows went up. "Okay, Nancy, but you did. Hear that chap? You did hurt somebody. This won't go easy for you. Whatever possessed you to shoot him?"

"Well, I was ..." Nancy began, but Lew burst in.

"When we pulled up, that harridan Barnswallowper was hollering her ass off at the poor guy. He was coming toward her in a gesture of surrender, like this ... " Lew spread his arms wide and had to stagger to get his balance. "Like this, and she hollered that if he took one more step, she'd shoot him. He kind of waved his hands, you know, like to say 'hold on a minute' and he lifted his foot and she shot him. Right in the other foot. He went down like a lead balloon."

"That's when we called 911," Fourier interjected helpfully.

"It was self defense," Nancy muttered.

"Self defense!" Garrett exclaimed, as a shout came up from the slope below. The EMTs had apparently begun to cut the boot off the injured foot, and the victim was objecting. "Don't cut that! Hey, wait! Don't cut ... Those boots cost a fortune!"

They cut the boot.

Bagly began working over the foot, fussing over the blood,

Baby Skulls and Fowl Odors

and pulling splints and bandages from a medical kit by his side. Tiffany was back up the hill and had extracted a gurney from the ambulance. Struggling to a more level place along the hillside, she parked the gurney and took out the soft cot that was nestled on the gurney bed. Fast downhill strides took her back to Bagly and the annoyed, moaning, and mumbling victim.

"Permission to assist, Chief?" Now, that was the old McCracken. Garrett could almost feel her invisible salute. However, when he responded, "Sure, go ahead," and McCracken propped the gun against the cop car and started down, the whole crowd started down the hill behind her, including Nancy.

"Whoa, Nancy! You get on back up here."

"But Sheriff! I wanna help 'im. Seems to be bleeding pretty bad."

Garrett was at the end of his rope. He pulled on his mustache and said, "Of *course* he's bleeding pretty bad. You shot him in the foot at close range with a .22 rifle! Probably has broken bones, and sure as hell you made a hole clear through." Thus reminding himself, Garrett yelled down the slope, "McCracken, bring that shoe up when you come." Turning back to Nancy, he continued, "Now I need you to stay here and tell me why you did that. Why did you call it self defense? Was he going to hurt you?"

Casting a worried glance down the hill, Nancy turned back toward the sheriff. "He was gettin' ready to. He was trespassin'. He was gonna dig up a bunch of my land. You know what this land means to me. Diggin' it up, you know, that's like violatin' my real person. I was just out rabbit huntin', gonna get me a little meat for supper, and I hear that backhoe over there." She gestured to the old feeder road that had served as the driveway to Mac and Alice Biedermann's tepee.

Sure enough, a big yellow backhoe was parked there, barely visible in thick brush. One of those half-relevant questions that flickers like summer lightning and then disappears traversed Garrett's brain. Where did Mac Biedermann, the son of Reider, last year's corpse, and Victoria ... where did he go, anyhow? Was he off dealing in drugs somewhere else now? He didn't express the thought. Instead he pondered aloud, "Ain't it a little early to be diggin' anything yet? I figure the soil's still froze here."

Nancy extended a foot and pushed thoughtfully at the earth near her. "Nah, it's an early spring, warm, this is just a late, wet snow. I've already started workin' ditches on the upper end of the place."

The crowd of assistants had gotten the victim transferred to the gurney, and now it had arrived back up on the road after much huffing and puffing from the various lifters. Tiffany removed her jacket, and Garrett could see her wiry muscles from where he stood. Lew was wheezing out, "Come on, Lucky. Hurry up." Apparently Lucky, although dead and potentially fast, hadn't achieved a slot at the side of the gurney and was lagging behind.

Turning her head to watch with Garrett, Nancy added, "But that S.O.B. there, he already had his shovel out. He was digging right over there." She eyed the hill and gave several worried sniffs, like a dog, as if indicating to Garrett that the scent would guide his eyes to where the gunshot victim had dug.

Struggling with his straps, the man raised his head. "Ms. Barnswallowper, I keep trying to tell you—this is *my* land! I just want to be good neighbors. I bought this place last fall and I want to build a house for me and Sienna right over there. That's why I was starting to dig."

Nancy reddened, her dander rising again. "And I tell *you*, Mr. Fowler, it ain't your land. This is my land. I got interests here."

They were lifting the gurney into the ambulance, but Fowler, still struggling, squeaked out, "Look, I can't go to the hospital. Please. Hold on! I don't have any way to get back, and I promised Sienna I'd pick her up from school. We're new here. I don't know anybody."

Aggravated, Tiffany said, "Are you refusing transport?" but Fourier had leaned in. Patting Fowler's shoulder, he said, "It's okay, neighbor. You need to get that foot looked at. I'll drop Lew and Clint ... and Lucky ... off at their place and then come on down to the hospital to check on you. If they say you can come home, it'll be easy to bring you back. Or else I'll get ... who? Senna? Your ... daughter? to you. No worries."

With that, Tiffany gave the gurney a vigorous shove into the back of the ambulance and climbed in after it while Bagly

Baby Skulls and Fowl Odors

firmly shut the doors. Garrett turned to Nancy and said grimly, "Nancy Jane, you know we have to take you in." And to McCracken, "Secure the damn gun off the side of the car, McCracken, and load Nancy up." Then to the others, "Thanks, people. You've been helpful." He suddenly thought to be courteous and added, "You, too, Lucky."

All the men looked dubious, and Clint, rubbing at the back of his neck, spoke for the first time. "Ain't so sure about Lucky."

Working their way down the mountain past the Barnswallowper place to their right, Garrett watched Nancy's face in the rearview mirror. She looked sad, but more, she looked worried. She saw him watching and said, "Damn it, Sheriff, this ain't right. It just ain't right. Spring work and calvin' comin' on and all. He was trespassin', and there's laws about that. You heard of 'make my day,' right?"

Nancy knew better. All Garrett could think to say was, "I'm sorry, Nancy." What he didn't say, as the three continued to drive silently toward Peaseford, well, silently except for the snorts being emitted by McCracken's phone ... What he didn't say was that Nancy hadn't convinced him. Even if she was right, and that was her little nipple of land on the other side of the road, it was kind of a useless piece, not agricultural, dry, no irrigation, mostly stubby, nasty cactus to poke into your ankles if you didn't watch out. Why had she gotten so stirred up about it—so upset that she shot that guy? Even for Nancy, that was radical. He pursed his lips, pulled at his mustache, and glanced at McCracken, who was fiddling with her phone.

That brought up another mystery for him to ponder. When Tiffany had texted McCracken to say that Jenny was safe after the Cowpath Saloon fire, she had said Jenny was going out with somebody named Xyster, a Black guy. Then she had added, "LOL." Didn't LOL mean "Laughing Out Loud?" What was she LOLing about? Did she think it was funny that Jenny, an older white hippie, would go out with a Black guy? Garrett felt aggravated, protective of Jenny. Was this Tiffany racist? Or a mean little gossip? He wanted to ask McCracken, but he couldn't, not with Nancy Jane sitting right there in the back seat, biting her lip and frowning out the window.

4

THE ONLY WOMAN who had ever called Garrett 'Patrick' was hanging up her light spring coat when she felt it. Jenny Threewinds stopped dead still in her little bedroom at the east end of the trailer. She'd just gotten home from the Cowpath, having put in several hours at locating and dealing with smoke-damaged items, but now she sensed it, something wrong. The juniper outside the bedroom window, moved by the gentle evening breeze, scratched lightly at the glass, making her stomach knot. What was it?

Spot looked into her face and whined. Roughneck jumped onto the bed and tried to reach her hands for a welcoming lick, and as she glanced down at him, she saw it—the empty space. Her doll was gone! Oh, my god! Oh, my god! My doll is gone!

Jenny's coat slid unnoticed to the floor and she sank onto the bed and stared. Nothing could help her process this. Her doll, the one thing—she was always there, always waiting, secure against the pillows, for Jenny to come home, ready to be snuggled into the little chair by the dresser, ready to say good night. The doll had helped her get through it. She couldn't be gone! How could she be gone?

After casting her eyes frantically around the bedroom, Jenny hurried into the main part of the trailer, searching desperately. It was only when she got to the little alcove that formed an entryway that something suddenly clicked. The box ... the box of old toys was gone. Oh, no! Brady! He wouldn't have, would he? She sank into a nearby chair and covered her face with her hands. "Oh, Brady Xyster, what have you done?"

5

FOR GARFIELD FOURIER, the trip to the hospital in Riversmet to pick up Chuck Fowler was calming and pleasant. It was a long way, well over an hour, but Honey wouldn't be back until tomorrow, so he had all the time in the world to hum to himself, wool-gather, and admire the warm burlap of the 'dobies as they folded into mysterious, shaded blue canyons, distancing themselves from the highway. He was glad to see patches of snow still holding on the north sides of the hills, because snow always meant water in this country, and equally happy to see hardy grasses struggling to green on the south slopes. He wanted to explore the canyons sometime, but he knew they would only yield to his curiosity by way of unmarked side roads, using ATVs or shanks' mares. The fact that the term "using shanks' mares" crossed his mind to describe walking into the canyons pleased him. It was an old-time term, and Garfield loved old-time things. He loved the idea that he and Honey were settling under Fourier Ridge, which had been named for his ancestors, and that he could now retire from his overseas contract work and settle into an old-time, real American, community, engaging in old-time enterprises. It felt to him that it would be healing after the stresses of working in a war-ravaged foreign country.

Of course he would use engineering skills he had developed in Iraq to work his place; for example, he could study the irrigation system, maybe install more pipe, make elevation refinements, and so-on, but for the most part he would respect what the old-timers had accomplished, and he would respect the land. Yup, old-timers. They were really something!

Honey — well, actually, Honey was none too happy with all this. She missed the city, the restaurants, plays, cinema, activities ... her friends. Even now she had gone to visit friends in Denver, trying to get her courage up to break free of the urban life. Sure, she was feeling uncomfortable here, but he had faith in her. She was an adaptable woman, and there was much here for her to appreciate, once she got involved with it. Nature and community. His mind leap-frogged pleasantly past Honey's concerns and again took up his own dreams. They could raise cattle. They could grow potatoes. Or hemp. Now that Colorado's marijuana laws had loosened, would hemp be a possible crop? People needed hemp for industrial use, and America had to import it, right? He'd have to research that. About the legality, and the soils and climate and all.

It was a pleasant drive, but his peaceful daydreams ended abruptly by the time he'd gotten a pale and hobbling Chuck Fowler loaded in the front passenger seat of the SUV, his crutch propped beside him. Garfield eased the car into traffic and attempted to open a conversation, picking his favorite topic.

"You know, Chuck, it sure is a pretty day, isn't it? Springtime in the country. Honey and I are sure looking forward to living here. You know, my ancestors were some of the first ones to ..." Chuck Fowler, his eyes fixed tiredly out the window, emitted a soft, involuntary moan.

Thinking a moan would be a natural reaction to pain, Garfield decided to forge ahead, maybe help distract the man. "That ridge just south of your place and above mine, that's Fourier Ridge. My great-granddaddy logged off that ridge with a team and wagon. Family camped up there all summer, every summer. Of course, now that I own it, my priorities will be more environmentally friendly. I hope to protect the trees and ..." Fowler pulled a handkerchief from his back pocket; the movement to reach it made him gasp. He mopped his forehead while Garfield looked at him anxiously. He seemed kind of gray; was he crying?

Forging lamely onward, Garfield said, "So, I have big dreams for that piece of land, all right. What do you have up your sleeve for your property, neighbor?" At this point he could see that Fowler was looking at him and shaking his head. His lips moved, but nothing was coming out. Alarmed, Garfield blurted, "Are you in pain? Should we return to the doctor?"

This, finally, elicited words. Continuing to shake his head, Chuck Fowler said, "No no no! No broken bones, and they gave

Baby Skulls and Fowl Odors

me pain medication. Just healing time. What I don't have." He blinked. "I'm sorry. I just ... I've had a rough week, and I'm having trouble focusing on what you're saying. We ... I ... I just don't know how I'm going to manage Sienna and me and keep up with my work, my plans for her and that place ... I'm really sorry, Mr. Fourier. I appreciate you picking me up, but honestly, I feel like my troubles have just begun, and I barely heard a word you said so far."

Now, this Garfield could handle. In fact, he was thrilled. He immediately waxed hearty. "Oh, no problem! No problem! And I'm not Mr. Fourier to you — please, call me Garfield. It's me that should be sorry. I should have realized that having an injured foot and being alone in the country, plus brand new here! Why of course that would make you worry, especially with a kid to take care of, but hey! We're neighbors! Honey and I are right next door, so to speak. You just call on us! In fact, I'll just make a point of coming over first thing in the morning — I can make short work of those chores, and Honey can pick up supplies for you and the kid. Hey, old buddy, we've sure got you covered there. No worries!"

Garfield, driving and immersed in his new plans, didn't notice the clouds of anxiety that were crossing Fowler's face as he talked, particularly as he mentioned taking over Chuck Fowler's chores. All he heard was the mumbled "Well, thanks. That's good of you," and he accepted it as an appropriate response under the circumstances. As they rode silently for the remainder of the way to the school in Peaseford, he had the urge to start humming to himself again. He could think of so many things he could do to help this poor guy and get him back on his feet. Foot. It wasn't until they picked up Sienna, in Peaseford, that the atmosphere in the car again turned unpleasant for Garfield. Unpleasant or worse — maybe just plain sour.

Sienna flounced into Garfield's green SUV and slammed the door. "Where the hell have you been, Chuck? I had to wait here nearly a half hour with this bunch of jerks!"

"I'm sorry, sweetheart. I ... I hurt my foot. Please say hello to Mr. Fourier, our new neighbor. He was kind enough to bring me from the hospital."

With narrowed eyes and a touch of sarcasm, Sienna turned to the front and said, "Well, hello, Mr. Fourier. So kind of you to run after my clumsy *parent*."

Garfield's eyebrows went up, but he turned in his seat and offered a friendly hand. "Hello, Sienna. I'm glad to meet you. You know, your father wasn't clumsy. Ms. Barnswallowper shot him in the foot because of a land dispute."

Making a grim mouth, Sienna took the proffered hand, gave it a limp shake and dropped it like a smelly dead fish. "Barnswallowper, too? They're all like that around here—everybody is a bully! I told you, Chuck. Patsy pulls my hair on the bus, and that kid Brandon calls me an ugly little slant eye." Her voice had gotten thick, and Garfield realized she was just short of tears.

While Fowler said, "I'm really sorry, Sienna, we hurried as fast as we could," Fourier turned to the front and put the SUV in gear, saying, "It's gonna to be all right, Sienna. I think you'll meet some decent people after you've been here awhile. Right now, we'll get you and your dad home as soon as we can."

Sienna mumbled something about just not getting in such a rush that you slide us off the damned icy redneck dirt roads, then curled into what appeared to be a fetal ball, although a brief glance in the rearview mirror told Garfield that she had pulled out a phone and was messing with the apps.

After they'd driven awhile, Chuck Fowler said softly, "I apologize for her manners. The move has been hard on her. She's only 12, you know."

Garfield emitted a forgiving, "Oh, no problem," while a sullen voice from the back said, "Almost 13, really."

After that everyone was quiet until they pulled up in front of the shabby trailer that now sat where Mac and Alice's tepee had been. Sienna bailed out, dragging her heavy backpack behind her, while Chuck struggled to extricate his aching foot and manage the crutch. Garfield rushed to help him, but Chuck was looking up to watch Sienna headed for the trailer steps. "Sienna," he called, "Don't forget your chores. And you could give me a hand here, too, you know." Turning to Garfield, clearly embarrassed, he said for the hundredth time, "I really am sorry. She's had an awful rough time since her mother left."

With that, Sienna became a whirlwind. Slamming down the backpack, she shot down the trailer steps, yelling, "Just *say* it, damn it, Chuck! Why won't you ever just say it? My mother didn't leave, she's *dead!*" Turning to Garfield, she shouted, "Dead, you

Baby Skulls and Fowl Odors

hear me? He just won't admit it!" And back to Fowler, "Mom would be here if she could, and she would never have ignored the problems I'm having with this awful place." Both men had stretched out their hands to defend themselves against the approaching dynamo, but she screeched to an abrupt halt in front of Fowler, making him sway on the crutch, and said in a menacing voice, "Plus you know very well that I would *never* forget my chores. They are my chores, a sacred trust that my mother left me — left *me*, not you! — and I would do them no matter what, even after what has happened. Even after that big secret mess!"

Spinning toward Garfield, tears on her cheeks, she gritted out, "You bet I'm a slant eye. My mother's name was Xi Feng Ling, and I'm proud of it, and she's dead, and I will do my chores for *her*." Turning, she stomped to the trailer, leaving the men to struggle, speechless, with foot and crutch across the uneven terrain and up the steps.

Driving home, Garfield was no longer daydreaming. The episode had left him thoroughly disturbed. The little girl was clearly half Chinese, but whatever had happened to her Chinese mother? Where was Xi Feng Ling?

6

JENNY THREEWINDS HEARD the crunch of Brady Xyster's tires as he pulled up the gravel drive; she met him at the door. "Xy, I left that box right here and ..."

Holding up a cautionary finger, he pointed to the cell phone by his ear, then waved his hand at her, a shushing motion. "Uh huh. Uh huh. Look, I *told* them it wouldn't move that fast. No. Well, there have been complications here, too. Right. Right. Sure. I'll get back tomorrow." Popping the phone into his shirt pocket, he gave Jenny an apologetic shrug. "Sorry, Jen—just business stuff. Now, what were you ...?"

"It's okay, Brady, but about the box that ..."

Linus strummed the piano from Xyster's pocket, cheerfully playing the Charlie Brown theme, and Xyster made a grab for the phone. "Hi, Chuck, my man! S'up? Right. I just talked to Megan. No, listen, they have to understand, seriously. I can't pull this shit out of thin air. I don't care if it's been done before and you tell me anyone can do it." His voice had gone up, sharpening. "No. Seriously. You listen to me—maybe at this point people are starting to catch on to what's really happening, right? So, I *am* moving it along, damn it, Charles. Right. Right. When I can, okay?"

Phone back in pocket, forgive-me look directed back at Jenny, whose brain was still trying to finish the Charlie Brown sequence started by his ring tone. Nodding, she said, "So, anyhow, Xy, the box here, this morning ..."

Xyster delivered a blank look. "Box?"

"Yes, Brady, box. The box that was sitting right there!"

Following her gesture toward a place in the corner where there was no box now, Xyster scowled, then his expression clarified. "Oh, *that* box. The one you wanted to go to the dump

Baby Skulls and Fowl Odors

or somewhere." He scrubbed at his forehead. "It's been a long day."

Her own soft voice starting to take on an edge, Jenny said, "Xy, you didn't take it to the dump, did you?"

Shaking his head as if to clear it, Xyster laughed. "No, no, no." Teasing. "It looked like dumpster stuff to me, but you told me that while I was 'out running around,' as you put it, I may as well do something useful and earn my keep around here. You told me to drop it off somewhere it might do some good, so I did. I even looked around for other stuff that needed to go. I left that old stuffed rabbit on the porch because I think it belongs to the dogs, but I threw in the big old doll in the chair by your bed, kind of looked like an Indian kid, thought you forgot to get it, and I threw in that ugly old ceramic vase from the corner over there. Couldn't imagine you wanting to keep that. So! Now you feel better? I done good, huh?"

He was dancing from foot to foot, anxious to get past Jenny, on into the house, grab a drink, put up his feet, but Jenny had gone pale. She hadn't noticed the urn missing. "Brady, for god's sake! That 'ugly old vase' was the urn with my mother's ashes in it! *Where* did you take that stuff!"

"Oh, crap. Looks like I'll be sleeping in the dog house now." He pulled his lips down in a mock sad face. "You gonna kick me out?" His pocket grated out the Dalek battle cry, "Exterminate," followed by a deep trash-bin burp from a Dr. Who scene called "When Plastic Attacks." Xyster's hand went for the phone, but Jenny was faster. She pounced, snatched the phone, and hit talk. "Look, *Who*-ever you are, this is Ms. Who, Dr. Who's secretary. Who's busy, and he'll call you back in a minute." She punched "end" without waiting to hear the caller's baffled noises, and mumbled to herself, "And, I might add, Who's on first," then narrowed her eyes at Brady. "Now, Mr. Xy, you just focus for a minute. Where did you take my stuff?"

Brady was staring in shock at the phone still in Jenny's hand. "Jenny, that was my boss! The big, bad *boss!* I have to talk to him! Damn it, Jenny, give me my phone."

Jenny didn't soften. Gripping the phone tighter, she said, "Damn it yourself. This will just take a minute. Brady, where did you take my stuff? Where did you take my *mother* and my... my doll?"

Agitated and still staring at the phone, Brady said, "Look, I thought you'd be pleased. You said it wasn't stuff that was worth much in the real world, just sentimental value, but you thought maybe somebody else could get some good of it." His eyes were shifting from her hand to her face and back. "So far, this hasn't been my most successful day, okay?"

Taking a deep breath, Jenny gritted into his flow of speech. "Right, bad day. I get it. Now, *where-did-you-take-my-stuff?* A C.S.I. theme started on the phone, and Jenny cut it off.

Brady's hands had gone wild. "Lots of places, Jen! I took your junk lots of places. I was trying to make sure that it got where you wanted, where it could make somebody happy. And I'm not kidding. I have job worries. You know, things aren't easy for people like me in this area ..." Jenny's face had become menacing as she took a step toward him.

"Brady, this involves dead people. *My* dead people! I have to get the urn and ... and the doll back. Where specifically did you leave them?

"I don't remember."

The sigh that escaped her didn't begin to express her frustration. "Try. Try and remember. Please, Brady!" Shoulders drooping, she tossed him the phone.

"No, seriously, I'm trying to tell you. I've run into stuff around here. I'm distracted. The best I can remember for you is the thrift store in Croysant and the Catholic church in Peaseford. I had some business at the court house in Riversmet, so I tried the hospital, but they wouldn't take any stuff, some kind of hygiene rules. Oh, yeah, and the retirement home in Peaseford. I don't know which places took which stuff; I was just trying to spread it around a little." His eyes were still on the phone, now in his own hand, and his expression was so distressed that Jenny softened.

"Listen to me, Xy. Don't get so stirred up. And you don't mess with that phone while you're driving—you'll kill yourself and somebody else. Really, all I wish you could remember is where you left the urn and the Indian doll."

"Honestly, Jenny, I don't know. So much pressure—I can't get anywhere with this deal, and ..." he raised anxious eyes to her face, "... And I really don't want to think it, but I'm starting to wonder if it's because I'm Black. Small town rural prejudices."

Baby Skulls and Fowl Odors

Jenny started to respond, but the phone played the theme song from Jeopardy. Dum da dum da dum da dum ... Xyster hunkered over it, mumbling, "Hey, Marco. Been awhile. Yeah. I know. I know. Sorry. Soon as I can. Yeah ..."

7

NOW *THIS* WAS WHY these women attended Community Club. Some might call it the gossip factor, but the more discerning among us will realize that it has to do with networking, community relationships, and the vital flow of information needed to maintain values and underwrite economic issues. Today, the members hit the mother lode: first, here was Jilly Brown, appearing for the first time ever in skirt and ruffly blouse instead of her regular uniform of jeans and a casual tee. Her rambunctious twins were at last in school (poor Mrs. Harris) and the skirt and blouse were elegant and stain free.

Here she was, all right, the youngest president in the history of the Oozle-Onion Valley Club, and conducting a flawless, business-like meeting. She had googled Robert's Rules of Order, and she meant it. She even kept Alma gently in check, Alma who loved to talk and who drifted into other worlds as the meeting moved forward.

Second, here was Honey Fourier. What a lovely woman, but what a contrast to Victoria, the previous occupant of the big house up Oozle Road! Victoria had been so blond, so slender, so white-complexioned, and, well, so beautifully Swedish. Honey was shorter, dusky, long, straight, silky dark hair bobbed to drift along her shoulders, great brown eyes framed by the kind of lovely, lacy lashes that cost real dollars when you bought 'em in a store. They couldn't, unfortunately, talk about her today, her being right there and all, but the as yet unspoken consensus was that she was a large cut over the disappointing Victoria Biedermann. Why, Honey's husband was practically an old-timer here, having descended from the local Fouriers for which Fourier Ridge was named. He had been in Iraq. Maybe he had found Honey there. While this could mean that maybe she was

Baby Skulls and Fowl Odors

one of those A-rabs that gave America so much trouble all the time, they were ready to forgive her this. No doubt she loved America or Garfield wouldn't have married her, and besides, she couldn't help what she was. They needed to account for her somewhat brown foreign look, but they were willing to let it rest for now. Her real origins would surface as she and Garfield settled into the community.

Everyone was pleased to have Tiffany Gallenas there, too. She was such a busy girl that she didn't often make it to club, but she was Hallie's niece—poor Hallie, gone now, and missed, but her family always welcome. Besides, they wanted more detail from Tiffany about the Cowpath Saloon fire, as they had heard she was one of the first emergency responders. Donna Caswell elbowed in first, to ask her, in a leading fashion, "Well. I heard you were at that fire at the Cowpath the other night? You had to pick old Lew Harris off the ground? But he was okay?"

Tiffany, mindful of her HIPAA privacy oath, said, "Something like that. Lew was there with Lucky." Tiffany frowned down at the leash Donna was clutching, which had woven itself tightly around her ankles and was now giving jerking motions. "New dog, Donna?"

Her face solemn, Donna gave what had become, at this point, a practiced response. "Yes, Spit finally could live no more, poor baby. Only old age could conquer him. My dear, blessed darling. Impossible to replace." She knelt to untangle Tiffany's ankles, not noticing glances from women nearby which indicated that they wished Spit really had been impossible to replace. Spit had begun life as a fierce little Chihuahua who barked so hard he spit, and who didn't hesitate to yap during meetings and clamor at the women's legs, his own leg raised. Finally, oh, finally! in his old age he settled down, sitting out club meetings on Donna's lap. When he went to his great doggy reward in the sky, all would have been well, but an old friend in Riversmet helpfully located the appropriately named Yip. When the friend compassionately gifted Donna with the little bug-eyed monster, what could Donna do but graciously accept?

Yip now made his way to Honey's fashionably clad feet, where he sucked in his belly and began to heave. Tiffany leaped forward to make a grab for him, but Donna beat her to it. Snatching him up, she said, "Oh, my poor baby! Oh, little Yip—

what has mommy fed you that was all wrong?" Making a frantic dash for the door, she glanced hurriedly over her shoulder to gabble, "I am so sorry to rush off! I'll see you next time! Oh, my poor, poor little Yippy!" all accompanied by gagging noises from the dog and the squeaking of the old clubhouse door closing behind her.

After an exchange of glances, the conversational murmur began again. Tiffany sat down beside Honey and said, "I'm just relieved to get out of the house for a while. The kids drive me berserk, even though they're a heck of a lot older than Jilly's. Do you have kids?"

Smiling, Honey said, "Not yet. Now that Gar is back from overseas, we do want to try, though."

"Well, that's cool. Yours will be mellow. Me, I'm a single mom, and my boys can really be a pain. Luke is 17, and he's got some of the big ideas of his deadbeat dad, and then Larry's just 12. He follows Luke around like a sick sheep, big adoring eyes. Hero worship. Luke even finishes Larry's sentences, and that suits the little suck-up just fine. Excuse my language."

Clearly not bothered by the language, Honey chuckled. "I know that a little, I think. I have a twin brother, born 20 minutes before me, but you would think he was born years before. He's a big bustle butt—excuse *my* language—always busy, self-important, and ... well, he finishes my sentences, too. The family calls him B, and they call me Honey, so the two of us are Honeybee, always buzzing around. But it's really B that buzzes, not me."

All this interested Tiffany and the nearby eavesdroppers very much, but Jilly, Robert's Rules at the ready, pounded the table with a carpenter's hammer she'd found in Billy's tool kit, calling the meeting to order.

It was after the meeting, while Frieda and Doreen were serving fat slices of angel food cake smothered in fresh strawberries and buried in whipped cream, that the third wonderfully exciting, gossip-stimulating event occurred: Nancy Jane Barnswallowper exploded into the clubhouse, shouting, "He's got chickens, I tell you! The S.O.B. is claiming *my* land and he plans to build a gawd-damned factory chicken farm on it. I will not allow this! You've gotta help me—it is your gawd-damned, gawd-given duty to this community!" Surely she was a little

Baby Skulls and Fowl Odors

drunk. She didn't say "excuse my language." Her usual ranch attire was even more rumpled than usual, and she staggered as she waved what appeared to be a fist full of picket signs.

Tiny, gentle Doreen, always first to the rescue, rushed forward, holding up her hands and waving them to stop Nancy Jane's onslaught. "Oh, Nancy, honey, you must calm down. You must sit and tell us what has happened that upsets you so."

"Don't just set me down, Dory! You gotta hear me out!"

Agnes Michaelson, tripping on Honey's toes, had reached Nancy Jane's side and begun to guide her to a chair, but Tiffany was standing, eyeing Nancy's hands. Was she armed? "Look, Barnswallowper, I thought you went downtown with the sheriff. How'd you get outta jail?"

Doreen swiveled, fluttering, toward Tiffany. "Oh, Tiffany, you mustn't talk so ... so cranky to Nancy Jane! She is among friends here."

Still squinting at Nancy Jane, Tiffany loosened her knees, ready to spring if necessary, but in a quieter voice she repeated, "Didn't Sheriff Garrett take you in yesterday?"

Brandishing the signs and shaking her head 'no,' Nancy Jane said, "Yes, indeed, he did, ma'am, but the sheriff, he's a good man. He understands spring work and watchin' mother cows that are tryin' to calve, so he helped me see the judge right away and I am now free of my own recognizing."

"Recognizance," Tiffany mumbled.

"What'd you say?"

"I said, the word is not 'recognizing,' it is 'recognizance.' It's okay. Just let it go."

"Recognizing, ree-cog-nah... nah... whatever. It just means I'm free till next week, then the judge will hear me out in court. And no guns till then. He made me promise that, but he says he'll hear me out. So it's okay."

Agnes Michaelson was frantically patting Nancy Jane's shoulder. "Oh, good. Oh, good, then, honey. So you can just sit right down here and have some cake and tell us what it is that's got you all stirred up." The final pat was heavy, more of a push, and Nancy Jane finally released her locked knees and sat. All the club members had converged into the main room; Honey had pulled her vulnerable feet up onto the chair rung; Alma was shifting her walker about, feeling that she must somehow be prepared for action.

Putting the signs down, Nancy Jane nodded, frowning, then pulled a little .22 revolver from the belt under her shirt. Everyone gasped, leaning back. "I brought this to help us out. I would think the judge just meant rifles; he surely wouldn't want a lone woman off up Oozle Road to not be protected. This means you know you'll be safe when we all go up there. We wouldn't want to go unarmed around that snake."

Doreen, her tiny back straight but her face pale, said, "So where is it we are all going, Miss Nancy Jane? You must catch us up to your thinking."

"Yeah, yeah, Dory, I'm glad you asked. Of course, you know that we are going up to that damned Chuck Fowler's." Doreen flinched on the "damned," language which hadn't been excused, but nodded encouragingly. "See, after the judge let me loose, I figured to just do a little research while I was in town. I ran up to the county clerk's office, and Tammy Sue—you all know Tammy Sue, right? Used to live up South Peaseford Mesa before she married that Riversmet guy ... well, anyhow, she helped me look at recent land use applications, and I'll be go to hell, there it was."

A brief but weighty silence ensued. Finally, Tiffany said, "There what was?"

"The evidence of that bastard's land grab!" Again, Doreen flinched, 'bastard' not being excused, but Nancy Jane was on a roll. "See, here's what's gonna get you all fired up." She took a bite of the cake that Frieda had slid onto her lap and spoke, muffled, around it. "See, that S.O.B. is planning a chicken factory right here. A chicken factory farm. On what is really my property in the first place!"

Tiffany interjected. "Wait! How is it you know this?" But Nancy Jane just gave her a sideways glance, stuffed another spoonful of cake into her mouth, and kept talking, words still muffled.

"You know what this means? You realize the stink of a place like that, stench rollin' down the hill toward my house? Chicken shit and shit dust everywhere? And them big trucks blockin' the road to load up chickens, unload feed and shit? And those poor damn chickens. Poor devils, squashed in tiny cages, shot up with them hormones! We gotta stop this! It is our civic

Baby Skulls and Fowl Odors

duty!" Nancy Jane jumped up, handed her partially eaten cake to Honey, and picked up her signs, ready to give them out. As nearly as the club women could see, the signs all just said, "No Chickens," scrawled in heavy-handed black Sharpie.

Raising her voice to command mode, Tiffany said, "Are you saying that Chuck Fowler's name was on a land use application for a factory farm? For chickens?"

Her own voice edged with sarcasm, Nancy Jane said, "No, Miss Tiffy, not exactly. Don't be so damned litrell. It was for 2432 Oozle Road. That's Fowler's place except for the part that's mine. And it didn't have his name. The application was for Tinker Chicken. He's plannin' to let Tinker Chicken onto that place."

Hesitantly, Honey said, "Tinker Chicken! They're a huge company! They are all over the country, maybe even overseas, and they really do run factory farms. I've read about them, how they contract with small farmers to build big facilities on their places and the small farm families put in the money and do the work, but it's a losing contract. They hardly get enough to survive, while the big company scoops up the profits. If poultry disease hits, they often lose the old family farm and everything. Maybe ... maybe that's what poor Chuck Fowler has gotten himself into?"

"Poor Chuck Fowler, my ass," Nancy Jane burst out. "If he does this, you can bet your sweet ass I won't be the only one smellin' chicken shit. The merry little breezes'll boil it right on over those hills to your place and Johnson's and ..."

Doreen's hands had flown up, fending off too many 'asses.' "Nancy, Nancy! This isn't good, but really! What do you expect us to do?"

Expelling a heavy breath, Nancy Jane said, "Isn't it obvious? You all gotta get in your cars and follow me up there. Take these signs and we'll picket the bastard. We need to get my land back and get him stopped ..."

This caused a general turmoil in the room, the women milling around, someone saying, "Well, I wasn't expecting this," while someone else was saying, "No, this is out. I need to get to town before supper," and Alma struggling ineffectively to raise herself with her walker, saying, "Kick at? Kick at? Who do we have to kick at?"

At this point Jilly Brown, realizing that she was, after all, the president, and that it was up to her to take control, brought the hammer down sharply on the table. This caused a cracking sound, as the table was old, and the blow split a board, but everyone did fall silent. "Ladies, ladies," Jilly said, "Let's have order. I don't think we know enough yet to go picket Chuck Fowler. I think we need a committee. A committee to go see what's happening up there." She took a deep, authoritative breath. "I shall appoint a committee."

Several women nodded, and Alma ceased to struggle with her walker. "Who's Chuck Fowler?" she exclaimed. "I never heard of any Fowlers around here. What do you mean, kick at him?"

No one answered. Nancy Jane scowled, muttering, "I already know about Fowler," but Jilly overrode her. She said loudly, "Raise your hand if you want to volunteer for a committee to go with Nancy Jane to investigate what is currently happening at the Fowler place, so we will know what needs to be done."

Alma heard this. Her hand shot up; she loved to be in the thick of things and to know what was going on. Agnes Michaelson gently pressed it back down. "No, no, dear, I'm your ride today, and I need to get you ... to get home now. It's time to cook supper, you know."

Looking disappointed, Alma said, "Oh, okay," No one else's hand went up. Nancy Jane's scowl deepened, and Jilly said hopefully, "Maybe someone who lives nearby should go?"

Hesitantly, Frieda's chubby fingers wiggled at the room. "Honey and I came over together. We are the nearest neighbors, except Nancy Jane, of course. I guess we could go on up with her to check it out."

Honey's feet slipped from where they had been balanced on the chair rung and hit the floor with a clunk. Sitting up straight and handing Nancy's cake dish to Tiffany, next to her, she said, "I, uh ... I ..." but Jilly was feeling empowered. "All right, then. That sounds like a great plan. In fact, I am president, so I will go along, too, and we can just drive up and see what might be happening there. After what Nancy Jane has contributed so far." She smiled across the room at Honey's appalled face. "Really, I don't think it will take all that long."

After the other club members had left, a bit more quickly than usual, Nancy Jane piled into her truck, impatiently telling

Baby Skulls and Fowl Odors

the three women to "come on," then pulling out and disappearing around the corner in a cloud of dust. Jilly waited solicitously for Frieda and Honey; when she saw they were in their car, she, too, shot ahead. Frieda, plump and pleasant, exited the parking lot and drove sedately far behind, letting the dust settle in front of her.

"How do they drive so fast on this gravel road?" Honey asked. "It feels dangerous!"

"It really is rough, isn't it? Like a warsh board." Frieda was navigating wildly to avoid the worst of the corrugates and pot holes, while Honey held the bar above the door to maintain her balance as the car swerved, her rich, dark hair swaying from side to side. She was trying to visualize a wash board, and wondered whether Frieda had ever used one. A "warsh" board. She smiled to herself; she rather liked Frieda.

As they approached the turn to her own house, which Garfield had exuberantly labeled "Fourier Lane" with a large sign that swung over the entrance and displayed silhouettes of deer and bear cut from the rustically stained wood, Honey said hopefully, "Frieda, if you'd like, you could just drop me here and save yourself the drive back. I don't mind walking down the lane."

Frieda chuckled warmly. "Ah, save your nice shoes. I don't mind the drivin'. We can't leave poor Jilly up there with old Nancy Jane. Who knows?" She kept driving, going past her own driveway and turning up K-4 while Honey looked back wistfully, her hopes of early release dashed. She wondered what that meant. "Who knows." Who knows what? Meanwhile, Frieda's car, having turned right, angled purposefully up the steep hill, around the sharp corners, and found its way to a small pull-out near Fowler's driveway. Jilly and Nancy Jane were already out of their vehicles and looking thoughtfully toward Fowler's trailer below them on the hill.

It was completely quiet. Somewhere in the valley far below a crow cawed. Jilly shaded her eyes, peered toward the trailer, and said, "I don't think anyone's here. Plus, it seems like if he's starting a chicken farm, we'd see some building activity, or maybe hear chickens."

Frieda had folded her arms to rest across the plush pillow of her bosom. Expelling a thoughtful breath, she added, "Look,

Nancy Jane, there ain't nobody here to picket."

Her mouth in a grim line, Nancy Jane's hands formed fists around the signs she was carrying. "Why the hell does that application for chicken torture have the number of this place on it, then?"

"I don't know, but nobody's here, see? It's all quiet down there, not even a vehicle. What do you expect us to do?"

"Maybe the lazy little coward is just layin' low. We need to go down there to that trailer and confront him."

Jilly, annoyed, put her hands on her hips. "Nancy Jane, you already did that, and see where it got everybody? You shot the man in the foot, for God's sake! If he is there, he's probably just resting his foot."

Honey glanced with some anxiety at the surrounding trees. "Uh, maybe we can come back another day," this tentative.

Her arms crossed even more tightly on her chest, Frieda said, "Seriously, Nancy J. No chickets to picket." She chuckled, relishing her own word play.

From just behind the trailer, a rooster crowed. This was followed by a series of loud squawking noises such as chickens make when they have crowded into each other's territory. Just as abruptly, everything fell quiet again, including all four women.

It didn't last. Nancy Jane dropped the signs with a clatter, reached under her shirt, and pulled out the .22. "I told you," she said. "I told you. I told you. I told you. Now, by damn, we are gonna go in."

Her jaw set like a rock and her eyes narrowed, Jilly shot in front of Nancy Jane, blocking her. "Oh, no, you don't, damn it, lady. You drop that gun. You know better. You didn't drag us up here for this. We got no interest in your damn guns and confrontations."

Surprisingly, Nancy Jane stopped, but Honey had wheeled on her heel, saying, "You people do what you want. I'm going home now." Politely she added, "Thank you for the lovely afternoon."

She had taken a few steps down the road when Frieda, unfolding her arms, said, "Wait. It's okay, Honey. Wait a minute, and I'll take you." It wasn't clear whether she was using 'Honey' as the proper name, or as a familiar term intended to comfort, but Honey stopped. Frieda continued in her rich, comfortable

Baby Skulls and Fowl Odors

voice, "Nancy Jane, you really do know better. You know the sheriff didn't just mean rifles. Now, give me that pistol." Frieda rolled forward, her hand extended, and Nancy Jane dropped the gun in it, her face working.

"It's about the land, gawdamnit! Frieda, you and Little Pete wouldn't want Fowler to grab a hunk of *your* land. Not for a stinkin', shitty chicken farm. And here, right here where I am standin'? This here's my land." She seemed to have shrunk, and there were tears in her voice.

Honey hadn't realized that her own hand had extended and opened, but something about the matter-of-fact way that Frieda thrust the pistol at her had left her holding the gun. Suddenly aware of what she was doing, her eyes grew enormous and she held it away from her body with her fingertips, a hot potato. Gathering Nancy into her ample embrace, Frieda said, "Aw. Aw, honey, of course not. We gotta get these land claims straight."

Jilly nodded. Time for another executive decision, and she was on it. "Hey, Nance. I'll tell you what let's do. Let's put these signs out on your part of the land here, and then go home and just see what happens, okay?"

So that is what they did. While Honey gingerly held the pistol, barrel shakily pointed down, Nancy Jane, Frieda, and Jilly gathered up the signs, a dozen signs saying bluntly, "No Chickens," and, walking gingerly to avoid cactus, put them out among the pinion, junipers, and sage on the piece of land that Nancy claimed as her own.

8

WITH EACH PASSING DAY, Alma withdrew further into other worlds, following her heart as it sought to rejoin those who had left her behind: her husband, Doug; her parents; cousins and siblings; Hallie; maybe even crazy old Lena Larson. Sometimes she would even speak out loud with them as she drifted there. Thus it was that when Jenny slipped quietly into the room, she found Alma home from club, resting in Doug's old recliner, mumbling softly, her face vague, her bare feet with the knobby bunions stretched out before her on the foot rest. Her home health care nurse wasn't expected for another hour, and she was alone and tired. When Jenny bent to place a light kiss on her forehead, Alma realized for the first time that someone had entered her house. She focused her eyes on Jenny with some puzzlement. In a voice weighted by impending sleep and old age, she croaked, "Well, hello there, young lady. I didn't know you were here."

"I'm sorry. I didn't mean to alarm you. I mostly just dropped by to say 'Hi.'" Jenny knelt by Alma's feet and began to gently massage them as her eyes took in the room with its collection of toys perched on chairs and along couch backs. She wasn't sure how to approach this. It had been a long day. Xyster left early, but she had to do desk work and chores before she could tackle her search and rescue mission. When she finally started, the process was maddening. The Croysant thrift store had closed for the day. She drove on down to Peaseford, where the volunteer at the Catholic Church was friendly, quite chatty, in fact. First came the "how-are-you's," the aches and pains. Then, of course, the weather. "Well, the rain is good for the crops, but does it have to get so darned cold for this time of year?" Finally, Jenny found her opening to explain why she'd come. The volunteer's eyes widened. "You mean he was just

Baby Skulls and Fowl Odors

going to throw your good things in the trash?"

"Oh, no, no," Jenny protested, "That was just teasing. And they aren't all that good." This realization made her a little embarrassed, so she added, "I'm sorry." Then she added, "It's just the urn and doll, you understand. My mother's ashes. And her ... uh ... gift. The doll." The volunteer was nodding vigorously as Jenny stumbled over the words, then turned briskly and gave an ear-shattering blast through an adjoining door. "Father Terry! Could you come here? Come here a minute, Father." Jenny was making shushing motions with her hands, and the volunteer shrugged. "Father doesn't hear as well as he used to."

Jenny started to say, "But you don't have to bother the Father," but just then an older chap in jeans and a bright Hawaiian shirt popped into the room. " 'Tsup, Katy?"

Speaking several decibels up, the volunteer said, "This lady's friend, a Mr. Xyster, brought in a donation for the poor yesterday. Were you here when he came by?"

"A shyster?" puzzled the priest, causing the volunteer to look askance at Jenny, thinking it might have been she who had misheard.

"No, no," Jenny shook her head. "Xyster. Brady Xyster. But it doesn't ..." The priest was leaning in, bending his ear toward her and cupping it with his hand. Jenny raised her voice, aiming it right at him. "It's Xyster. Sounds like Z-Y-S-T-E-R. But that doesn't matter. It's just that he brought things I didn't mean to donate, and now I need to find them." It strained her vocal cords to keep her voice at that intense level. Katy had crossed the room to a large basket by the door and was pawing through it.

"There's nothing in here, Father," she shouted. "I mean, nothing like what she's missing."

The priest was thoughtfully holding up his finger. "Oh! Oh, now I remember. Big Black fellow. But we couldn't take the things because they were all used, and we only accept new items for our 'Market Basket for the Poor' over there. So I am sorry. I don't think we can help you."

The volunteer was nodding with him as he spoke, and Jenny, trying to control her disappointment, shouted, "That's okay. Thank you so much anyhow," and turned to go.

Just then, the priest said, "Oh, wait. There was one thing. A beautiful vase." Jenny whirled back. "A vase?" and the priest, oblivious to her response, meditated, "Ah, yes, such a fine vase. I didn't think anyone would mind if I kept it for my own use. It had been donated, after all. I've put some of those early tulips in it to bring out the yellow shadings of the pattern."

Jenny's mouth had come open, but the volunteer said, "Uhh, didn't it have anything in it, Father?"

"Oh, it was full of dirt and dust. I thought maybe someone had tried to plant in it. I poured the dirt out under the lilac bushes in back and washed the vase up, good as new." He smiled to himself, quite pleased.

The women stared at each other, and Katy managed, "but ... but ..." while Jenny silenced her with a hand motion. "It's okay. It's okay," she said softly. "I understand my mother wasn't Catholic, but ... well, I think she will rest just fine here."

Father Terry was looking anxiously from face to face, trying to lip read the soft-voiced exchange. "Who wasn't Catholic?" he frowned. "I will be happy to go get the vase if you need it, Child."

Both women shouted, "Oh, no! no," and the volunteer said, "No, Father, she says she wants you to keep the vase. She says she isn't Catholic, but the vase has found a good home."

Nodding happily at Jenny, Father Terry said, "Well, thank you. Thank you. I will cherish it. It's such a beautiful piece."

Back in the car, Jenny said to herself, "So there, Brady. And you called my mother's urn ugly." Turning the car in the church driveway, she glanced back and whispered, "Bye, Mama, I love you. I think you'll be happy here—you always loved lilacs." She began to chuckle—what next from life? She was still recalling the Father's unexpected move and chuckling when she reached the old folk's home.

Which turned out to be difficult, and not as amusing. The head nurse recalled Brady and his offering very well. She had sent the toys to the laundry room with instructions to wash all the ones which were washable, and the ones which came out okay were to be distributed among the patients who might appreciate them. "I saw a stuffed rabbit in there," she said. "Mrs. Tavonscic in room 147B has collected rabbits for years, so I thought she might enjoy that. That sort of thing, I thought."

"So ... where are the toys now?"

Baby Skulls and Fowl Odors

"Our people are very busy," the nurse snapped defensively. "This would not be their first priority. The things are probably still in the laundry room."

Hesitantly, Jenny said, "So, may I go look in the laundry room? I just wanted the one doll back. For sentimental reasons."

"Of course. Go right ahead." The nurse turned to her desk and began to fill in forms from a large stack. Jenny stood looking at her back, uncertain what to do next.

Behind her, at the level of her shoulder, a chunky nurse's aide squeaked past a lip ring, causing her to jump and turn. "I heard. The laundry room is in the basement, and I have literally about thirty seconds. Come on, I'll take you."

The toys were stacked on a folding table, a couple in a nearby trash can. It didn't take long to look through them. "None of these?" the girl squeaked, hopeful. She was clutching a sock monkey from the pile.

"No," Jenny said, her voice trailing off. "No ... it's a large, stuffed doll ... "

The girl was smiling at the monkey. "I have one just like this at home. This could be its twin."

"Then you should take it," Jenny said kindly, and began to look in each washer and dryer. The girl sighed, "Thanks," smiled, and stuffed the monkey into the front of her uniform shirt, considerably enhancing her bosom size. Patting her chest, she said, "Josh'd like this," then, "gotta go."

Jenny wandered up the stairs after her, crossed the parking lot, and sat disconsolately in her car. She'd been everywhere. Now what could she do? Closing her eyes, she leaned her forehead on the steering wheel. Just as tears began to burn behind her lids, she heard knocking on the car window. A tall woman with glasses secured on a chain motioned her to roll down the window.

"I have something to tell you, but it must remain between you and me. Can you keep this quiet?" Her whole face had entered the window, forcing Jenny to lean away as she nodded. "We are not supposed to distribute contributions until they have been cleaned and examined, but among those toys you brought was an Indian doll. I've known Alma Weinant for years; she loves dolls, and she makes dolls somewhat like that one. I examined that doll thoroughly and it was in good shape except for very mild wear and tear. Thinking Alma would enjoy it, I took it for her before someone else could get their hands on it. She was supposed to be here for quite some time, for therapy, but apparently the plan changed. They checked her out yesterday, and I think the doll went with her."

"Oh!" Jenny gasped. "Oh, I know Alma, too! I can check for the doll—it must be with her. I need that doll ... it ... it wasn't supposed to be donated. Xy ... oh, the doll means ... "

The woman straightened up, settled the glasses firmly on the end of her nose, and growled, "Just to be clear. You do not tell anyone what I told you. You do not know how Alma got the doll, understand? It's between you and me. No one else. Right? My job could be at stake."

Now Jenny's tension did erupt into tears. "I won't tell anyone. I promise. Thank you! Thank you so much!"

"They don't think I hear anything," Alma sighed, her bunions begging for it to never stop, those gentle pinches and pushes being administered by Jenny. Nestling deeper into the recliner, she continued, "They don't think I hear, Jenny, but I hear a lot, and there was something wrong with that doll. I didn't make that doll, you know. Maybe Lena made it; she used to make dolls like that." At this last, Jenny's eyes widened and she dropped one of the feet as her hand shot to her mouth, but Alma merely wiggled the offended foot impatiently and kept talking. "I know there was something seriously wrong with that doll. Gritty and Carmen were close-mouthed about it all, but I thought I heard them say it was full of gelatin! Now, that certainly does not make sense, does it?"

As long as she massaged, Alma talked, so Jenny had returned to the offended foot. Still, she was now the one left speechless. "Gelatin?" she iterated. Saying it out loud, however, brought it home. Gelatin. Skeleton.

"That's what I thought they said, but you're right, it doesn't make sense. Does gelatin go bad? Is that why they said they were going to bury it? Never in all my years have I heard of gelatin going bad like that."

"*Bury* it!?" It was all she could do to keep her hands from shaking. Steady, girl. "Are you sure they said they were going to *bury* it?" Her over-stressed mind was tumbling. Would that be

Baby Skulls and Fowl Odors

the logical thing to do if you found a skeleton in a doll?

"I'm sure that's what she told me."

Wait. This was getting ... what? "...she told me"? Jenny studied Alma's face. Her eyes were droopy, tired. "Alma, honey, who told you?"

Alma's gaze wandered. "Why, Hallie, of course. Just the other day." A little defensive. "Hallie told me that they had to do something with him after she shot him, so they buried him. They figured no one would miss him."

"Alma, Hallie ... " Jenny started, then stopped. She couldn't say it. It was better that Alma didn't recall that her dearest friend was now dead. Still ... Alma was almost mumbling now. "You know, Hallie told me that I was the only one, the only one she would ever tell. Honestly, I think it tickled her to shoot him and get him out of the way. But I shouldn't have told you. You won't pass this on, will you? You're a good person, so I think I can trust you."

"Oh, I ... I would never tell, Alma. This is yours and Hallie's secret." Jenny felt as if her brow were getting a permanent worry furrow; too many secrets to keep. And the doll clearly wasn't in this room. She ventured, "But Alma ... Do you recall that we were talking about a doll someone sent with you from the retirement home?"

Alma smiled fondly. "Oh, yes. They put that doll next to me and the first thing I did was try to eat a baloney sandwich and get catsup all over her face. Patty brought her home—you know Patty, don't you? She's my home nurse—she brought my things because she knew I was coming home, and she stuck that doll in with my own dolls, but I didn't make that doll, you know. But she was pretty, like one Lena might have made. Gritty and Carmen came over to clean up my things, then Duz got me and brought me home, and I guess ... Oh, maybe it wasn't catsup. You could just sponge off catsup. I think they said the doll was full of gelatin. Red jello, like catsup. That is why they had to bury her."

This last long speech sent Jenny's head spinning. She heard a car entering Alma's drive, probably Patty, back to bring dinner and tuck Alma in. The last thing she wanted was to get into a discussion about the doll with Patty. Too many questions! Trying to keep her voice steady, she asked, "Is the doll here now?"

"Oh, no, dear, of course not. Like I keep saying, the girls said they had to bury it." The nurse's footsteps could be heard on the porch.

Desperate, Jenny burst out, "Where? Where did they say they were going to bury it?"

From the entry, the nurse called out cheerily, "Hi, Alma! You got company?"

Alma called back, "Just come on in, Patty. We're just chatting." Jenny lay the pampered feet on the foot rest and stood, biting her lip, her hands hopeless at her sides, but Alma continued, "I'm pretty sure they said they'd go up and bury it by the tepee. It was Gritty said, or maybe Hallie."

The nurse came in, smiling. "Oh, are you talking about all that fuss up at the tepee, well, not a tepee now, but that new guy's place? I can't believe that crazy Nancy Jane would shoot him in the foot."

Frowning, puzzled, Alma said, "No, it was something else. A doll. Somebody bur ... "

Jenny overrode her. "That's what we were talking about, but I have to go now, and we've had a good visit, anyhow, haven't we?" She bent to kiss Alma on the forehead again. "You have a good night, Almee, and sweet dreams."

When she reached the doorway, Jenny beckoned the nurse to follow her to the porch. "Listen, Patty, I think she may be overtired from club," she whispered. "Kind of hallucinating. She's been telling me things she thinks Hallie just told her this week. I just let it go—I can't remind her that Hallie's gone. You know."

With an understanding nod, Patty whispered back, "Poor old blessed dear. I'll give her a peaceful tuck-in."

Exiting Alma's driveway, Jenny turned right. "What am I doing?" she asked herself. "I need to get on home. Jenny, girl, you know nobody buried anything up by that new guy's place." Still, the car headed left at the next turn, taking Oozle Road. Jilly Brown passed on her way back from somewhere, waving cheerily, and Jenny waved back, wondering absently where Jilly had been since club had adjourned. Fighting the potholes and gravelly corrugates, Jenny twisted on up K-4 Road and pulled out at a bend near Fowler's. Cutting her engine, she hesitantly stepped out.

Baby Skulls and Fowl Odors

She hadn't been here since the tepee had been removed. Now there was a little trailer instead, just down the hill, but everything was quiet. She didn't know what to do next. There seemed to be no one around to ask permission to ... to what? Look for a buried doll? This was ridiculous. Reluctantly, she took a few furtive steps, then a few more, which took her onto the property itself. There were several odd signs scattered all over. What did Fowler mean by that: "No Chickens"? He must have his reasons. They looked so bizarre that in some odd way it gave her courage. I'm not the only weird one, she supposed. She began to look around purposefully.

Had the earth been disturbed anywhere recently? She couldn't tell—pinion, sage, rocks, maybe some loose adobe soil piled a little closer to the trailer, but she didn't want to go that close. It gave her the heebie-jeebies. What about over there, to her left? Was that something out of place, maybe dug at? She heard a motor approaching from the valley below, far down, the sound carrying up the clear air from Oozle Road. Even if it turned up, it would take a while to get here.

Hurrying, dodging cactus, she walked the other twenty feet along the slanted hillside to stare at the pile of mounded dobie soil. Yes, someone had dug here not so long ago! It looked as if the soil had barely been turned, then rocks stacked like a marker near the disturbance. The little mound was part of a larger, slightly depressed area. She wanted to claw at the mound, bare-handed, down through the difficult earth, but the sound of the approaching vehicle stopped her. She had forgotten to listen for it.

Sprinting for her car, she jumped in and shot ahead, pulling up around a concealing turn in the road just as the school van set its blinkers and pulled to a halt, unloading Sienna at the top of her drive. Chuck Fowler emerged from the trailer, hobbling on his crutch and shielding his eyes from the sharp sunlight. "Hey, girl, I'm glad you're home. I just woke up—that pain medicine knocks my pegs out. Makes me sleep like the dead." The van lurched forward, turning off its blinkers to allow the approaching car to pass, Jenny driving and waving innocently at the van driver. A rooster crowed behind Chuck and he grinned. "Well, old buddy, you're as bad as I am. You feel like it's morning, too."

9

SIENNA WAS A LITTLE trapped weasel, her back to the van window, her mouth partly open, teeth bared. This happened every time she rode the bus home. Once they turned onto the Oozle loop from the highway, the few kids remaining on the bus took the opportunity to tease her mercilessly. She wished she could die. She couldn't scrunch away from them, because they changed seats until they had her surrounded. The van driver, whistling an absent-minded little ditty, seemed oblivious to the torture occurring at his back. Sienna took this to mean he was secretly in cahoots with her tormentors.

The big ones did the taunting, while the little ones just leaned in and leered, watching to see what reaction each verbal goad would produce. Brandon said, "Your father deals drugs, doesn't he? He's just like that slimy bastard that lived on that place before you came. Sheriff caught that S.O.B. with every kind of shit all over that tepee, cocaine, Mary Jane, the works, and ain't nobody heard from him since. Mac Biedermann. Sheriff sent the S.O.B. packin.' Nope, ain't nobody heard from the slimy squirrel since. Except maybe your daddy. Yeah, I'll bet your daddy's his agent. Fronts for Mac Biedermann, big drug dealer." Brandon pushed in close and added, "He is, isn't he?"

Patsy butted in. "You have slant eyes. You're a slant eye. Where you from?"

Tiffany's youngest, Larry Gallenas, shifted in his seat. He didn't like this mean stuff. He wished Luke was here, but now that Luke could drive, he stayed after school to do physical training with the other kids interested in the military. This made their mama furious. She didn't want Luke in the military, at least not just yet, but military recruiters swarmed the high school and their career promises and stories lured the poor farm kids like

Baby Skulls and Fowl Odors

the sweet grain that lures in calves that are being weaned from their mama's teats. Larry gazed out the window at the new calves in the fields and pondered what he'd heard the recruiters tell Luke, and how his mama felt about it, and tried to decide how he himself felt about all of this stuff.

Meanwhile, the torture continued. Someone said, "You know your old man's a land thief. Old Barnswallowper wouldn't say it was her land if it weren't. She's a old-timer, and she's honest."

"You got slant eyes. You ain't even American. Where you from?"

"Too bad Barnswallowper didn't aim a little higher. That woulda' solved the whole problem." At this, the smaller kids snickered, pleased to have decoded what aiming higher meant, but Larry turned from the window.

"Lay off her, you damn bullies. Quit pickin' on her." Immediately he regretted it, and regretted it more when one of the pipsqueaks sang out, "Larry's got a girlfriend!" He reddened from his scalp to his collar.

One of the big kids picked it up, saying, "Yeah, little chink jap land-thievin' girlfriend. Real cute choice, Larry."

They had turned up K-4 Road, almost home, but Sienna shot off the seat, kicking, hitting, spitting, and yelling. "Larry isn't my boyfriend and I don't need anyone talkin' for me and you leave me alone and you leave him alone." The driver continued to drive, negotiating turns, and the kids, trying to escape Sienna's fury, were thrown around like livestock in a tornado. Patsy gagged out "eeeooo," wiping frantically at a glob of spit in her hair, while Brandon held his ear, ringing from the impact of a well-directed fist.

"Do I have to stop this bus?" The driver was scowling into his rearview mirror and, at last, his voice was raised. "You kids sit down. Right now. I mean it."

They all sat, but the van was turning the corner just before Sienna's stop and she sprang back to her feet, facing them, panting. "You *shit* asses. Chuck Fowler *bought* this place. It's *our* land. Barnswallowper is a liar. We have buried my *mother* here, my *mother!* And we are going to build a house right next to her grave. Her ghost will keep our house holy, and she will protect us from *shit* asses like you." Her arm rubbed across her face, dragging tears and snot with it, then she dropped down the van steps, everyone staring after her as the driver placidly said, "Now, Sienna."

Chuck Fowler had come out of the trailer and seemed to be smiling and greeting her happily, but she ran past him, giving him a shove, and disappeared behind the trailer. Chuck staggered, grabbing a juniper limb that hung over the path to steady himself on his crutch.

As the bus chugged to a reluctant, mountain-climbing start, Larry continued to look out the window, back at the sad-faced man standing in front of the little trailer. Then he saw the signs. Squinting, he made out "No Chickens." Huh? What did that mean, "No Chickens"? He wished Luke was here.

10

BILLY BROWN, NOT COMPLETELY washed clean of the grease and rust he accumulated during the day while repairing neighbors' farm machinery and personal vehicles, but clean enough, by his calculation, cracked an eye at his wife, sitting propped against the pillows beside him and skimming her fingers briskly across the annoyingly bright, disruptively blinky screen on her iPad. She loved the damn thing, but at 11:00 at night, trying to get some sleep, he seriously regretted having gotten it for her birthday. How did she do it, anyhow? First the morning chores, then the club, then restraining the housewrecking, rowdy twins for a homework session, then twins arguing and falling and needing sympathy and bruise repair, all merging into dinner and baths and teeth, and now on into the night with that thing. Just thinking about it made him tired; his stamina had given out long ago. All he wanted at this point was to spoon around her tough little body and soak himself in sleep.

Looking over, Jilly spotted his slitted eye. "Ah, good. You *are* awake." Pointing her finger at the screen and shaking it slightly she said, "Nancy Jane and that new Fourier woman, they call her Honey, they are just absolutely right. It's all right here! You should read this. Tinker Chicken is just an awful company. They restrain those poor animals in tiny, tiny spaces; they even put their necks in little handcuffs, well, I guess you could call them neckcuffs, so that they can't move. All they can do is sleep and eat from the day they are hatched until the day they are brutally slaughtered." Jilly wiped away tears, thinking of her own fat, contented poultry wandering freely around the farm, searching for bugs, flapping their wings to stretch them, basking in the afternoon sunlight as they kicked to cover their happy, feathery bodies in the dust of the corral. How could Tinker *do* that to a chicken? She tried to show a picture of a confined chicken to Billy, but he had closed his eye again, wishing it was he who was in handcuffs so that all he had to do was eat, and, more importantly, sleep, but Jilly was undaunted. She continued.

"Just listen to this! Even their slogan is disgusting: on every package in the supermarket that contains those poor, tortured animals it says, 'We TINKER with your chicken till it's tender for your tummy.' Ugh! Cannibal bastards." Jilly knew this wasn't a great comparison, since chickens weren't people, but she was getting worked up. Billy sighed, opened both eyes, and rolled toward her as she persisted.

"And Honey, or whichever one of them said it, was right about that poor Fowler. The contracts the small farmers sign with that big, greedy company don't get them any profit, just all the work. And wherever the little farms are will be stinky and dusty and maybe spread disease, just like Nancy Jane said."

Knowing he shouldn't go down this road, but figuring he may as well get it over with, Billy said, "But there's nothing you can do about it, is there?"

For a minute Jilly was silenced, but thinking, then her mouth set in a grim, determined line. "Yes," she declared, "Yes, there is. We can organize. Tomorrow, while the kids are in school, I will get letters off to all the papers, local and even in Denver. And I will contact animal welfare groups — the Humane Society, and, you know, like PETA. They will help us protest. Don't you tell me, Billy Brown, that one person can't make a difference in this world!" Then, as if it were he who had been keeping her awake all this time, urging her to talk, she said firmly, "Now Sweetie, we really shouldn't be staying up this late. I need to get some sleep. I have a lot to do tomorrow. Roll over, okay?"

Obligingly, Billy took a side and Jilly snuggled in behind him, her arms around his wiry chest and her knees pushed up under his butt. For the first time this evening, Billy smiled.

The Browns weren't the only ones awake past their bedtime. By late evening, Sheriff Garrett had come to the realization that although he hadn't known what to expect when he slit her little chest with his pocket knife, it certainly wasn't this. At 9:00 he had been sitting innocently on his patio, trying to soothe himself with Beethoven's "Archduke" piano trio — he loved classical music — and a tall, stemmed glass of good Merlot, but nothing about the previous two days was right, and he couldn't rest. Pat Garrett was a man of powerful intuitions. He knew that the correct thing, the legal thing, would be to turn that doll in to Forensics and let them check it out, but some irritating, indefinable hunch was holding him back. He realized that the problem wasn't going to yield to reason. Even so, why had the Croysant area, which had been quiet since the Biedermann case, suddenly become a beehive of unusual activity? A doll with a skeleton in it? A fire at the Cowpath Saloon, maybe endangering Jenny? Rumors of a possibly illegal chicken farm? There couldn't be a connection, could there? He pulled a footstool toward himself and raised his feet. Reason told him that the only thing with which he should concern himself was the dratted doll. The fire had been explained as an accident, and the chicken farm was just a rumor. The doll, however, was lying on the couch in his living room. Right. It was clearly the doll that made him restless.

Yielding, he got up and ambled back into the house. He turned on the light and stared down at the little stuffed creature, whose lopsided face, like anyone's face, now hid her skull once again. Like anyone's face, except hers was held in place by safety pins. Except for the red smear on her cheek, she was a pretty little thing. He ran his finger along the smear; he was more and more convinced that the stain was movie blood: catsup. This suspicion fed his intuition that there was not something criminal going on here, but something innocent. Still, he felt guilty. He knew he should take it to the lab for analysis.

Sighing, he sat beside the doll and pulled down the top of the carefully decorated little white leather dress. Her exposed body was a taut, chubby tube. Sighing again, he mumbled to himself, "And just how many times has curiosity killed your cat, Garrett?" Pulling his knife from his pocket, he opened the slender blade he always kept sharp and added a phrase he'd heard his daddy say. "Guess they can kill me, but they can't eat me." Pushing the tip of the blade in where an upper rib might be found on a real person, he began to make a short, careful slit.

What had he expected to encounter—a rib bone? A chunk of commercial toy stuffing like what women use from a craft store? A wad of kapok? He found none of these. He had barely begun to cut when a fluffy substance the brownish color of half-pulled taffy oozed out at him. He stopped cutting. The slit had only reached four inches long, but the stuff, under pressure, kept leaking out. It was as soft as eiderdown or the fur of a baby bunny, its fluffy aspect punctuated by tiny bright lines which looked like short-tailed comets in a cloud nebula. He was pretty sure he had encountered stuff like this when he was a kid, hunting blackbirds in cattail-filled swamps near his house. What was it doing in a doll? He tried to push it back and it did compress, but then followed his fingers back out as he removed them.

His big bald head shining in the lamplight, he rubbed his nose in bewilderment. Some of the stuff had clung to his hand, sending him into a vigorous sneezing fit, the air bursting from the sneezes wafting puffs of the stuff away from the slit and across the room. Recovering himself, he said, "Well. Sooner started, sooner done." Taking a deep breath, he shoved his thick index finger into the tiny chest. He felt like a cardiac surgeon. The finger tip encountered a hard object. Now he tried in vain to hook whatever it was with his bent fingertip. No such luck.

Sighing yet a third time, he stood, dusted the clinging fluff as best he could from hands and face, and began a foray around the house. Somewhere he had a pair of long tweezers—damn it all, where had he left them? He searched the kitchen, then had a revelation and opened the door to the back porch. A brisk evening breeze had come up, cooling his cheeks, but glancing back, he realized that the down released from the doll's chest was blowing around the entire room. Grabbing the tweezers from the shelf, he hurried in, pulling the door shut hard against the rising wind.

As he struggled to bring the hard object out of the chest and into the light, fluff stuck to his hands, clothing, ears, and hair ... Like Lady Macbeth, wracked with guilt and the uncertainty of unexpected consequences, he sneezed forth the words, "Out, damned stuffing!" Finally, the hard object succumbed, allowing itself to be pulled past the muffling fluff. It was, indeed, a bone. He knew it would be. His money was on it being a rib, part of the rib cage of a small child.

He returned as much of the fuzzy stuff to the inside of the doll as he could and awkwardly pinched the wound shut, securing it with duct tape. Then he pulled out the vacuum and chased floaters for a while, a game, the vacuum exhaust blowing the many hither and thither even as the suction tube took in the few.

Baby Skulls and Fowl Odors

Finally, feeling very tired, he pushed the vacuum aside, promising himself to finish in the morning.

Lying in bed, he still felt that same sixth sense that he shouldn't report this. But why? What was blocking him? What was it, after all, that he should do? Sleep wouldn't come. Jenny drifted inexplicably into and out of his mind. Pointless. She had a boyfriend now — he needed to let her go. As if he ever had her. But ... back to the doll ... what a weird, but strangely appealing, community, was Croysant. His eyes were closed and he felt himself drifting into that lovely, pre-sleep state. Behind his lids he saw the Croysant church sign. He always looked for the church billboard when he drove up to that area; usually he was rewarded with a spicy or amusing new saying. Yesterday ... was it yesterday? ... yesterday the sign had said, "Weather report: God reigns, son shines." Behind his lids he imagined the sign blinking quietly off and on, off and on, like a commercial neon sign in the city, or like a busy iPad. It was soothing: blink blink weather report blink blink God reigns blink blink son shines blink blink God rains ... rains ... rains ... His lids flew open. It was raining, the earlier sharp breeze having brought in a little weather. Drops splattered on the roof, and the room was cold.

Suddenly, it was clear to him what he must do, but not now. In the morning. For tonight, he must do something else. Heavily, the big man unfolded his long body from his bed and padded back to the living room. His large ears jutted in the pale light, and the heavy scar that ran from cheek to chest shadowed his rough face. Fumbling along the couch back, he found the blanket Carmen had sent with the doll when he brought her here from Alma's. Gently, he shook it open and then spread it across the little thing, making sure her tiny, toeless feet were covered and that the blanket was well up under her chin.

"Nighty night. Don't let the bed bugs bite. And I pray the Lord your soul did take."

Only then did Garrett pad back to bed and finally slip into a deep, dreamless sleep.

11

"**CAN I COME HOME** with Luke?"
"6:30 latest"
"K"

So. No Larry on the bus. Tiffany dropped her phone in her pocket and glanced furtively up the supermarket aisle. Shopping in Peaseford inevitably meant encountering friends and neighbors. Did they really all want to visit, or did they just think it was you who wanted to talk, so they stopped, compelled to be social, and nattered endlessly away, gossip and weather, while you looked hopelessly at the Cocoa Puffs you needed, unreachable just beyond their left shoulder. Whatever, she thought. Anyhow, sometimes she enjoyed chatting. It was just that tonight she was really drained. Part of supporting her family involved cleaning motels in Aspen two days a week, and this was one of those days. The drive over the pass was a back killer, but that wasn't the real source of her exhaustion. The last couple of days had brought up serious problems, and she needed down time to mull them over. It was going to help having the boys come home later, if she could just make it out of this store unimpeded.

She eased into the dairy aisle, saw Frieda loading butter and cheese into her basket, backed up and started to take the canned vegetable and pasta route, noticed Gritty at the end, talking to Patty Harris, reversed again and lurked at the end of frozen foods. A friendly stocker flattened a packing box and greeted, "Hi! Finding everything all right?"

"Oh, sure, fine, I am," she smiled, and fled. Further down the aisle, she examined her cart, distracted. *Had* she found everything? Maybe. Snagging two large all-meat pizzas and a gallon of ice cream from the display, which had lights that went on and off disconcertingly as you passed the doors, she thought, "There, that's supper," put the cart into high gear, made it past a helpful clerk at the front, and did her own check out.

Pulling out of the lot, she wondered idly why Luke let Larry ride with him. Usually Larry's status as a twelve-year-old was far beneath Luke's elevated seventeen-year-old horizons. Did Luke need to extort gas money from his little brother again? Then she dismissed it. Aloud, she said, "Damn it all, Nancy Jane." She shook her head, feeling stymied by the woman.

Traffic was bad today, a truck and trailer with hay bales in front of her and two cars behind. The truck slowed her, the cars tailgated. Passing the church, she glanced at what the billboard had to say this time. "Hell is totally not cool."

"Tell me about it," Tiffany mumbled. Just then, the farthest back of the two cars shot past them all, barreling over the yellow line and up the hill. Tiffany shrugged. "Go to hell," she urged. "That wasn't cool." She knew the driver, a distant uncle, a drinker, the kind of guy that sent her EMT button into overdrive.

Everyone in these darned little communities was related. Nancy Jane, for example, was Tiffany's second cousin, or was it first cousin, once removed? At any rate, Hallie Flute had been aunt to Tiffany, her sister's child, and great-aunt to Nancy, the age discrepancy accounted for by Hallie's first brother being so much older. Foof. When Hallie died last year, the family all agreed that Tiffany, as a closer relative and favorite niece, should inherit the property, but it was no big favor. The old ranch house was falling down, and the whole ranch was mortgaged up the ying/yang. As she pulled into the drive, Tiffany surveyed her ramshackle home with a mixture of fondness and resentment. Now she was stuck here, struggling with this old family legacy, and money had become a big issue. She had loved Hallie a lot, but it was that attachment that had gotten her in the wrong place at the wrong time, creating this big problem with Nancy Jane. Tiffany knew why Nancy was so upset with Chuck Fowler, and it didn't have to do with chickens.

Hallie's kitchen had old-fashioned cabinets, the kind with some of the shelves forbiddingly tall for height-challenged people like Tiffany. Rather than get a stool, Tiffany set aside some items for Luke to put away when he got home: Luke, who suddenly and shockingly had to bend way, way down to hug his strong little mama; Luke, who was becoming a lot like his father in some ways, but not as easily disposed of. Not that that had been easy. Not that she wanted to dispose of the kid. Kurt had been so full of belligerence and control, but she put up with it until he hit their daughter, the boys' older sister, Lisa. At that point, she was out of there. She tried to refuse all financial aid from that man, hoping to get him completely away from the kids and out of her life, but Social Services caught up with him, anyhow. Once in a while, apparently when the man wasn't in jail and was actually working, she would get child support checks that had been collected by Social Services. It was never even close to enough. The real bills were paid by her working her tail off at whatever jobs she could get.

Now Luke was exhibiting the same stubborn tendencies as his father, bent on the military despite her objections, bossing Larry. What the hell? Was it DNA? How do you deal with hating the father and adoring the damned sweet kid? So, is it DNA? Couldn't be. Luke wasn't even close to being like his father. He was just a teenager, testing his strengths, pushing boundaries. So she must believe.

Popping the tab on a can of Coors, Tiffany put her feet up. She berated herself. "I need to let all that shit go. Old news. The real problem has nothing to do with the kids. It's Nancy Jane." The little hot head was taking the wrong approach and had been from the first. Tiffany didn't want to fight the sheriff and the neighbors and march around with "No Chickens" signs. That was just stupid. She was glad to be living here; she liked the people and fresh air and open spaces; she just wanted to get along in the community.

She glanced up at the clock. 7:45. Where were those two yahoos, anyhow? Give 'em the mother's five minutes, then worry. Picking up the paper, she glanced at the headline: "Steel Valley shuts down Pitman Mine." Yeah, right, that's why she didn't want a coal mining job—you just got going, then there was a cave-in or a mine fire or the economy shifted, and whoops! Back out on the street. If you were lucky, and not squashed. Or blown to hell. Not cool. Better to clean motels and home care the old folks.

The mother's five worked. It did every time. At 7:50, the boys burst in the door with their "sorry, moms." It seemed they were low on gas, as usual, and "had to run into Peaseford to get

Baby Skulls and Fowl Odors

a couple gallons." This excuse was one of the more amusing that she had heard. If you were already low on gas, why would you drive over twelve miles to another town to get "a couple gallons"? Plus why didn't they get it when they were actually in Peaseford when they left school, thus saving time and pocket money? Of course, she knew the answer. She could smell the Dr. Pepper on Larry, and Luke's drink would have been a Monster. She didn't bother to nag. She figured that kids need to hang out.

She started to go into the kitchen to pull the pizza from the oven, but Larry said, "Wait, Mom, we ..." and Luke finished, "... wanted to tell you something." Continuing past them, she said, "Okay, talk. I'm here." What now? She couldn't see his truck from the window. Had Luke put a new dent in it? You'd never know — it would be camouflaged by the dozens already riding with the kid.

Larry started, "It's about that ..." and Luke finished, "... new guy up Oozle Road, Chuck Fowler."

She pulled the pizza. "Okay, so. What?"

"I guess we were ... " Larry began.

"Kind of snoopy ... " Luke finished. "But Fowler's daughter, Sienna, gets bullied on the bus." Tiffany looked around sharply.

"Oh, that's no good. Those Clayton kids?"

"Yeah, some of it, but it's not about them. It's about ... " from Larry, "... what she said." From Luke. "I wasn't there, but Larry told me the kids called her slant-eyes."

"Slant-eye," Larry corrected.

"You said slant-eyes when you told me," from Luke.

"I did not. I said they called her a slant-eye."

"Well, when you told me, you said slant-eyes."

"I did not. That doesn't make sense."

"It makes as much sense as slant-eye, and it's what you said."

"It is not. Having slanty eyes is different from being A slant-eye, so I didn't say slant-eyes, I said ..."

"You're just mixed up. I heard you say slant-eyes ..."

Tiffany, her forehead bonking in her hand, said, "Oh, you people, please! It doesn't f—ing matter, okay? Shut up and tell me what you're trying to tell me."

They were at the table, having sat, as a unit, during the altercation. Larry, speaking through a mouthful of pizza, started,

"Well, anyhow, they bullied her. So she got really mad and started ..."

"Kicking and hitting and spitting and ..."

"Shut UP!" Larry's voice, not yet changed to a male bass, suddenly gave an unexpected rumble and squeak. "Shut up, Luke, you shit ass. This is *my* story."

"But you said. You told me, and it was me drove you up there."

It was like watching a tennis match. Tiffany interjected, "You took him up *where?* Why?"

Somehow, Luke managed to emit words as he chewed a huge bite of his fourth slice. "Because when she freaked out she said ..."

Fighting weak and unmanly tears, Larry started to stand. "Luke, this is *my* story. I'm not gonna sit around here and listen to you piss-mangle it. I'm gonna kill you."

Putting a hand on both boys' arms, thus restraining the youngest from homicide, Tiffany said, "No, you're not. Don't even talk that way. And Luke, let him tell the damn story. Just shut up a minute, okay? And Larry, clean up your shitty little mouth. You don't need to cuss about everything, damn it!"

Mollified, Larry said, "Luke's right. She did get freaked out. So when she got off the bus she hollered at everybody and told them ..."

Luke couldn't hold it in. "She told them they had buried her mother on that place so that she could haunt it and protect it from everyone."

Tiffany frowned. "Oh, come on, guys, you don't really believe that, do you? They've only been there a few weeks, and there's never been a sign of a mother to even die."

"They probably brought her corpse with them," Larry said enthusiastically.

"Oh, no, kids, I think that little Sienna was just upset. I don't think it's even legal to bury somebody on your property. She had to say something to make herself sound big. We just need to see what we can do about the bullying."

"But Mom," Larry began, and Luke continued, "Mom, we went up there. Larry whined and begged, told me something weird is going on there, and talked me into driving him up there. He said there were weird signs about chickens and everything, and he wanted to see them and see what was going on, so after he kept *whin*ing I told him I'd take him, and sure enough, we saw Sienna by a grave."

Larry's arms were folded across his chest and he had slumped into his chair, eyes narrowed, grumping, "I didn't f—ing whine. You told me you wanted to go."

Tiffany's reaction was more marked. She'd gotten very quiet, and now she said slowly, "By a grave? What do you mean, by a grave? Just what, exactly, did you two see, anyhow?"

Fixing Luke with a shriveling, silencing glare, Larry said, "I will tell you what we saw, Mom. We saw Sienna in that yard by a pile of dirt, you know how dirt looks when it's been all dug up? It was like that. And she was holdin' flowers. Leaning over, like to put them on that dirt. And Luke slowed way down and she looked up, and I'm pretty sure she was bawlin'. Tears, I think, but she saw us, you know, so..."

"I had to speed up and get the hell out of there." Satisfied, Luke wrapped it up. "But it really is a weird place."

Tiffany's face had taken on a strange look, and though she was staring at the boys, they weren't sure she was seeing them.

12

THE PROBLEM WOULD BE HONEY. As for himself, Garfield Fourier loved life; he loved America; he loved Croysant; and he loved his property and big log house. When he had completed his contract obligations in Iraq, he couldn't wait to get back home and be part of his country again. He loved standing in this high-beamed living room, the tang of the spruce logs always permeating the bright air, the firewood in tidy stacks beside the massive rock fireplace. Savory aromas from Honey's cooking were now wafting toward him, cheese stuffed meat loaf, collard greens, and some innovative fruit compote designed from fresh blueberries and frozen peaches. His mouth watered and his belly rumbled in contented anticipation.

Sure, the guy who had lived here before them had been murdered, but that didn't bother him. According to what people said, Biedermann had been a bad apple and probably deserved it. Garfield had seen death more than once in Iraq; one dead no-good was no worse than another. He sipped his chai and considered human misery in general, feeling charitable. One should start with one's neighbors was his philosophy. Take Fowler over there. That poor man, with his aching foot and his cranky daughter, hurt by some family emotional upheaval. Garfield planned to go to Fowler's again; he wanted to help. So far, the man kept insisting that they, he and Sienna, were doing just fine, but Garfield could see that he was dealing with a loner. The man was in pain, just too proud to accept neighborly assistance.

He gazed out the huge window at the mountains that rose in increasingly elevated sequences, peaks and shoulders appearing behind closer peaks and shoulders until the eye was lifted on into the sky. Right square on in front of him was Fourier Ridge, almost just a foothill compared to the mountains rising behind it,

Baby Skulls and Fowl Odors

but he didn't care. His chest swelled just to think of it, that it belonged now to Honey and him. His heritage. Where his ancestors stopped their rolling wagons and set up their lumber business, the forest free, the Utes just departed. It was holy to him; he would be sure it was preserved, honoring the Native Americans who had been uprooted from this place, making sure old-growth juniper and pinion, and higher up, aspen and spruce, were not disturbed. The wildlife here would be safe, too, on his watch. He could see the little access road from here, trailing from their driveway to disappear into the sage, and, he knew, to climb the mountain on into heavy timber. He planned to use that road regularly, to make sure all was well there.

There was even a fine little stream running through, South Oozle, 'Oozle' being misspelled, as often happened with the early settlers. They had intended to name it after the little water bird, the ouzel, that dipped and bounced in and out of the sparkling stream. How green they looked, the mountains, already this spring. Locals complained about drought, always fussing about irrigating water. This did irritate Garfield. They should see Iraq, damn it, if they wanted to see dry. Take care of what you have, was his philosophy. Nurture your neighbors and your own forest; that's what he believed.

"Ten minutes, Gar," Honey sang out. Jolted from his reverie, Garfield bit his lip. Yes, it would be Honey who was the hitch in all his dreams and plans. Honey. She loved him, so she was putting on a brave front for his sake, but he knew this place jarred her. What could he do? How could he help her shift to his own joy in the area?

Strolling to the table, he put out napkins and plates, one of the few things she would let him do in her kitchen. He ventured, "So, sweetheart, how are you feeling by now about this community, now that you're getting to know them?"

He noted the slight hesitation, then she said, "Well, they seem like good-hearted people." A pause. "Most of them."

"Most of them?" he smiled. She was no doubt right about that.

"I'm not sure quite how to explain it. Remember how yesterday I got left holding Nancy Jane's gun? You know how I feel about guns. Still, I don't sense that Nancy is a bad sort. On the one hand, she seems to feel the need to be armed, but on the other ... well, she's certainly not one of those cultish militants, either. Maybe she's Tea Party. Or maybe she just has a valid point about that Chuck Fowler. I really don't want a chicken farm this close to us, either." The greens were on the table, and meat loaf slices were being carefully placed on a fine china platter. Honey continued, "I haven't seen *anybody* of color around here, unless you count Mexicans."

"They say Jenny Threewinds has a Black boyfriend."

"They say. I haven't seen him. And from what I hear, Jenny is a little more ... well, more easy-going than some. Honestly, Gar, I think there may be a lot of racial prejudice here, if you run into it."

Sitting down and unfolding their napkins on their laps, they took a few bites in thoughtful silence. Then Garfield said, "Well, I hate to admit it, but I stopped to help some guy with his calves yesterday. He was vaccinating them, and whenever a black one would stop and fight the chute he'd swear at it and call it a 'damn stubborn little nigger.'"

Before he could continue, Honey burst out, "Yes! That's what I mean. The prejudice is like a bad spice in the broth. There's an underlying bad taste. It ruins the soup! The other day at Coffin's Country Store I heard some woman going on at length about 'Obama, that damned nigger.' Gar! She was talking about our president! The president of our country! How can people do that?"

The food had lost some of its allure. Garfield slumped in his chair. "I don't know. I really don't know. I have never understood intolerance. Surely the people we are talking about don't represent the real community values. Not this beautiful community we have adopted."

Honey had stopped eating. She was looking into his eyes unconvinced, disturbed. "Oh, Gar, you are such a good man."

Wanting to commiserate, he leaned toward her to put a consoling hand on her shoulder. Then he forgot, and his fingers began to rove, gently stroking her head. Honey immediately stiffened and snapped, "Not the hair, Gar! You know better than that. You must not touch my hair!"

13

HILLBILLY LILY was a cowboy poet divorcée. She held a guitar decorated with spurs, coyotes, the bleached skulls of steers, and a violent splash of pink roses, all painted randomly across the shiny white guitar body. As for herself, she, too, wore a flowered white lacquer of good cheer. It was the age-old story. She loved Gene, but he drank too damn much and she had to kick him out, meaning that her life thereafter must be marked by a determinedly happy front. Right now, she was shouting out her poetry at the assembled crowd, ending each verse with a vigorous, discordant strum and a hefty slap at the guitar. Perhaps the hapless instrument was Gene.

The poem she was reciting was called "Shootin' Up the Herd." Jenny, parked in a seat at the back near the door, squirmed and squinted toward the window, trying to see if it was dark outside yet. It looked dark, but then the room was bright, so you couldn't tell. The evening seemed to last forever.

> We headed up all them cows
> Damn sure cranky old sows
> And we said, 'Boys, let's go make some hay.'
> TWANG! THUMP!
> But ol' Johney Boy Bob had his gun
> We never knew he was on the run
> Till he shot in the air and hollered, 'Whoopee Ti Yi Yay!'
> TWANG! THUMP!

The little white-haired chap at Jenny's left elbow leaned in to whisper, "Whyn't they ask you? You ain't never played that bad at the Cowpath. I mean, I don't mean you play bad. Your guitar playin' is real purty. It sure isn't as bad as Lily's." He still wasn't sure he had said what he meant, and started to explain more, but Jenny shook her head toward him, smiled, and shrugged a meaningful, eyebrows-raised, "I don't know."

She did know. This was a fund-raising potluck to raise money to help restore the old saloon after the fire, and they had asked her to play for them, but she just felt too distracted to do it. She simply had to find that doll. Tonight, she'd brought a platter of vegetables, nibbled a few bites of someone's spicy casserole which boasted cheese and burger with Fritos crumbled on top, and tried to mingle with the neighbors. She hoped that was enough. Would it ever get dark?

> *We'll get us a good ol' stampede*
> *Erase all my tracks like I need*
> *And keep the damned snoopy sheriff away.*
> *TWANG! THUNK!*
> *The night she were hot and real sultry*
> *Them cows they just scattered like poultry*
> *And little Roy cried, "We all got hell to pay."*
> *THUNK! THUNK! TWANG TWANG TWANG!*

Cowboy Lily stepped dramatically toward the crowd for the grand finale, something involving frightening lightning, but Jenny had escaped. Her nerves were in shreds; she could sit still no longer. The night, quiet under a sliver of moon, was a sharp contrast with the bright, bustling community room. Disoriented, she reassured herself, "You gotta do what you gotta do." The doll just couldn't be there, but she needed to get this step out of the way. She had to be sure. She'd seen the mound of soil, maybe recently dug. She had to look, then she would decide what to do next.

By the time she turned up K-4 Road, it was good and dark, the quarter moon shimmering toward her from above the mountains, only occasionally silenced by a small, drifting cloud that would then busily skitter on by, releasing the pale light again. "I don't suppose Lily's poetry is all that bad," she thought. "Rhyming 'sultry' and 'poultry' was kind of an interesting choice." She pulled out into a flat place on the verge, far below Chuck Fowler's trailer. The sound of a lone engine would carry in these mountains. Trudging up the hill by the faint moonlight and swinging the shovel as she walked, she almost felt like whistling a happy tune, then the shovel slipped from her hand and clinked loudly on the rocks as it hit the road. Pouncing, and throttling the delinquent shovel, she held her breath, listening,

Baby Skulls and Fowl Odors

but nothing stirred. What would she say if Chuck Fowler or his daughter really did see her on their place? Or was it Nancy's — she didn't know. Maybe she should say, "Nancy Jane dropped her gun and she sent me to pick it up." In her adrenalin-charged state, this witticism struck her as incredibly funny. She snorted and stopped walking until she could control the fit of giggles that was overtaking her.

The "No Chickens" signs were still there, shining wanly in the moonlight. The trailer was dark, no lights, no sounds. It was difficult to get her bearings as she cast the beam of her flashlight around among the bushes. Once, the light reflected off the window of the backhoe parked in the brush to the east. Jenny cringed. Had someone turned the light on in the backhoe cab? She protectively hit the switch to black herself out, and the cab light went off, too. "Seriously, Jenny?" she lectured herself. Steadying her breath, she tried working her light systematically across the terrain, searching for the area that had taken her attention in the daylight. Where had she seen that disturbed dirt? A few steps in, move the light, look again. Step in more, sweep the light across, now look. Some of the heavy clay soil had been shaded by foliage and was still damp from the storm earlier in the week. She felt it clinging persistently to her shoes, and bit her lip. Her tracks would be all over out here. What did she think she was doing, anyhow? She meant no harm, but she had to face it. Here she was, an adult, trespassing. She wished she could just ask permission, but how? "Mr. Fowler, could I see if somebody buried my doll on your property?" Yeah, like she could really get a long way with that! She took another hesitant series of steps, and the brush opened out.

There it was, the slightly depressed cleared area she had seen yesterday, the mound of freshly turned earth next to it, the rocks on the mound — just as she remembered it. With a sigh of something like relief, she propped the flashlight so that the beam illuminated as much as possible of the small clearing. She would tackle the mound and if it was all a false alarm — oh, she was so sure it was — she'd restore it just as she found it and get the hell out of here. This was creepy. Admittedly, not more creepy than the original circumstances surrounding her doll, she thought wryly, but still, creepy.

She lifted the rocks off the mound. There was a flat stick in them, like the sticks used to mark off rows in a garden. Poor Fowler! She was probably tearing up his first planting of the year! She held the stick to the light and made out the letters SEF, tidily printed in black. SEF? Sunflower Blank Blank ... Sick Elfin Fairy ... what did SEF stand for? Who knew. She tossed the stick to the side and picked up her shovel. There wouldn't be a doll here. Alma was just a confused old woman. Still, she had come this far ...

Gently, she pushed at the soil on the mound. Yes, it had been dug recently. It was very soft. That jerk who had lived over there with Alice, in the tepee, before Fowler came, that Mac Biedermann, had grown a lot of pot and stuff. And everyone knew he hit Alice. Surely that wasn't what Fowler was up to. Not hitting Alice, but growing pot. With marijuana legal in Colorado, did he plan to have a pot farm? This train of thought made her nervous, and she picked up the flashlight and cast the beam around herself, an entire circle. After all, Mac's father had been murdered. Drug dealers scared her.

Nothing. Everything still as ... still as death. She gave herself a firm mental shake. Back to work. Quickly, now. The whole mound excavated, down to the rocky base. Surprise! No buried doll. Hurrying, she started shoveling dirt back to make it a mound again. It didn't seem as high as it had been. It always seemed like the dirt you took from a place never equaled the dirt you needed to put back. Trying to loosen soil next to it to add to make the mound higher, she cringed as her shovel again hit a rock, clanging loudly. Darn. All the area around the mound was too hard and rocky, except for the depressed area. It would be easier to get all the dirt from there, and what did it hurt? Whatever dirt she used was going to be noticeably out of place if Fowler happened to look out here, anyhow, and her tracks were everywhere. She stepped down and took a generous spadeful of the looser dirt in the depression, hoping she wasn't digging up Fowler's radish seeds or something. A second scoop. One more should do it, and she could leave. She was feeling silly. And very alone.

A slight wind whispered down her collar, tugging at the hair along her neckline, raising goosebumps. She shivered. The trailer was still dark and quiet, although she thought now that she could hear a shuffling sound from the area behind it,

Baby Skulls and Fowl Odors

perhaps an animal. There was a drowsy "pluck pluck." Was it a cluck? Fowler's mythical chickens? Trying to kid with herself she muttered, "Probably Nancy Jane, lurking over there ready to reclaim her land." It wasn't funny this time. She knew she had been digging on the land that Nancy said was hers, and Nancy Jane Barnswallowper had been known to carry a gun.

Jenny stomped heavily on the shovel, striving to get the blade deep, anxious to finish. She pulled out a final scoop of dirt and tipped it on top of the mound. Just as she said, "Okay, then," something white caught the faint moonlight. Frowning, she brought her flashlight beam to bear on the object. Just a bone. No big deal. Bones were common in the country—maybe a gnawed deer leg, left here by a busy coyote. She knelt and brushed the dirt away to get a better look. It looked like ... well, it looked like a human hand. Skeletal. Maybe a little tissue still attached, not much. No, seriously. It couldn't be—a hand? She felt herself pale; a heavier cloud covered the moon, darkening the hillside, causing the wind to intensify and throwing out a mountain nighttime chill. No, this was too creepy, too unreal! It had to be a paw. A dog, a coyote ...

She picked up the bones to look more closely and something loose fell, hitting a rock on the mound with a soft clink. She jerked the light beam toward whatever had dropped. A ring! Coyotes ... Coyotes don't wear rings. She shuddered. What else was down there? Cautiously, she set the bones back down and turned her head, staring over her shoulder at the depression from which she'd removed the dirt. Her own hand was shaking. No, her whole body was shaking! What had she gotten herself into? What should she do?

If she left it, someone could take it. Then no one would believe her. But would they need to? Of course not—she'd just walk away, take her shovel and flashlight, head home, and not tell anyone. She wouldn't be involved at all, right? But you couldn't just not report a human hand, could you? Her head swam. "Keep the damned snoopy sheriff away. Twang. Thunk."

Making a frantic grab for the bones and the ring, she gathered them clumsily together and dumped them back in the hole. Snatching at the rocks, she jammed them on the mound, cramming the stick haphazardly in their midst. With her foot, she shoved dirt over the bones, then covered the disturbed hole with a rock. Gripping the shovel and light as if they were struggling to break free and race her to the car, she headed for the road, heedless of the crackling sounds she made as she pushed the underbrush aside.

Then she stopped. "Damned snoopy sheriff?" What was she thinking? Patrick wasn't snoopy. She visualized his big, ugly face with the shiny, shaved head. Ugly, but wise. Wise, hard-working, and kind. And way too shy. Pushy or snoopy? If only.

Sighing, she turned back toward the mound. She could never dump on Pat Garrett. As she unearthed the skeletal hand again, she told herself, "I'm really going to have a lot of explaining to do. I really am."

14

EDITH OVIEDO HIT the 'send' key, then looked up to acknowledge her boss. "What's up, Sheriff?"

"Look, A-deet, I need a few minutes private time with Deputy McCracken and Asa. No phone calls, no interruptions, no pizza deliveries, okay?"

When Garrett had first learned that Edith wanted the Spanish pronunciation of her name, it had shocked his tongue, but by now the 'Adeet' came easily, as did the light-hearted kidding. Responding to his request, Edith said, "Not even pizza? So who's bringing the reefer, ay? Can I join you?"

"Not today, señorita. And I'd advise you to keep your mouth shut to the D.A. about this little get-together." Although he grinned at her as he turned to go, she could see that his heart wasn't in it. For some reason, the man was serious, and he was preoccupied.

When he reached his office, Garrett wasn't at all surprised to find Detective Asa Hobbs slouched in the disreputable earth-brown easy chair. After all, one reason Garrett kept this example of seating dereliction was because he knew how much his old friend liked to sit in it. He also was not surprised to see McCracken's wild red-haired mop bent over her cell phone, her fingers swirling across the screen as the creature in her hand emitted occasional snorts. It was as if she were frantically conquering a small, viciously unruly animal. He gave a disgusted snort of his own, moving his nicotine-free wintergreen chew back and forth against his lower lip.

His deputy had sure changed over the past year since she discovered Red and texting. He used to wish she would quit calling him "chief" and greeting his every move with her over-wrought expectations. She'd acted as if he were Superman, ready to save the world, and he had felt set up, unable to fit the hero mold she'd picked for him. Now she was always texting, and most of it seemed to be with the man she had at first called "Red, that big lummox of a kid." Garrett wasn't sure what the attraction was, but if he had to guess he would have said that McCracken was enjoying having gained control of someone a lot larger than herself. Her rare conversations with her boss now were peppered with comments of the "I just told Red to do that" and "I just sent Red there" variety. Since her control of Red as a boyfriend hadn't so far interfered with Garrett's need to keep his two deputies in line, he let it all go.

Both Asa and McCracken looked up questioningly as he entered the room. He was pleased to note that McCracken even ignored a snort from her phone to ask, "What's up, Chief?" He closed the door behind him, and to the surprise of his deputy and detective, he turned the lock.

"I asked A-deet to keep it quiet for us for a few minutes. This is a personal and private matter. I need to talk to you two as friends. Not official capacity. Trusted friends." He emphasized 'trusted.' Now he really had their attention. Garrett was known as a lone thinker, rarely confiding in anyone. They could see that the effort to do so now was making him uncomfortable. As he said "trusted friends" his color had risen, painting his face scarlet from scar to shaved dome. McCracken, eyes wide, clicked the 'off' button on her phone.

Garrett ignored his desk and sat on a folding chair beside them, causing the already small office space to feel even more crowded. Clearing his throat, he pulled at his skinny mustache, then took a snuff box from his shirt pocket. "Like I say, this is a personal problem," he repeated, then cleared his throat again. "I don't want what we talk about today to leave this room. Consider it privileged information." He opened the snuff box, pinched something between his thumb and index finger, and handed it to Hobbs. "Asa, do you know what this is?" McCracken crowded her chair closer and leaned in, peering at the material in Hobbs' hand.

Asa Hobbs was a miracle in a hefty, toadlike body. He had an eidetic memory. Garrett had never known him to forget names and faces, and he seemed to keep at hand a rich supply of other facts, too, stored from deep in his childhood experiences as

Baby Skulls and Fowl Odors

well as from information gleaned from copious reading, gobbled like candy. Now he rubbed the stuff between his fingers as McCracken scowled, puzzled. "Well, sure, Pat, I know what it is and so do you. It's cattail down. So, what's up?"

"Cattail down." Garrett nodded as if confirming a suspicion. "Cattail. Found everywhere, or just certain areas?"

"Found everywhere in this country, swamps, shallow water ... so what's this all about, Pat?"

"Cattail have lots of uses?"

Asa Hobbs closed his eyes, thinking. McCracken looked anxiously from one man's face to the other, baffled. Secretly pleased that he had her puzzled, Garrett mentally labeled his sense of satisfaction as petty, and was careful not to let his face betray it. Meanwhile, eyes still closed, Hobbs began to mutter, as if drawing from some deep well of trivia lodged inside his brain. "*Typhaceae*," he said. "*Typha angustifolia* and *Typha latifolia*. Beautiful plants. Damn right. They're useful."

He opened his eyes, contemplating the downy fur between his fingers. "Indians used 'em for everything—used the dry stalks to make mats and bags, mixed this down with animal fat to make poultices to heal cuts, bruises, burns ... and they ate it. Every part of this plant is edible. Euell Gibbons, that great naturalist, he called the cattail the 'supermarket of the swamps.' You eat the first shoots; you eat the core of the young plant, both like salad, or asparagus. Eat the pollen spike, like corn-on-the-cob. Shake the pollen off into wheat flour to enrich the protein content, or just dig up the roots later to make your own flour. Dry 'em, peel 'em, and pound 'em up. Very nutritious.

"You can twist up the leaves to make really comfortable and durable rush seats." Hobbs glanced at his friend. Garrett seemed poised, waiting to hear something more, but Hobbs said, "I guess that'd be about all, what I can recall."

McCracken's eyes shot to Garrett's face, seeking enlightenment. He twisted his mouth, mauling his chew. "That's quite a lot of rememberin', Detective Hobbs. Good plant." He pulled more of the fluff from the snuff box and fingered it thoughtfully. "Kinda pretty, this cattail down. You ever hear about anybody usin' it to stuff anything?"

Hobbs narrowed his eyes at the sheriff. What did he have up his sleeve, anyhow? He paused, then responded, "Well, you're right. It did slip my mind, but it can be used to stuff, well, you know, things like winter coats, for insulation, keep 'em warm. Heard it's good to stuff in life preservers, light, makes 'em float. Oh, and you know, I think a lot of old-timers used it when they were making toys. Early settlers, they couldn't afford much store-bought stuff, or they didn't have access, so they made their whistles from willow sticks, stuffed their dolls with cattail down, that kind of thing."

A slow smile had appeared on Garrett's face. "Old-timers. Makes sense. Awful messy, though, wasn't it? Flew around the room ..."

"Oh, yeah, I remember my granny complaining about it, getting in the nose, sneezing. I don't remember if they had any special tricks to control it or not."

Now everyone was quiet, but as the silence filled the room, Hobbs' cheek gave an involuntary, impatient twitch. McCracken was studying her boss. Finally, Hobbs said, "What I wanna know is, why do you care?"

McCracken broke her silence for the first time. Still contemplating Garrett, she said, "I think I have an idea, but I sure don't have the whole picture."

Pleased with her, Garrett nodded. "You're right. And that's the problem. I don't understand, myself. I should have sent it to the lab. Yesterday."

Now it was Hobbs' turn to be baffled, but Garrett was ready to move forward. Standing up awkwardly in the small space, he headed for his desk, narrowly avoiding McCracken's toes. Reaching into a box stowed behind the desk, he pulled out the doll, leaned over, and handed it to Hobbs. Her eyes following the motion, McCracken saw the duct tape and said accusingly, "Chief, you cut her open!"

Grimly, Garrett said, "Yeah, I know."

Hobbs, holding the doll, said, "What is this? What's goin' on?"

With one voice, Garrett and McCracken replied, "Unpin her face."

His stubby fingers surprisingly agile, Hobbs undid the pins, then laid the face over. He said, "Oh." A long pause, then, thoroughly examining the skull, his fingers across cheekbones and jaw, he said, "It's real, isn't it." It was a statement. "Why is it here? What's going on?"

Sighing, Garrett said, "You tell him where it came from, Mac, then I'll talk."

After McCracken had narrated their visit to Alma's in Croysant, dragging it out, a good cop, the details all in place, Garrett cleared his throat. "So, the long and short of it is, this doll should be in the lab, and there is no logical reason for not sending her there." He pulled on his mustache, uncomfortable. "Just my intuition. I think something subtle is going on here, and if this thing gets caught up in the cogs of the criminal system, well ..." He struggled for words. "... well, someone that shouldn't be might get hurt. Some old lady who didn't do anything that she thought was wrong. Or maybe some old lady trying to make something right that had gone wrong. Something like that. I just don't want to throw someone under the train until I find out more about what happened here."

"But, Chief! It's a skeleton. Some kid died ..."

"I know. I know, Mac. It worries me, too. In the end, we gotta find out, but ... "

Hobbs interjected, poking at the duct tape. "You ain't much of a surgeon, buddy. The whole dead kid in here?"

McCracken cringed at that, but Garrett said, "Probably. I found a rib — over there in my desk drawer right now."

"So what do you expect me and hot shot here to do?"

"Keep your mouths shut and your noses clean and your eyes open ..."

Hobbs was grinning. "That's a whole face. You figure there's any skulls or brains under it all that we could use?"

Not amused, Garrett said, "I need you two as sounding boards — I know about my reputation, but I can't always do this stuff alone. And you might need to do some leg work. But I don't want you to get hurt. Professionally. If it looks like somehow the word got out about me doing this private investigation here, don't get caught up in it. Heat starts coming down, you point your finger at me and let me take it from the commissioners and the voters — I can handle it. Technically, I got the right to conduct this investigation for a little while on my own. No reason people should get their wind up."

The detective's affable face was thoughtful as he turned the doll over in his lap, studying her beaded dress and moccasins, examining her construction. "Only Indian I actually know about in this valley is your girlfriend, Ms. Threewinds. Of course, it's probably not an Indian, and there's no doubt lots of old ladies around here made dolls."

Garrett's face had reddened again. "She ain't my girlfriend, and she ain't an Indian. She's a hippie."

"Yeah. Well, point is I'm not sure where to start, but I'm willing to keep my head up." Hobbs struggled with the old easy chair, standing, mumbling, "Musta stuffed this piece a' junk with cattails. Old enough."

McCracken was biting her knuckles and thinking of what she'd seen on the church billboard while out on patrol this morning. It read, "Ready or not, here I come. Signed, Jesus." Okay, ready. Be ready, don't be wishy-washy. Standing up, she shook loose her hair. "Well, I'm ready, Chief. I'll try to see what I can do." Garrett had mentally left the room. He was in a zone somewhere, and had been since Hobbs mentioned Jenny. Whatever. Quietly, she added, "And thanks for taking me into your confidence," before following Hobbs out the office door and closing it softly behind them.

15

COFFIN'S COUNTRY STORE had been called "Coffin's Calamity" by those looking for items of the more plastic variety, such as flash drives, talking baby toys, or coffee beans not yet ground. Coffin would respond to such urban inquiries first with a prolonged, upward-curving "Ehhhh?" then with a high-pitched salvo of words saying something like, "I ain't intendin' to run no Walmart here." Recently, he had updated this to, "What you think I am, a cock-eyed Sprouts?"

Nevertheless, local ranchers, as well as most bemused newcomers, found Coffin's place to be invaluable. The really old-timers referred to it by its original name, Peaseford Feed and Seed, and they felt it could be relied on to fill all their basic needs, be it poultry mash, all possible varieties of nuts and bolts, good cheap white bread and bologna, chew, Coors, fishing tackle, cracked corn, well, what have you. Coffin had it. Honey had fallen in love with the place at first sight. She made excuses, some of them lame, to stop here whenever she could. It reminded her of her grampy's old store in Virginia, maybe minus a few items, such as the shoo-fly pie her grammy brought every morning from home. That pie. It always sold out before the end of the day, but never before Honey had snagged a piece for herself. She smiled sadly, reminiscent, as she fingered some swatches of cloth displayed in a back corner of the store. Lost in memory, she jumped and whirled when a male voice behind her said, "Hey! Honey!"

Honey gasped. "What are *you* doing here!"

A mocking drawl: "Just a' buyin' me some chicken feed." He chuckled. "I thought you'd be glad to see me."

Stepping forward to hug him, Honey looked over his shoulder, taking in the empty store. Even Coffin was away from the counter. "Well I ... Well, I am. Of course, I am, but you ..."

"... I surprised you, that's all."

"Yes, you surprised me and ..."

"... And my being here makes you nervous. Let's go on over to The Harvest Apple and hide behind their ferns. I need to talk some business with you."

"No! No, B!" Honey blew an abrupt, frustrated whoof of air out her nose. "I thought you planned to ..."

"... Stay in Denver? Well, plans change, pretty much whenever the big boss says. And my new plans need to involve you."

"You're going to ruin everything!"

"Oh, come on. Don't be so jumpy. We just need to get together for a little private tete-a-tete, that's all."

"You plan to blackmail me."

"Honey, you dope! Get real. I don't want to blackmail you. I just want to talk."

The bell on Coffin's door jingled as Jilly Brown entered. This made Honey increasingly agitated. "Damn it, B, get away from me. I don't want to be seen with you. You f—ing win, as usual. Garfield is getting supplies in Riversmet tomorrow for Chuck Fowler. He'll be gone by 10:00. Come to the house then and we'll ... we'll walk to the foot of Fourier Ridge. That's a private place."

They could hear Jilly humming, moving in their direction, gathering cans of pinto beans and a stack of Big Hunk bars as her eyes explored the shelves. Honey was wringing her hands. "Our Fourier Ridge—Gar is so proud of it. Now get away from me, B! Get completely away! Just leave!" She gave him a shove toward the next aisle, out of Jilly's shopping path.

Faking a secretive, spy voice he edged back and whispered, "I'll be there, little sis," as he reached out to pat her head. Eyes flashing, she shoved his hand away. "Don't you dare touch my head, B. You know better. Now, get out."

Turning down the Jilly aisle, he gloated to himself, "Finally, a break. Couldn't be more perfect." Whistling a little tune, he pulled his phone from his pocket while nodding at Jilly as he passed her. "Howdy. Nice day."

Engrossed in examining a display of potato chips and jerky sticks, she nodded back absently and mumbled, "Hi. How ya' doin?"

Baby Skulls and Fowl Odors

As he left, B was saying into the phone, "Okay, I think the eagle has finally landed. I'll get back to you by noon tomorrow." Meanwhile, Honey was slipping into the liquor area behind the freezers, aiming for an alternate route out, but Jilly glanced up just before she could disappear.

"Oh, hi, Honey. Sure is gettin' hot for this time of year, isn't it?"

16

PAT GARRETT WASN'T THE ONLY one to be plagued by a healthy dose of intuition. Asa Hobbs was deeply troubled by the idea of someone's having put a child's skeleton in a doll. Once he left the sheriff's office to cross the hall to his own, he closed the door, placed himself stolidly in his desk chair, and stared absently at his screen saver: floating pieces of pie, cake, and cookies, deliciously presented in vivid color. He was still holding the pinch of cattail down between his finger and thumb, rubbing it back and forth, shredding it. *Threewinds Threewinds Threewinds* — the word wouldn't leave him. It echoed pointlessly around his skull, trying to beat its way out. He knew his friend was sweet on Jenny Threewinds; maybe that was what held Garrett back from pushing an open investigation. An Indian doll, stuffed with cattail down and a skeleton, and Jenny Threewinds, supposed to be a hippie, but the only person he could think of with that Indian-flavored name. No, too farfetched. No real connection. Even as he thought it, his detective curiosity had bullied its way to the front and his index fingers began to poke at the keyboard. It never hurt to get information, he told himself. What he often told himself. "That's why," he muttered, "That I'm a god-damned detective. I'll just look this up. It can't hurt Pat."

He tried "Indian burials." Nothing very specific there. "Indian." Not a very good word, anyhow. Should think in terms of tribes: Navajo. Ute. Shoshone. Sioux. And weren't you supposed to call the Navajo *Diné?* And the Sioux ... was that derogatory, originally a French word? Maybe Lakota, or Dakota. Or something. He relaxed and let his mind and fingers wander as they wanted, then suddenly he stopped, squinting at the web site that had randomly appeared. Hmmm, he thought, hmmm.

Baby Skulls and Fowl Odors

Two more keyboard pokes and a contact number appeared. He reached for his phone. While the number rang, he burrowed into his memory for a map. South Dakota. The Lakota nation: Pine Ridge to the west, Rosebud east of it, others north. Nebraska to the south. Someone picked up. The answering voice was pleasant and friendly. "Oglala Lakota College. How may I direct your call?"

Hobbs cleared his throat. "This is Detective Asa Hobbs in Riversmet, Colorado. I work with the sheriff's office here. We have a problem. Someone has unearthed a skeleton in a rather unusual place, and it would help our investigation if I could learn a little more about tribal burial practices."

Except for a brief pause, the response was noncommittal. Hobbs was relieved. He had expected curiosity, or worse, to be told where to put his nosy questions. Instead, the courteous voice said, "Dr. McDonald may be able to help you. Please hold the line while I connect you."

Hobbs tried to interject to ask for McDonald's number; he hated being told that he was being connected, because usually they just lost you in phoneland and you ended up with a dial tone. Besides, McDonald didn't sound very promising as an Indian name. The human at the other end of the line had disappeared, however, so he brushed breakfast crumbs off his chest and pushed shredded cattail down off his desk, and waited.

The voice, when it finally arrived, was female and soft. "Detective Hobbs? I'm Ramona McDonald. May I help you?"

Hobbs frowned at the phone. "Thank you. Maybe. I was hoping to speak with an actual Sioux ..." he choked himself off from saying Sioux Indian. Nice save, he told himself. Probably insulting. He cleared his throat. "You sound young. I was looking for an old-timer who might know about Lakota burial practices, probably from a few years back. We're trying to figure out what happened with respect to a skeleton that has been discovered here in an unusual place."

Now the voice contained amusement. "*Ramona McDonald* doesn't sound very Indian, does it? I still might be able to help you; I married into the Tribe many years ago. My married name is Fights Red Bear. And I'm not such a spring chicken, either. I've got kids and grandkids, all raised right here. Was your question about scaffolding? Or maybe I should ask you to tell me first where the skeleton was found?"

Hobbs hedged. "Scaffolding is where the remains of the deceased are placed on a platform, right? In a sacred place?"

"That is correct, Mr. Hobbs. I must tell you, however, that that type of burial is very rare in modern times. Most of our burial ceremonies are different now. Let me describe them for you. What we do now is that first the person is brought into town from whatever funeral home (off-Reservation) prepared the body. Family and mourners meet the hearse at a junction a few miles out of town and follow the body back in to wherever the wake is being held. The wake can be one, two or four days. Food is provided and people can sing and talk about their memories of the deceased.

"On the morning of the funeral, there is time for viewing — usually there is an honor song by a drum group during the formal viewing just before the service. There is a book to sign and a program. Cakes and memorial objects like pictures, trophies, newspaper clippings are on display around the casket with the flowers from various people. Star quilts are hung around the walls. During the viewing mourners process by the coffin, then go through a line to shake hands with the family members, or hug and say consoling things to them if they have a closer relationship. Casket bearers are six to eight young men who are given ribbons or pins to distinguish them, and they sit in one of the front rows. The family is the last to view and say their goodbyes.

"Then services, which may be Christian or not, then the casket is closed and the body taken to the burial site. The mourners load all of the flowers from the church or hall into the hearse or their cars. Everyone follows the hearse to the cemetery. The hole is dug, but all of the non-Indian hydraulics are not used. It's just a bare grave with a mound of dirt next to it. Words are said by whoever gave the services, and family members throw in a handful of dirt. Once prayers are done, the casket bearers pick up shovels and fill in the hole. This is a long, hard task, and other young men present will take turns at it. Once the grave is filled in, the ladies and children take the bouquets and arrange them to cover the grave.

"Once that is all done, the mourners and family go back to the church or hall for a meal. At the meal, the family has a give-away, which is usually the star quilts for the casket bearers and baskets or bundles of household items, such as hand towels, rubbermaid containers, for elderlies first and then other people, if they have enough to give away."

While she talked, Hobbs had ambled down the hall and procured coffee and a donut from the food station by Edith. This is a nice lady, he thought. She is trying to get me pointed in the right direction with respect to Native American ways. Once the narrative stopped, and when he was sure she was done, Hobbs said, "Thank you. I appreciate that description. It sounds like a very thoughtful ceremony ... well, a little like a white guy's funeral. Do you ever cremate?"

"Lakota families frown on cremation."

"Are there other ceremonies? I've heard of 'Keeping the Spirit' ceremonies. Are there any occasions when the family might want to retain some of the remains of the deceased? Like maybe take the bones off the scaffold after a period of time to keep for something sacred?"

Again, there was the pause. Then Ramona McDonald said, "You know, Detective, Catholic people who carry around pieces of saint's bones as 'relics' would be considered to be absolute nutjobs by Lakota standards. Once the deceased is laid out on the platform, they are never touched. If they are scattered by the wind or fall off the platform, they are not disturbed. It is expected that they will return to the earth with time. The Lakota don't pack around pieces of dead people."

"Well, that settles that," Hobbs began, but then Ramona McDonald interrupted him.

"Not quite settled, I don't think. You didn't answer my own original question. Where did your people find this mysterious skeleton?"

Secrecy obligations to Garrett aside, fair was fair. Hobbs cleared his throat. "You have to realize that we are really stumped by this, or I wouldn't have bothered you. The skeleton ... the skeleton is a child's skeleton, sewn inside a toy, a doll that is dressed in what appears to be authentic Indian clothes, that is, a beaded white buckskin dress, moccasins and so-on, and embedded in a cattail down stuffing."

This time there was no hesitation. Dr. McDonald gave a snort of disgust. "Look, Detective, only a super crazy white person would put a child's bones in a doll—it's horrifying! No Lakota grandmother would ever allow such a thing to happen."

Settling his round frame back against his desk chair and tapping his pen thoughtfully on the desk, Hobbs nodded. "Well, thank you. Thank you, Dr. McDonald. Frankly, you've erased all doubt from my mind in this area of the investigation." He paused, thinking, and she was quiet, sensing that he might not be finished. McDonald, he thought. Like Garrett's Jenny, not a real Indian. But this one ... this grandmother had been around for quite a while. "Dr. McDonald?" he said, tentatively. "Maybe just one more question? If you have time?"

Again, the pause. He had decided it was a cultural thing, if not a personal mannerism. "Sure, then. Go ahead."

"Did you ever know an Indian named Mike Threewinds? This would have been twenty, maybe twenty-five years ago."

"Oh, Mike. Yes, of course! All of us back then knew Mike — he was all over the Rez. He wasn't an Indian, though. That name, Threewinds, that's not a real Lakota name, especially not the way he spelled it. If it were an actual name, it would be two words, Three Winds. But I think he just made it up.

"He did kind of look a little like an Indian, though. I think maybe he had some Asian in his background. Everyone here liked him a lot. He was a lawyer, and he wanted to help our people. I wish he was still alive — he'd be all over this Keystone XL pipeline dispute. If anyone could save us from that disaster, he'd have been the one."

This massive injection of unexpected information sent Hobbs' brain into overdrive. "But he's not ... he's not alive?"

"No, he died sometime in the late eighties, him and his little girl. He was headed over to Rapid City for some reason, out on 90, and some jerk, drunk, we heard, swerved into his lane. Rolled the car. Neither of them survived."

"A little girl! She died, too? How old was she?"

"Just a toddler. Her mother, I can't remember her mother's name, but she had a lot of respect for tribal tradition. When the little girl was born, she let the name stay Threewinds, like her and Mike, but she spelled it right, separated it into two words, Three Winds."

"Uh ... respect for tradition. Did ... what kind of burial did Mike Threewinds and the little girl have?"

Again, Ramona McDonald sounded amused. "I can see

where you're going with this, and the answer is no, no platforms or relics. And now, as we've been talking, I recall the names. The mother was Jenny. She was devastated, of course, and right after the burial she returned to her original home, in Colorado. The little girl was Margaret. They called her Maggie — beautiful little thing, big dark eyes and full of giggles.

"I recall that Jenny told us that she would notify Mike's family, but that he had no ... I think the word she used was respect. He had no respect for his family — it was a bad relationship. Jenny said something about addictions. So, anyhow, Jenny asked if he could be buried here, among friends, and his little girl with him, because he felt as if the Lakota were his true family. It was the kind of funeral I described to you earlier."

Hobbs was hurriedly making notes as McDonald continued thoughtfully, "You know, a lot of this is coming back to me now. As I think about it, I don't think Mike did look particularly Asian. More maybe a Heinz soup ancestry. But where I got the idea, well, the crowd at the funeral was really big. Lots of people liked Mike, and lots of the Tribal members were helping with the hole digging and so-on. Jenny's parents had come up, and they helped her with the meal and the give-away ... well, I am just rambling now. Maybe you don't want to hear all this stuff?"

"Oh, no! No, I want to hear it. Uh ... I may ... I may know this Jenny."

"Okay. Well, anyhow, the grandmother, Jenny's mother, she brought three quilts. They weren't star quilts, just another design, homestead or something. But the gesture was good. But the reason I am saying this is that one member of Mike's family did come, and that girl was definitely Asian. Maybe that's why I was thinking Asian. For Mike.

"The thing is, memories can be wrong, but what I do remember is that girl was a teenager, maybe 16 or 18 years, and dressed bad, like a slut. Short skirt, long, stringy black hair, barely combed, low-cut blouse, tottery high heels. She was crying maybe even worse than everybody else, and it had her make-up all smeared all over her face. But Jenny and her parents went over and gave that girl the first quilt. That's maybe why I remember her now."

"So, who was the girl?"

"I'm trying to remember, to be sure. It seems like when

Jenny carried the quilt to her she said something like, 'Here, Zee. I'm sorry. I'm so sorry. Take this from me, to remember your brother.'" Ramona McDonald was quiet, trying to recall. "Then she said ... she said something odd. Something like, 'Don't let your damned father near that quilt. Mike can't protect you, but I'm still here. You know where I'll be if you need me.' And then the girl ... the girl hugged the quilt to her little bare chest. Let me think. What happened then. I really can't remember. But I do know that Mike and that little Maggie are in the ground down at Sicangu ... you know, Rosebud. I can guarantee it."

Asa Hobbs trudged down the hall to find Garrett's door open, him bent over the stack of files and bookwork that were the bane of his sheriffhood. "Hey, Pat, can I come in a minute? I been doin' a little snoopin' with respect to your issues of earlier this morning."

Garrett made a face. "Yeah. Close the door."

"Yeah. I hated to bother you, you bein' so damn busy and important and all, but then I got the impression you felt like the little dolly business was a big priority. Big question, interrupt you or leave you alone? Didn't know whether to shit or go blind."

Scowling, Garrett grunted. "So close one eye and fart. What the hell you got, Asa?"

17

GARRETT WAS ALONE in his office, mulling over Hobbs' story. So, the Threewinds guy was no Indian. He hadn't known that. Did it matter? So, Jenny had an Asian sister-in-law. News to him. Whatever—it didn't seem relevant. Plus, Jenny had had a little kid and lost her. Big news to him. Poor little kid dead and buried on the Rez. Hobbs seemed to think that knowing the kid was buried in South Dakota cleared Jenny of something. Garrett frowned. Why would he have ever suspected Jenny? The doll was in Indian dress, sure, but that had nothing to do with Jenny. All he really felt was sad. Sad for her that she had lost that little girl. She must still mourn her, even though it was so long ago.

A soft knock on his door interrupted his thoughts. Looking guiltily at the stack of papers in front of him, a stack which hadn't lowered at all since he first sat down here, he sighed and said, "Sure, why not. Come on in."

Jenny appeared in the doorway, very pale. She stepped inside, closing the door behind her. "Oh, Patrick! Oh, Patrick! I need to talk to you." She was holding out a tissue box, which confused him. "I need to talk to you in private. I have dug something up."

Sheriff Garrett's stomach gave a lurch and he half stood from his chair, large hands on his desk. "Oh," he said. "Oh, all right then. Have a seat ... maybe I better get us some coffee."

Jenny sat. Feeling absolutely awful, she held the tissue box on her lap while Garrett went for coffee. She really wanted this damned box and the responsibility that went with it far away from her. It belonged in Garrett's capable hands. She knew that once he took over, everything would go right again. But before she could get to that point, she had to explain what she was doing digging on Chuck Fowler's property, and that was not going to be easy. It didn't help that Brady X. had almost done it again this morning, rattling her already rattled psyche. She just couldn't believe that man!

When she drove home late last night, the moon was popping in and out of the clouds in front of her, a mountain breeze panting down the road in pursuit of her fleeing car. She had slipped, trembling, into the dark house and sat at the kitchen counter, trying to think clearly. Brady was snoring away, no fear of waking him! Even so, she hated being alone in the dark with the bones. She had used a tissue to keep them together this far, and that gave her an idea. She pulled over the tissue box that she normally kept on the counter, removed all of them, and pushed the skeletal hand to the bottom. Replacing the tissues in one clump, she sat staring at the box, struggling with her thoughts. What should she tell Garrett?

She didn't hear Brady until he sneezed explosively near her ear. The sun was up, and he was trying to loosen a tissue from the wad at the top of the box. Her head shot up from the pillow her arms had made on the cabinet as he said, "Damned allergies. I may as well just take this whole box with me." He'd turned it over to shake and pry at the stubborn wad as he said, "Oh, hi, sleeping beauty. You got any allergy drugs around here? These things are stuck ... "

Jenny's arm shot out like a cobra, snatching the box. "Oh, Xy, don't mess with this box. Must be a company screwup—the tissues are all in a lump. I'll have to shop for a better brand." She was babbling, but no problem; the ominous Dalek battle cry ground from his phone before he could react to what she said. She dashed into the bathroom to emerge with another box of tissue and some Loratadine, slapping them on the cabinet, as he was saying, "Yes, I told Charlie, I have an idea." She said, "Here, take these," then turned and ran back to the bathroom. "Sorry, Xy. Gotta go. Sick."

He followed her to the bathroom door. "Need help?" and her voice, muffled, "No, I think the worst has passed. Just go on to work." A shrugged "Okay," and the sounds of sneezing, a couple of sniffles, and the door closing. Only when she heard his car crunch the gravel, going out the driveway, did she re-appear, clutching the box. Within minutes it was riding on her lap as she drove to Riversmet.

Garrett eyed the cup he'd placed in front of her on the desk. "Do you take cream or sugar?"

"Oh, no, Patrick. I ... I really ... Thank you for the coffee. Didn't get any yet today. But I need ... I need to explain something. I hope you under ... I hope you'll try to understand. It's such a ... such a long story. And kind of, well, kind of complex."

Garrett sat behind his desk, putting the desk between them. This situation was making him distinctly uncomfortable. He needed to hear what she was going to say before he discussed anything with her, but this was Jenny, and he felt two-faced. It was tough to stay in his sheriff role; he wanted to commiserate without feeling shifty about it. "I guess just ... try me."

She took a sip of coffee and her eyes slid sideways as she started to speak. "It's about my little girl. I had a little girl once, a long time ago, why, she'd be a grown woman now! But I lost her."

This was it, then; here it came. Garrett waited, wanting her to get it out, wanting to find a way to console her, but Jenny didn't continue. The thoughtful, gray-flecked blue eyes which sang to Garrett of cool and misty mountain forests now seemed lost, gazing into a middle distance. She sat, the comfortable padded body stolid and silent, until at last he gently prodded, "Jenny, was there something in that tissue box that you wanted to show me?"

Returned to the present, she focused on his face. "Oh, yes. Yes, Patrick. But I need to explain. You see, I told you once about Mike, my husband, Mike Threewinds, and that he was killed in a car accident. But I didn't tell you about Maggie. Our little girl. It just hurts too much, even now, to talk about her. But she was killed, too. Killed in the same accident. Just a little thing, so innocent. She never even got to live."

Tears had formed in her eyes, bringing a lump to Garrett's own throat. "I'm so sorry." Now he expected her to take a tissue from the box, but instead she continued.

"I was so sad, you know, and I ... I know this sounds silly, but ... but to comfort me, someone, well, my mother. My mother made a beautiful doll. Of course it wasn't Maggie, and it didn't even look like Maggie, of course, being a doll, but it was a symbol. She had ... she had big brown eyes and my ... my mother dressed her like I once dressed Maggie. Lakota clothes. I loved the doll,

Patrick. She wasn't Maggie, of course, but she represented how my mother loved me and her tiny grandchild. My mother died not long ... not long after that."

A crease had formed along Garrett's bare forehead, and he began to tug at his mustache. He had interrogated many accused felons in his career, and even if he hadn't had a highly suspicious, bone-stuffed doll burning a hole in the box right next to him behind his desk, he could tell that what Jenny was saying was off kilter, not right somehow. Was she going to continue, now, and tell the truth about this doll, which apparently had little Maggie's bones stuffed inside? Or didn't she know about the bones? His sheriff's instinct told him that she did, but his training warned him about jumping to conclusions.

Jenny took another fortifying sip of the weak, sludge-ridden office coffee, wishing it were brandy, then continued in a rush, seemingly resolved. "So anyhow, that guy that is living with me, Brady Xyster, thought he would do me a big favor. He took a box of my old toys around to give out to thrift stores and such, which would have been fine, very sweet, except he didn't just take the toys I asked him to take. He put my doll in there, too."

At the mention of Brady Xyster's name, Garrett stiffened and grimaced. She was just so casual about a live-in boyfriend! All he said was, "I see."

"So you see, I had to go looking for my doll, and I hunted all day, because, you see, Brady couldn't remember where he'd left her. You'd have to know Brady—he's kind of scatty. And this weird thing happened. Somebody told me the doll might be at Alma's, so I went to Alma's and she told me ... she told me Gritty and Carmen had buried the doll at Fowlers." The words were tumbling over each other now, and Jenny was looking more and more miserable. "Patrick, this is the part you probably can't understand. I don't know why! I don't know why I believed her, or thought she might be right, or anything, but I drove up there, up to Fowler's, and there was ... there was a place or two where someone might have been digging. Hard to tell, with the rocky soil, but Patrick, it bothered me, and I just had to see!"

Garrett was now looking at her with startled eyes. He didn't want to believe that this woman, the one woman in this whole valley that he wished he could cherish, that she might be unbalanced. Insane?

Jenny caught his glance and read it. It caused her to hunch into herself, arms protective over her stomach, but she was resilient, and she persisted. "I know it sounds crazy, but I just had to see. If Alma was right and for some reason they buried that doll, why, I couldn't imagine, but if they did, then good, I'd have her back. And if not, then I could look somewhere else with a clear mind, without feeling as if I'd left something dangling."

The explanation might have made sense if the context hadn't been so off-the-wall strange. Garrett said gently, "Jenny, you realize that Alma is an old, old woman now. Sometimes she's clear, but more often she's quite addled."

"I know. That's what I do know." Jenny met his eyes, hers pleading. "Worse, Patrick, I didn't tell anyone. I trespassed. I snuck onto Chuck Fowler's at night. Late last night."

Baffled, he said, "You ... you what? Jenny, why?"

Now Jenny sighed and shook her head. "Oh, Patrick. Look how much trouble I'm having just telling you this. And you are the person I trust. You understand things. But Fowler? I don't even know Chuck Fowler. If even you think I'm crazy, what would some stranger think?"

Her miserable appearance. Her trust in him. Garrett needed to melt — or run. Elbow on desk, hand propping forehead, he squeezed his eyes tightly shut and drew in a deep breath. Then, pulling at his mustache, he said quietly, "So where is your little girl now?"

Startled by the shift in the conversational direction, Jenny sat up straight and stared at him. "Why I told you! She is dead — she died with Mike when the car rolled."

"And did you have a traditional Indian burial?"

For the first time, Jenny seemed to soften, a ghost of a smile tracing reminiscent across her face. "Oh, yes! Yes, that was the one beautiful thing. So many Lakota loved Mike and Maggie — the wake lasted three days, and the drum group did an honor song that brought us to our knees. My parents were there, and we threw dirt into the graves, Mike's and little Maggie's, sending them back to the Mother, Mother Earth. And after they were buried, we had food and a beautiful give-away. You can't feel good about burying your husband and baby, but I always believed we sent them away the best we could. Mike felt like the

Lakota were family, you know."

Carefully, Garrett probed. "I thought Mike was Lakota."

Jenny looked surprised. "Oh, no, I thought you knew. Mike was an Indian wanna-be, the kind of hippie you think you don't like, Patrick, like me. But he was a good guy. He wanted to help the tribe, and so did I." Pat Garrett was stopped momentarily in his tracks. He had never explicitly told her that he didn't like hippies and especially Indian wanna-be hippies. Had he? How could she read his mind like that? Collecting himself, he said, "So, then, were any of Mike's real family there, at the funeral? His biological family?"

"Oh, Patrick, Mike hated them, at least his stepfather. He had loved his real father, Ed Jones, who died, but I think he was angry with his mother for taking up with the stepfather after she lost Ed. He felt the stepfather was a scum bag. He wouldn't talk about either of them; he only told me that the stepfather was an addict of some kind, and when I tried to ask, Mike would just say that dysfunctional was not an adequate term to describe some families.

"I did meet his little stepsister a couple of times, though. She was messed up, way out there. Mike and I worried that her father, that would be Mike's stepfather, was abusing her, and we tried to help, but we could never get close to her. She came to the funeral, though. The poor kid was so devastated. I kept wishing I could give Mike back to her. All I could give her was one of the quilts my mother made, a quilt to remember him by."

"I see." Garrett didn't see. What was going on here? This was like a splinter you couldn't get at. The more you dug at it, the deeper it burrowed under your skin. "Sooo ... let me be clear on this. You buried Maggie on the reservation, too? And you came back here? You didn't want to stay there, or at least bring Maggie here, to be with you?" Watching her face, he added, "Jenny, I'm not trying to criticize this bad situation, the grief. I'm just trying to understand."

Jenny nodded. "I know. Maggie and her daddy were very close, and I felt they would rest well together, somehow. Somehow, well, maybe console each other? Kind of care for each other. And me? What could I do? I'd lost them. It felt like I'd lost my reason for living. Then my parents became ill, one and then the other, and I came back here to care for them. I guess, like they say, God works in mysterious ways. I'm related to nearly everybody in this valley by some crooked connection or other, marriage and so-on, the old-timers, even the newcomers like those people over on Oozle Road, and the community became a support group. They helped me with my parents, and once my parents passed, I felt like I wasn't so alone, that I had friends in this valley, and that I could make a life here."

Garrett had submitted. He had melted, and he knew it. Still, he must ask. "So, you didn't find your doll at Fowlers, is that right? And you came here to ask me to help find it?" He was resisting tugging the toy from the box at his side.

"Oh, no, Patrick! I came here because when I was digging I found something else." She pushed the tissue box across the desk toward him.

Garrett frowned, and she nodded a go-ahead at him. Clumsily, he dug at the wad of tissues. The skeletal hand, entangled, pulled loose and the pieces dropped on the desk in front of him. Looking up at Jenny, he shook his head and said, "Oh, boy." Then, reaching for the button on his desk, he spoke wearily into the intercom. "A-deet? A-deet? Send in McCracken. I need to see her at once."

18

MCCRACKEN ROCKETED into the room. Shooting a questioning glance at Jenny, she pulled herself to attention and said, "What is it, Chief?" After all, there could be no happier moment in her life than to have her boss send for her to appear "at once."

Looking up with a wry smile, Garrett expressively expelled a lump of air. "Well, Mac, it ain't even noon, and have a look here at what Jenny just brought me."

"Oh, whoa!" Doing a double take at the little pile of bones on Garrett's desk, McCracken missed the troubled expression that had appeared on Jenny's face. "Wow. These are human! It's a hand. Where did you find these, Jenny?"

What could she say? Jenny's mouth came open and stayed there, but Garrett, watching her, overrode anything she might have offered. "Oh, Jenny just wanted to see the spring calves up at Barnswallowper's and Weinant's, so she went out for a drive. She saw that the bluebells were already out, then she turned on up the mountain at K-4 Road. She told me she loves the scarlet globe mallow and the cactus blooms, and she wanted to see if any of those were out early, too."

Jenny's expression had changed from one of possibly shocked betrayal to one of amazement. She was not a person who named flowers. She didn't even know what scarlet globe mallow was!

Garrett continued on smoothly. "When she passed Chuck Fowler's place, she saw what she thought were, oh, I guess they're wild phlox or something. My mother used to call 'em pinks. Anyhow, she got out to have a better look, because she was thinking it was early in the year for them, too."

Jenny was starting to like this story. Feeling she could be helpful, she interjected, "It wasn't fenced or anything, so I wasn't thinking of it as private property. I had my eye on those, uh, pinks, when I suddenly realized that I was closer to the Fowlers' trailer than I had meant to be." Working on her story, her voice having taken on a dramatic edge, she continued, "Also, I noticed that there were several signs, kind of picket signs, set up around the bushes where I was. They all said, 'No Chickens.' I don't know what that meant for sure, but it made me really uncomfortable, and I decided I'd better get out of there. Right away."

Scratching at his large ear, Garrett was regarding Jenny with an expression of mixed admiration and amusement, but McCracken was nodding solemnly, commiserating. "You did right. That's a dangerous place. That's where Nancy Jane let Fowler have it in the foot, and she's still layin' claim to that corner of land."

"Oh, is that right?" Jenny widened her eyes, and Garrett's lips twitched up as he watched her get so thoroughly into her role. Now she shuddered. "I didn't know that, but I must have felt something was amiss, because I turned and almost ran, back toward my car. I wasn't paying attention to how I was going, and that's when I tripped on a mound of earth and I ... and I ... " She turned the beam from her lovely blue, lash-fringed eyes toward the sheriff. Perhaps the moisture they exhibited was incipient tears, and Garrett realized he was being given his cue. He took up the story.

"Anyhow, Mac, she told me that there is a place there, kind of sunken like a grave gets after it's set for a year or two. Jenny, I thought you said it was a rock you tripped on?"

"I don't know! I really don't, Patrick. I shouldn't be ... I shouldn't have gotten so rattled, I know that."

"Well. So." Nodding tolerantly at her, Garrett continued. "So you lit on your hands and knees in the sunken area, and that's when you saw the bones, right?" What was it about the woman, anyhow? Garrett knew he shouldn't be spinning this big whopper of a lie to his deputy, but the truth was, he was having fun acting out this charade with Jenny, and it almost seemed as if Mac was into her own role, too. At any rate, he'd dug himself in so deeply that he had to continue. He'd have to make it up to Mac once he got things sorted out.

Now McCracken probed. "Was it just the hand?"

Wisely, Jenny's answer was brief. "I was afraid to look further."

Game over. Briskly, Garrett said, "At any rate, her first instinct was right. She brought the bones directly to us, and now we need to see what's going on. Mac, I'd like you to get a search warrant to forestall any objections from either Fowler or Nancy Jane, then gather up a crime unit and meet me up there."

"Yes, Sir, Chief. I'll get 'er done asap."

"Yeah. And Mac? I'm gonna save the department a little gas money and impose on Jenny to drive me back up to Fowler's to show me the exact place she found those bones. Would you bring me back here when we get done, so that Jenny can go on home from there, since she lives close?"

"Good as done, Chief," and she was out the door before Garrett could unfold himself from his chair. He wasn't saying anything. Reluctant to go back to the real reason she had trespassed at Fowlers', Jenny was quiet, too. They passed down the hallway, and Garrett stopped at the main desk.

"Hold the fort for me for a while, A-deet. Some more stuff came up, up at Fowlers'. Literally. I need to get back up to Croysant to check it out."

"*Sí*, so you say, *Señor*. I know a *muchacha bonita* when I see one. You're just makin' a excuse to hang out with the lady and buy her *una comida.*"

Edith was grinning at him and dancing her shoulders, but Garrett scowled. "What the hell is oon ... oon-uh-combita?"

Unable to restrain her own smile, Jenny said, "*Una comida.* A meal. It's noon, Patrick, and Edith was just suggesting that you might buy lunch."

"And for me, too, sheriff. *Tengo hambre.*" Edith's eyebrows bobbed up and down.

Garrett had heard *tengo hambre* before. Now he somehow managed to scowl, looking stern and playful at the same time. He growled, "You don't talk about bein' hungry in this sweat shop, Ms. A-deet. You just work and eat the lunch you brought and tend to your business. Whether I decide to take some lady to Sonic for a burger, well, that is my business."

With a fake meek expression, Edith murmured, "Yes, boss," sticking her lip out in a mock pout. Turning her back pointedly toward Jenny and the sheriff, she began a barrage of fierce typing on her keyboard. As they turned to go, she spoke just loudly enough to be overheard. "Sure, it'll be Sonic. Be just like the old cheapskate." This, followed by a soft giggle.

As Jenny pulled out of her parking space, the sheriff said, "Well, at the risk of my being called names, how would you feel about pulling into Sonic for somethin' to go? I may be a cheapskate, but I'm also a hungry cheapskate in a hurry."

Jenny chuckled, but a glance at his gloomy face told her that the professed cheapskate was in fact a distracted law officer needing to move along. She gave her order quickly, and as they left, driving toward Peaseford, each downing fries, her sipping a cranberry slushy while he wasted no time with a java chiller, he was back to the old quiet, inscrutable Patrick that she felt she had come to know quite well. He seemed to have forgotten her long story about the doll. She crossed her fingers.

Finally, using one of the thin paper napkins to wipe milkshake froth from his mustache, Garrett emitted a sound resembling a low "hmmm." Jenny glanced over and returned the "hmmm" as "hmmmm?" It was now a question eliciting further comment.

"Yeah." The sheriff pulled on his mustache. "You know, Jenny, I wanted to ride up with you for a reason. I've got somethin' I been wanting to talk to you about."

Jenny's stomach, which hadn't had breakfast and was appreciating the food, had almost settled down, but now it gave a lurch. Uh-oh, here it came. He didn't believe her, not about the doll. Instead, though, he continued, "You were working, weren't you, the night of the fire at the Cowpath?"

Swallowing her relief, Jenny said, "Oh, yeah. Right. Yeah, I was."

"Can you tell me about it? Who was in the restaurant at the time; what happened; how did it start; did you notice anything suspicious ... I heard there were shots ... that kind of thing."

"Well I ... well, sure. I don't think there was anything suspicious. Cookie is usually pretty careful, but he must have had one of those accidents we all have. That's why they call them accidents, I think — they aren't expected. So anyhow, it seems it was just a really smoky grease fire that got started somehow. It kind of looked like he had some of those bar cloths you have around when you cook. His would have been greasy, and one got near the burner and started up, and it spread into the grease traps, and so-on. He'd gone into the pantry to get stuff, and the fire was going pretty good when he came back in. He hollered and started trying to put it out, and everyone cleared out of the restaurant. It was really smoky; it made a big stink, a big mess, but we all got out of there fast enough. No one hurt, no harm done, except just the stinking smoke smell on everything. I think we've got it cleaned up now. We had to dump supplies. One thing we do that's illegal—I'm trusting to tell you this, that you won't act on it. It could be a licensing problem. We always send our garbage over to the Likovitz farm. We hate to waste it, so at least their pigs get good from it. We sent the smoked-up food over there, and the Likovitzes were really grateful. I think they struggle to make ends meet."

Garrett nodded. He was working his chew. "Who all was in the restaurant at the time?"

"Oh, not too many. Let me see. Michaelsons were there; she was kidding around about their age and their anniversary. Sara and Jim from over at Peaseford—you maybe remember them. Sara always gets so tickled at Jim's corny jokes. A bunch ... well, let me see. There were a half dozen, because when they came in, I pointed them to the big booth in the back. That bunch of young people I didn't really know. They were out slumming from Riversmet. It was a mixed group, a couple Black guys, one cute little chick with a nose ring. I gathered that they were old high school buddies. Two were in uniform, and one of the women and the army guy next to her were flirting. The other woman was drinking a lot and got a little loud, I remember. They were talking about fishing and hunting, like everybody does around here, and that woman was telling the guy next to her, another one of the army guys, that he hadn't seen a rack until he saw what she planned to show him."

This brought a fleeting smile to Garrett's face. "We have to assume she meant deer antlers."

Jenny was smiling, too. "We must assume so. Anyhow, I guess the only other one I can think of was old Lew Harris, just having a quiet drink and taking it all in, kind of talking to himself like he does."

"Lew and Lucky?" Garrett assumed Lew's wife, the invisible, ghostly Lucky, would be there. He had never left her behind last year, when the sheriff and McCracken were investigating the Beidermann case.

Baby Skulls and Fowl Odors

"Lew claimed he tripped over Lucky when he was trying to get out the door to escape the smoke."

"He tripped?"

"Oh, yeah. Didn't you know? He stumbled on the steps going down from the door. He fell and hurt his poor old leg. We had to call 911 for him as well as the fire, and I give them credit. Tiffany was there so fast, just like lightning. You'd have thought she lived next door. She beat the ambulance, and it didn't take her long to get him comfortable. In the end, I guess, it wasn't broken. Just a nasty bruise."

Garrett was trying to digest the idea of tripping over a wife, much less a long dead one. They were both quiet for a while as the car rolled through Croysant, detouring around the Dog-That-Sleeps-in-The-Road, which got up with its habitual limp, cast them a sullen look, and drifted to the road side. As they passed the Cowpath, Garrett took it up again. "I thought somebody said they heard a shot while people were coming out of the building."

Jenny's hand came off the wheel and patted his arm tolerantly. "Honestly, Patrick, don't forget. This is Croysant. There are always shots. I just don't think anything criminal has happened at the Cowpath lately. I really don't."

Garrett emitted an "mmmph." His arm tingled disconcertingly where she'd touched it. They turned up Oozle Road, and Jenny sucked in a deep, fortifying breath. "Patrick, before we get there, I want to say 'thanks.' Thanks for covering for me this afternoon." There, she had said it. Garrett released another "mmmph" and shot her an inscrutable look. They were already approaching the K-4 turn. There was not time now to discuss her real story. The one about the doll.

Nancy Jane saw the sheriff and Jenny pull up and park in the turn-out. She saw Jenny point here and there, and saw the sheriff nodding thoughtfully as she pointed. She didn't have time to do more than hide and watch before two more sheriff's vehicles pulled into the other slots along the verge. McCracken got out and began to direct officers around the area; two of them fixed yellow crime scene tape among the sagebrush. It was circling the property—her property! Now she watched as McCracken approached the trailer, skittish as usual, her hand on the revolver in the holster at her hip. Good. Maybe she would shoot him in the other foot. But no. Fowler opened the door, leaning on his crutch, his expression surprised and friendly, nodding as McCracken spoke. All Nancy Jane could do now was shrink herself into the pinion shadow and watch.

Nancy Jane Barnswallowper had never been a woman to cry. It seemed strange to her now to feel her own tears crawling down her rough, chapped cheeks as she stared at the sunken place in the middle of the crime scene tape. The sheriff's people were swarming around the loop of property she knew was hers. She mouthed the words she'd seen on the church sign board last week, before this all started. It seemed so long ago. Softly she said, "Jesus came out of the tomb. So can you."

19

LARRY KEPT STRAINING to see Luke's face. Was he pissed off? Since Luke's truck didn't have a back seat, they were all jammed in the front, Sienna between the two boys, and Larry couldn't see much of anything past her little black head, which bounced and bobbled along as the truck swerved around corners and potholes. It didn't help that she was elevated, having sat on the pile of junk that was endemic to Luke's front seat. Finally, Larry just sat back and stared out at the scenery racing past. Sometimes he tried to decide if it raced faster when Luke was driving than when his mother was driving. Tiffany would have said it did, but Larry had concluded it was all about the same.

If Luke was mad at him, his jaw would be all hard and set, like it got when his mother tried to talk him out of enlisting. Luke wanted to join the army more than anything, but their mom wanted him to wait. She told him over and over that he needed to wait, that the army was too big a commitment to make at his age. Their arguments were frequent, loud, and passionate. "Stop and think, Luke! You aren't even eighteen yet. You can do this same thing later."

"I've thought it over, Mom. I did all the research. I need to do it now." Lots of guys in Luke's crowd at school were getting set up with the military recruiters. They needed parental permission to do anything before they turned eighteen, and Tiffany, her mouth clinched, refused to sign any papers. All she'd say was, "F'ing recruiters." Larry knew that the second Luke had his birthday he'd sign for himself, and it made him kind of sad. His mom was trying so hard to get them on the right path and take care of them, but Luke was stubborn as a donkey. He was focused on the paychecks and military support to go to college and lots of adventure, and well, when Larry thought about all that, it didn't sound so bad, actually. Still, he didn't think he could disappoint his mom, either, like Luke was doing.

The recruiters told Luke they'd help him get ready anyhow. They ignored their mom, and treated Luke like a future soldier, and several days a week gave him instruction and physical training after school. He was a big, opinionated kid, ready to get his own life, and Tiffany couldn't get it stopped.

Well, at least today there was no training, which was why Larry thought it was probably okay to ask Luke to drive Sienna home. He asked in front of Sienna, which made it harder for Luke to refuse. Which was why Luke might be mad at him. But he was still Larry's brother, so surely he felt as bad about those bus bullies as Larry did. It couldn't hurt to give Sienna a break for just one time, could it? Or maybe Luke was furious and had planned to hang with his buddies. But he would have said. Larry wondered what Luke would do to him when he got him alone. He tried to crane his neck to get a glimpse of his brother's face.

Just then Luke spoke for the first time since they left the schools. He made his voice loud over the rattle of the truck, and the unexpected utterance startled Larry, making him jump. Luke's question was directed at Sienna. "So, little Fowler Chick, does your papa really seriously plan to run a big chicken farm up there?"

Sienna snorted. "Not in a million years. Chuck's no chicken farmer. He wouldn't know a good chicken from his own ass hole."

Larry gaped at this outburst, complete with obscenity, waiting for Luke to respond, but he didn't say anything and they rode on in silence, detouring past The-Dog-That-Sleeps-in-The-Road in Croysant, speeding by the Lucky Lantern and the Cowpath. Just as they turned on to Oozle Road, it was Sienna who spoke.

"That was kind of random or crude or something. You know. I was just trying to tell you that we wouldn't mess with some kind of shitty Tinker chicken factory. Those aren't even real chickens."

She stopped talking, and after a long pause Luke said, "S'okay."

Taking a deep breath, Sienna said, "You know, you guys stuck up for me and all. You know, on the bus. And you're givin' me this ride home and everything. I really do appreciate it, you know. I guess ..."

Luke interrupted with "S'okay" again, and Larry interjected, "No problem," but Sienna continued. "I guess I oughta do something to show a little gratitude. We do have something ... well, this is a secret. I would show you, but you couldn't tell. Okay? What we have is something a lot classier than that sick old Tinker poultry, okay? If you can keep a secret, I'll show you. Because you don't treat me like shit. Okay?"

Luke ground the truck down a gear as they headed up K-4 Road, and Larry said, "You'll show us?" His curiosity trigger had been pulled. "Where?"

"Just ... when you get up here to my place, come out back with me and I'll show you. You gotta be quiet—I don't want Chuck to see us."

"I dunno. I'm kinda in a hurry," Luke said, but Larry was all over it. "Oh, come on, Luke. Please? It'll only take a minute."

There was no further time for negotiation. As they rounded the corner at Fowlers', they saw that all three near-by pull-outs were occupied by sheriff department vehicles. The "No Chickens" signs were still in place, but most of the property in the road loop was surrounded by yellow crime scene tape. A half dozen officers were there, two on hands and knees, apparently digging. McCracken, her red hair being lifted by a mild breeze, was in intense conversation with Chuck Fowler, who leaned on his crutch and nodded. Garrett had propped himself against a vehicle, watching, and as the kids passed they saw him expertly shoot a wad of spit and chew into the rocks nearby.

All three kids turned their heads to stare as the truck continued past. Larry said, "Wow," and Sienna said, "Oh, crap." Luke pulled around the bend and parked at the next wide place in the road. "Well, what do you suppose that's all about?"

Sienna was wiggling mightily, trying to extricate herself. "This isn't a good time. This is not a good time to show you my ... my stuff. Let me out. I can walk back."

Luke was regarding her through narrowed eyes. "Really? You sure? Now I really would kind of like to see your ... well, your stuff. Whatever it is."

She was trying to push free. "I can't take you now. You saw all those people. Maybe I am going to throw up. Let me out."

Larry was disgusted. He was curious, all right, but Sienna seemed really upset. Was his brother just another big bully? "Come on, Luke." Then he had an idea. "How about later? How about showing us later, after they all go?"

"Okay, whatever. Later. Now let me out. I gotta go."

Luke didn't give up. "So, later. When?"

She seemed less angry than just cornered again. "I don't know. I ..." then she suddenly seemed to gain her composure. "Okay. All right. Tonight. You be here at ten. Come in quiet. I'll watch for you—you'll see my LED light out behind the trailer. You come at ten, and I'll show you. But be quiet. Now, let me out." Larry moved, she bailed out, headed down the road at a trot, then turned and ran back. "Don't knock. Just sneak in the back. Behind the trailer."

Tiffany was still at her job, cleaning in Aspen, when they left. Larry didn't think Luke would go. He'd been cranky all evening, refusing to answer his little brother, and giving him a noogie when Larry said he didn't have to do Luke's share of the dishes. Still, it was kind of an absent-minded noogie, and maybe Luke was human after all, with as much curiosity as Larry. He'd been sprawled on the couch, texting his kajillion friends, especially the lovely Ginger, but a little after 9:30 he looked up and said, "Hey, Knothead, we better get going if we're gonna be up there on time for Miss Priss." Larry didn't even finish his game of Flappy Bird. Shutting his phone down, he stuffed it in his pocket and ran to keep up with Luke's long-legged strides to the truck.

It turned out to be more difficult than they thought. A couple of the sheriff's men were still there, doing what, that wasn't clear. Maybe just watching whatever was at the place where they'd been digging. Luke and Larry pulled on up, around the corner and out of sight, cut their engine, and hoped the officers didn't realize that their truck hadn't gone on up the mountain. Moving as furtively as possible for teenage boys, they dropped down the hill and cut through the brush toward the trailer. Larry could tell that Luke was pretending to be on a war maneuver. He kept looking around, stopping frequently to check for enemies. Larry's own primary concern was to avoid getting whacked in the face by one of the limbs Luke was catching hold of and

Baby Skulls and Fowl Odors

releasing back as he walked. Larry was also being careful not to grab one of those thorny bushes his grandpa used to call chaparral, or to have one of the ubiquitous cactus snag onto his sneaker. The dodge through the brush seemed to take forever. When they finally emerged into the little cleared area behind the trailer, Sienna's light jumped directly into their faces from six feet away, and they heard the sound of an engine starting by the road. Luke cursed. "Damn deputies are leaving — we could have just walked down the road."

Sienna grumped, "May as well have. And brought a marching band with you. You guys sneak like a herd of cows. Now, set your lights down here; somebody's going to see you."

Larry, rubbing a scratched arm, said, "I'm sorry," but Luke grumped back. "We did the best we could. So what's the big secret?"

Uttering a disgusted grunt, Sienna flounced across the cleared space behind the trailer to three wooden cages covered with chicken wire and sitting on short stilts. The stilts had been set in tin cans to prevent animals from climbing up them. "They're right here. I shouldn't show you, but I know you'll love them. They're awesome! Hold this light, Larry."

Dragging what appeared to be a very sleepy, somewhat bedraggled rooster from the first pen, Sienna placed him in Luke's hands as if she were Bilbo Baggins delivering a cache of dwarvish gold to Thorin Oakenshield. Both Luke and Larry stared at the treasure, open-mouthed. "But Sienna," Luke said. "This is a chicken."

"Not really," she snapped. "Hold on." Burrowing into the second cage, Sienna seemed to be involved in a tussle. There were annoyed squawks, then she emerged, dragging out a second rooster. It flapped and twisted, but she pinned its wings and handed it to Larry, who dropped her LED light with a clatter. She dived for the light as Larry said, "This is gonna wake ..." and Luke finished, "... up your dad."

Propping the light on a post, she said, "No, it's not. Chuck's still on drugs at night, claims it helps his foot. Wuss. He doesn't listen for outside stuff like he should, anyhow. He wouldn't hear a cougar if it ate his window screen."

Before saying more, she dived into the third cage, retrieving another flapping rooster. There were clucks and murmurs from all three cages, apparently from several disturbed chickens. She pinned the third rooster's wings and held him in the light for display. With satisfied pride, a little breathless, she said, "Aren't they beauties?"

The boys stared. Larry's rooster had feathers of many colors, black in the long tail, with white briefly appearing where the tail attached, golden and thick across the neck and wing, blue under the wing, and a ring of black and tan pointed feathers lying, like military decorations, from mid-back, down the shoulders, and across the breast. It had the most elaborate coloration of the three. Sienna's, a large fowl, had a huge black tail that draped across her arm to her waist, covering it, while its neck, back, and breast were thick with feathers in a rich, rusty red. Both of these two bright birds had little black eyes that glittered in the dark. Luke's was much simpler; it was black and white, its feathers comparatively thin over its body. After an uncomfortable silence, Larry said politely, "Well, they're real pretty, Sienna. They'd sure take a blue ribbon if you take 'em to the fair."

Luke said again, "They're chickens. They're ... nice, but they're just ... poultry."

Sienna was deeply disappointed. She knew she was doing the wrong thing, but she'd wanted so much to share these roosters with somebody. In the weak light from her LED, they saw her face pinch shut. She had thrown her gems before swine. Her voice tight, she said, "They are not. Can't you see? They are not just poultry. You are holding ... I am letting you hold prize fighting cocks. These that Larry and I have are pedigree game fowl from Hainan; they call them tail fighters, and they descended down from Green Jungle birds in Java. My grandfather bred them and fought them here in America, and they are mean, meaner than hell, just like he was."

This new information was having the desired effect on the boys. They both eyed the birds with new respect. Larry also eyed the one he held with apprehension, as it was staring directly into his face, causing Sienna to embellish. "You better be careful, or they might peck out your eyes."

Larry tried to resettle the bird facing away from his eyes, and it responded by stretching its neck, making a gurgling sound, and moving around to re-establish eye contact. Larry had put a silver ring in his ear, partly to annoy his mother, and

Baby Skulls and Fowl Odors

whenever the ring caught the light, the bird's eyes would leave Larry's face and he would tip his head to watch the ring. This was a little better, and Larry unconsciously responded by holding his ear toward the light.

Luke's rooster did not look as if it would attack anything. In fact, it seemed to have nestled dreamily into his chest, ready to return to sleep. Luke ventured, "This one doesn't seem too mean."

For the first time, Sienna smiled. "Nah, that's Xi Gong Ji. He's getting old now. He's so wonderful. He's a real, genuine Kaifeng fighting cock. My grandmother's ancestors brought his ancestors over from China, back in 1933. He's American now, like me—Xi Gong Ji means 'western rooster.'" She paused, then said hesitantly, "When we came here to the trailer, we also brought his father, Da Xi Gong Ji. That means big western rooster. But he ... he died."

Luke was smiling, too, and began to affectionately stroke Xi Gong Ji's feathers. Encouraged, Sienna said, "He and Da were my grandmother's birds. She wasn't mean like the old man. I heard that he killed my sister, then ran to Puerto Rico because it is the only place where cock fighting is still legal. Okay with Puerto Rico law, but still illegal according to the feds. That's what my mother said. And she said he was killed there himself, in a knife fight. She was glad."

"But this wasn't his rooster?"

"Not really. It came from my grandmother. I met her once, and she told me about the ancestor to this rooster. She said it was given to her father, but when you are given a Kaifeng gamecock, it is a really special gift, and you have to obey the rules. It is better than being given thousands of dollars. You can raise it, but you can't transfer it to others or breed it. If you can't raise it, you have to kill it and eat it, but give the head and feet back to the original owner. That shows you have good faith, because that first owner would rather give away his kid than give away his gamecock to someone who doesn't appreciate how it can fight."

Larry said, "Wow!", but Luke said, "That doesn't make sense. If your great-grandpa couldn't breed the first rooster, how did this one get here after all these years?"

"How should I know? Maybe he just ... maybe he just needed to start Kaifeng birds in America. People are always bringing stuff to this country, then changing it. It happens. Stuff happens in America."

Helpfully, Larry said, "Maybe he started some little chickens, then ate the first bird and mailed the feet back to China."

Both Sienna and Luke ignored this suggestion. Luke, growing increasingly skeptical, said, "But there seem to be hens in all the cages. They must be breeding anyhow."

Less and less happy about having revealed her special secret to the boys, Sienna said scornfully, "Oh, that's just Chuck for you. He says males get lonely without females around, so he got a bunch of hens and stuck them in there. We eat the eggs."

Still skeptical, Luke said, "So why is it all so hushy hushy? Why can't you just let people know you have some nice pedigreed roosters here?"

Sienna was shocked. "I *told* you! Cockfighting is illegal everywhere in this country. People have been ... people can be arrested for fighting cocks."

Luke started to ask if she was planning to fight them, but a distant rumble of thunder signaled one of those fast rising mountain storms, always welcome in a drought ridden country. Xi Gong Ji pushed his cowardly little head deeper into Luke's chest, but Larry's rooster suddenly scuffled in his arms and began to peck furiously at the ring in Larry's ear. Larry shrieked and dropped the bird, which caused Sienna to yelp and dive for it. Somehow, she managed to masterfully capture the dropped rooster while crushing the other Hainon cock under her arm. Luke, standing his ground with Xi Gong Ji, yelled, "Help her, damn it, Larry!"

Shoving the roosters back into their cages, Sienna said, "I think you people better go."

Larry said, "Yeah, sorry about this," and turned to pick up his light, but Luke's feet were still firmly planted. "There's something not right about this here. Sienna, you ain't bein' straight with us. Before I leave, I want to know what all those cops and 'No Chicken' signs are doing all over your property. Are you sure you aren't trying to start some kind of illegal chicken farm here? And I saw them digging—you told us you buried your mother there. Why would they be digging up your mother? What happened to her?"

Larry turned his light toward Sienna in time to see that she was spitting mad, like she had been on the bus. "My mother is absolutely none of your business. I said, get off this place. Nobody in this whole valley can be trusted, not even you two assholes. I let you know about the awesome fighting cocks here, and then you go back to talking trash, talking chicken factory shit and about my mother. I told you, my mother is dead. I told you that. And it isn't her they are digging up; it is some old prehistoric skeleton. So leave me alone. Just leave!"

There was nothing more to say. The deputies were gone, so the boys passed the trailer to go to the road, leaving Sienna with her back to them, fussing over the chickens. Much of the area inside the crime scene tape had been covered with tarp, which was a good thing, as just as the boys reached the road, the entire hillside was illuminated by lightning, followed immediately by a deafening clap of thunder. They ran. It was uphill, but they were young. They had almost gained the truck when the next flash and roar occurred, followed by a gush of rain so powerful that it sent water surging in rivers down the rocky ruts of the road.

Gaining the truck, slamming the doors against the rush of water that was coming in with them, Larry yelled over the din, "Gully washer," and Luke yelled back, "Cow pissin' on a flat rock." Hurrying to turn the truck and maneuver down the mountain before the road washed out, they swung right at Oozle Road to avoid the more common washouts that occurred in the loop just past Johnson's. As they passed Barnswallowper's, Larry, with his nose against the dripping window, said, "Slow down, Luke. That looks like Mom's car there at Nancy Jane's."

"If I go any slower, we'll grow roots," Luke growled, skidding around a sharp left. "And don't be stupid—we're already late. Why would Mom be up here at this time of night? She'll be home, and you better be ready. She'll be mad."

He was wrong on both counts, though. It was Lisa Marie, their older sister, who met them at the door, seething. Lisa was married and lived in Peaseford with her kid and her coal-mining husband. "Where the hell have you two been? Mom's been trying and trying to call you. It's storming on the pass, and she isn't going to drive over, too many slides lately. She finally called me, so now here I am, trying to deal with you two big babies. I thought I'd get a good night sleep once Trevon left for his graveyard shift, and the last thing I need is to worry about you two little snots."

Luke hung his head appropriately. "Sorry, Sis. Mom said she'd be late, so we were just bummin' around a little. Guess we lost track of the time. Got distracted. We're okay; you can go home now."

Larry, looking from face to face, echoed, "Yeah, distracted," but Luke was watching Lisa dial. She put in their mom's cell number, and he could hear Tiffany's voice. "Are they okay?" and Lisa replied, "Yeah, unfortunately. They're fine, the thoughtless little bastards." She and Tiffany talked a minute, but Luke wandered into the kitchen, pretending to search out food. He needed privacy. He needed to think—something was way off, way off about this whole evening. Their mom's cell didn't work in Aspen. Once you got over the pass, you lost reception. Lisa didn't seem to get it, but their mom wasn't in Aspen. That much he knew.

20

OLD LEW HARRIS WAS ACTING just about as cranky as Garrett felt. Lew had been thrilled to have unannounced guests, but the more he talked, the more he recalled gloomy events from his ranching days of yore, and the more he got out of sorts. As for Garrett, he was trying to be patient, but his last twenty-four hours had been a whirlwind of worrisome decisions, and he felt physically tired and emotionally drained. He felt as if one more time of having to nod sympathetically at the problem of the calf with water belly that had died over ten years ago might put him over the edge. "Hard to diagnose," Lew repeated for at least the third time, and Garrett figured that pretty much summed things up for his own issues, too. He tried to find an opening to break into the flow of reminiscences, but the next story had already started and he was forced to sigh, lean forward, and attempt to look attentive.

Last night, McCracken had driven him back to the station after the police work up at Fowler's was well under way. At that point, Garrett had been washed through with cold fury at himself. What had he been thinking, getting all cozy with Jenny, telling a big lie to McCracken, and losing every trace of objectivity and professionalism. That dark-haired hippie woman had bewitched him. He still had a case to solve. He was no closer to knowing how that skeleton had come to be in the doll than before the day started yesterday. While Jenny was with him, he had forgotten about the big Black guy, Jenny's Xyster, and he'd forgotten about Tiffany's catty comment on her text: "a black guy lol." Why didn't he pick up sooner on the fact that in the restaurant at the time of the fire there had been two Black guys. Why had Tiffany arrived on scene "as if she lived next door"?

Did Tiffany set the fire to smoke them out, then wait outside, hoping to shoot the Black guys? Was she that prejudiced? Everyone around here seemed to solve a lot of problems with guns, and now that he was not in the car with Jenny, he realized that he did, after all, trust his memory. Jenny had made small of it, but he was sure someone had told him they heard a shot as they ran from the door of the burning building. Maybe Jenny was in cahoots with Tiffany and covering for her. How did it all tie together, anyhow—fire, doll skeleton, buried skeleton? As he mulled this over, he decided he should go see old Lew. Lew might be dingy, but he might recall about the shot. Lew didn't have a hold on him, like Jenny did. He didn't want to admit it, but it was true. Despite everything, Xyster and all, Jenny still had a hold on him. It made his heart ache.

It was just then, heading into Riversmet, that McCracken tried to break the long conversational drought. "Jenny sure does love those wildflowers, doesn't she?"

"It would seem so," Garrett snapped, and they rode the rest of the way to the station in silence.

Driving home, he saw that thunder clouds were moving down from the mountains, bringing rain that hit his windshield with weak splatters, smearing the dust. He brought his mind up to spin and made himself think about what he had to do. A-deet would have to be included in this investigation. That would be his first step.

The next morning he called her into his office. Squelching her attempt at playful banter, he said, "A-deet, I have a big problem, and I need your help. I think I heard once that you are skilled with a sewing needle?"

"*Sí.* I sew a little, and *mi mama* sews good. What is it you need?"

"You can't bring your mama into this. This has to be kept under cover for a while. Can you do that for me?" With her curious nod of assent, he gave her the doll's background as carefully and briefly as possible, then he pulled the toy from the box by his desk. Even though she'd been told, Edith gasped as the facial flap fell aside, exposing the tiny skull.

"Here's what I want. I'm hoping you can stitch her back together, as near like new as possible." Edith started to object, but he said, "No, it doesn't have to be perfect. I think I'll take her to Alma, and Alma doesn't see so very well anymore. She probably won't even notice, if you stitch carefully." Now he gave her the old teasing grin. "Do this for me, and there is dinner in it for you, my lady, you and all your *familia*."

Edith grinned back. "How could I refuse, *señor?*"

Garrett waxed serious again. "Oh, and A-deet? They got most of that skeleton out of Fowlers' yesterday. We'll send it on up to the lab, the coroner will have a look, then maybe call in CBI. We're going to need identification. Anyhow, the team is still working. They may find more today. There's too much going on up at Croysant right now, and I want you to get on the horn to me if you hear anything new about that area. Private call. Not radio."

"You bet. Can do." Edith fetched a big black sack from supplies, carefully enclosed the doll, and carried her out. With the doll's exit, Garrett felt a quiet flush of relief.

He gathered up McCracken and they headed on up to Lew's, after which they would go to the crime scene. He felt so irritable at her texting all the way that he threatened her. "Mac, you know that texts are admissible evidence in a court of law, don't you?"

To his surprise, she set her phone aside and said, "Yeah. That's not good. I've been trying to think about this. You know, I made a mistake and texted Tiffany about the skeleton yesterday. That's a breach, I guess."

Garrett, still smarting from awareness of his own lapse in professional behavior, said, "Maybe."

"So Tiffany has been texting me back. She's not sure herself, what she should say, because she's not sure where HIPAA ethics come in on all this, what with her having been called out on Chuck Fowler's case and all, but she's pretty sure she knows who the skeleton is, and she has decided it is okay to tell me."

Glancing at his deputy with some annoyance, Garrett said, "Well, I'm pretty damn sure at this point it's also okay to tell me. Who the hell does she think it is? And why?"

"She thinks it is Xi Feng Ling, Fowler's wife. The reason is, one day on the bus the kids were bullying Fowler's kid, Sienna, and she started fighting back by yelling at them. She told them the land loop wasn't Nancy Jane's because her and her dad had buried her mother there, and they planned to build their house near the grave so the mother could guard it, or be close, or something. Larry—that's Tiffany's kid—was on the bus and overheard all that and then he told Tiffany."

Garrett's face had become stormy. "Mac, this isn't a HIPAA issue. She knows that. Why the hell didn't Tiffany come forward sooner?"

"I dunno," this said weakly. "I think she is just swamped, raising those rowdy boys and all, and you know. Kids say things. You're never sure."

"It still doesn't compute. Why doesn't Fowler come forward now? That skeleton is old, maybe as old as the one in the doll. Maybe not. But what in Sam Hill is going on here, Mac?"

They rode in sour silence until they reached Lew Harris's, where things took a decided turn for the worse. Recalling the courtesy they were expected to show last year toward Lew's deceased wife, Lucky, Garrett and McCracken remained standing when Lew asked them to sit. They didn't want to sit on Lucky, as they had done once before. Awkwardly, Garrett said, "Mac, I wonder if that's Lucky's favorite chair? What does she say?"

Lew stared at Garrett as if he'd lost his marbles. "Sit down, damn it. I don't let Lucky on the furniture."

The sheriff and deputy exchanged shocked glances, but obediently sat. Lew started to sit, too, then he creaked back into standing position. "You know, I think I'll put Lucky out. She isn't too well trained around strangers. It's okay, Sheriff—you don't have to pet 'er. She begs everybody like that."

With that, he walked through the kitchen to the back door, gave a sharp whistle, opened the door and rasped loudly, "Come on, Lucky. Come on, pooch. Get on out." Garrett and McCracken, both leaning out of their seats and craning to see, saw him give a brisk nudge with his foot, which almost overbalanced him because the movement was aimed at open space. With an air of satisfaction, he closed the door and tottered back toward them. McCracken couldn't resist whispering to Garrett, "Good lord! Lucky has morphed into a dog!"

Overhearing the dog part, Lew said as he sat, "Yeah, she's more than a fine dog, but she needs some work on her company manners. She's a good hunter, though."

Both McCracken and Garrett opened their mouths, but nothing came out. What was she, a beagle? A bloodhound? A

Baby Skulls and Fowl Odors

terrier? Finally, swallowing, McCracken asked, "What does she hunt best? I mean, what does she kind of, uh, like to hunt?"

Lew looked concerned, still not certain his two visitors were quite bright. "Well, she's a bird dog, as you can see. A pointer. She's good with pheasant, of course." While his guests tried to recall exactly what a bird dog looked like, Garrett taking his imagination to classical paintings of merry England and the hunting upper classes, Lew continued, narrowing his eyes at them. "I guess what you're trying to say is that she's obviously young, and you're right. She'll be better as she gets some experience." Suddenly, the old man shot up and began to shuffle rapidly around the room, shouting "ow ow ow ow ow!"

Both Garrett and McCracken were out of their seats. "What? What is it? What's the matter?" Garrett caught up and reached for his elbow, but Lew pushed him away, yelling, "Don't touch! Cramp cramp cramp cramp—vinegar! Kitchen! Vinegar!" He began a rapid hobble toward the kitchen, still yelling, "Ow! Cramp! Vinegar!" McCracken had reached the kitchen, too, and she was yelling, "Where? Where? Where?"

Shoving past her, Lew snatched a quart bottle of vinegar from the cabinet by the stove, tipped it up, and began to swallow. As the liquid rapidly disappeared, both McCracken and Garrett dived for the bottle, pulling it from his shaking hands. Garrett said, "Enough already. Give it a minute to work, Lew."

Lew embarked again, half hopping and half walking around the kitchen. McCracken got into his face, shouting, "Where does it hurt? Can we massage it?" to be answered with "No no no ow left calf … " then suddenly, "Ahhhhh. There it goes!" Lew turned to them with a smile. "Miracle drug, that vinegar. Pain all gone. Now, what was it you two wanted?"

This could have been promising, but before they could answer, Lew had launched into cramp stories, which led to cramps being worse in autumn, which somehow led to hunting stories about thoughtless hunters who scattered cattle because they didn't leave the gates as they found them, which led to bow hunting and an arrow-shot calf that had been eased out of the mountains, only to have its mother give up on it and it had to be shot with a gun anyhow, which cycled back to the water belly calf again. This was making them all increasingly gloomy. Garrett and McCracken tried occasionally to stop the word stampede by interjecting a "Well," or a "How about," but Lew was oblivious, and the words flowed on. McCracken knew she was losing it when she started wishing that Lucky would bark, or scratch to come in. And that is exactly what happened. Lew stopped mid-sentence and said, "I hate when that dog scratches that door like that. She's gonna ruin the paint. Say, did you hear about old Cliff Atcheson the other day?"

The sheriff and deputy had seized the break in the flow to stand. Without waiting for an answer, Lew continued, "Well, he had that stroke, you know, and they got him to the hospital. But what I wanted to tell you was the part that tickled me." Garrett and McCracken exchanged glances. Lew was struggling out of his chair. "See, old Cliff fell outta that hospital bed, and the nurse came in and found him flat on the floor." Lew chuckled merrily. "'Mr. Atcheson,' she says, 'Mr. Atcheson, did ya fall?' and from the floor old Cliff, flat on his back and purely helpless, he says, 'Oh, no, ma'm. I just thought I'd have a look, see what's under this bed.'" Lew's laugh was between a chortle and a wheeze. "Old Cliff. Always a damn good cowpoke, fine sense of humor. Now, what did you want to ask me?"

Did he still want to ask Lew anything? Would it get him started up again? Carefully, Garrett said, "Oh, we just wanted to know — that night you hurt your leg, when there was a fire at the Cowpath. I guess you tripped over Lucky. Anyhow, do you remember if you heard shots?"

Nodding wisely, pleased with the question, Lew said, "No, can't say as I do. Remember, that is. My memory just isn't what it used to be; barely know my own name sometimes, and sure don't recall that night. Now, if you two will let yourselves out, I need to get that dog in before she scratches my door to shreds."

21

LARRY HAD NEVER, EVER, ever, ever felt so shitty. Guilty, worried, and totally miserable, but worse. His arm had begun to throb with a terrifying insistence. He curled himself into a wretched, embryonic ball and knew he would have to tell his mother. But what? How much should he tell her? What could he say that wouldn't cast her youngest son in a horrible light? If he told just a little, she would think he was an idiot, but if he tried to give her the whole truth it would look as if he were trying to frame Luke. He didn't want to be a tattle tale. Especially not after Luke had told him why he had to keep his mouth shut.

He groaned and nursed his arm against his belly. Well, it was that stupid Luke where it had all started, wasn't it? It was his fault. Luke just couldn't resist; he had to tell the winsome Ginger about Sienna's roosters. He made it a big story, himself the hero. He made it sound as if he were wise because he doubted whether the birds were really legitimate fighting cocks. Larry overheard and was furious about Luke's betrayal of Sienna's trust. He got even by telling his own best friend, Cesar, and making it his own story. How stupid was that? He groaned again and went to the kitchen. The only thing in the freezer were five Marie Callender dinners. His favorite, meat loaf, was there, but he hurt so bad it didn't tempt him. He carried it back to his bedroom and curled up again, trying to press the cold against his arm. The box wouldn't bend right, and he wished for a sack of frozen peas, like his mom would have used. Actually, despite everything, he just wished for his mom. His shoulder had started to hurt worse now, too, where the fire had grazed it.

After listening to Luke's fighting cock story with big, googly, admiring eyes, and being told it was secret, Ginger had gone directly, do-not-pass-go, no morals at all, to her friend, Pewter. Larry hated Ginger. At least right now. Pewter, chubby and sweet of face, said, "Why, if they are soldier chickens, they will probably fight. Isn't that what soldiers do? When they see the enemy, they fight, right?" Her eyes caught Luke's, daring him. Behind that sweet face lurked pure evil; of that, Larry was certain.

They tried to cut Larry out of it, but he wouldn't hear of it. He stood up to Luke and told him that if they didn't take him and Cesar that he would tell Tiffany about the whole thing. Larry moaned and shifted, throwing the useless TV dinner on the floor, and wishing that he had been nobly and responsibly thinking of Sienna when he insisted on going, but in fact, he wasn't. He was doubly guilty. He wasn't trying to stick up for innocent Sienna at all — he just wanted to be in on whatever was going to happen.

Well, he certainly was. They went at 2:00 a.m.; that, they figured, would be late enough that even Sienna would be asleep. Creeping across the Fowler place, their lights held low, they passed the drooping crime scene tape and the "No Chickens" signs, now soggy and blurry from the rain. Luke held Ginger's hand tightly so that she would be safe and not trip into a grave or something, and the other three followed closely behind.

Since they had insisted on being there despite objections, Cesar and Larry had been designated as rooster carriers, but Luke, at least, did the actual heist. They all agreed to leave Xi Gong Ji alone, since he was old and too mellow; they just took the healthy, supposedly mean, Hainan fighting cocks.

"Now, be ready," Luke whispered, turning up his light and diving into the cages. The big, black-tailed cock came without a sound, and Luke pushed him at Cesar. The more brightly colored rooster that Larry had held before gave a sharp, surprised squawk, causing everyone to freeze in place. All of their eyes shot to the trailer, but it stayed mercifully dark; no lights came on inside. Luke had the bird's neck in a death grip and was hissing, "Douse your lights." As the trailer continued quiet, he released the rooster's neck. It gurgled, and he handed it to Larry. The bird struggled briefly, then its eye caught the ring in Larry's ear. He was just raising his glittery-eyed head to peck when Luke hissed at Pewter, "Give me your damn jacket." As

Baby Skulls and Fowl Odors

Larry twisted his head back, dodging the snakelike approach of the bright Hainan rooster head, Luke threw Pewter's coat over it and whispered, "Now, let's get outta here."

Larson's old barn wasn't far, just down by the club house, but Cesar and Larry were in the back riding on the hard truck bed, bouncing among Luke's various tools and collections of ropes, jacks, and other odds and ends, clutching the struggling roosters, and trying to keep their balance. The older teens in front were catching an adrenalin high, but Cesar and Larry were ready for the adventure to end.

Unfortunately, it didn't end there. At the barn, Luke, Pewter, and Ginger worked for some time dragging up old musty hay bales to make a "cock fighting arena." The younger boys tried to hand off the roosters to the girls so they could help carry bales, a far more manly task than holding chickens, but the girls refused to take them. Luke struggled with the heavy barn doors and Ginger, in the role of trusty helpmeet, shoved and pulled with him. Larry, neutralized on the sidelines with the struggling rooster, commented to Cesar that closing the doors was stupid. "You could still throw a cat out of a hundred gaps between those logs in this creaky old dump." Cesar agreed, but the two had to continue watching, powerless, as their elders set the place up.

When the ring was finally ready, everyone turned their lights on full beam in order to better see the battle. Pewter now said sweetly to Cesar, "Here, let me hold your rooster. I want to hug him, because I think he is the one who will be champion."

"Don't give him to her," Larry grumped, but Cesar shoved the bird into her arms and said, "Good. There's something I need from the truck."

Luke was relaxed and teasing, "Okay, wanna take bets? How about you, brat? Wanna bet on that long-necked earring pecker of yours? He's mean enough. He could win."

Cesar was pushing against the door to get out, but it wouldn't yield. Everyone started to argue as to whether they really needed to let him out, anyhow, but finally Luke pulled on it and with the effort of the two of them, the door opened.

Sullenly, Larry responded to Luke's earlier question. "Sure, we're already illegal as hell anyhow, stealing chickens, having a cock fight. We may as well gamble, too." He'd about had enough of this whole thing; he couldn't wait to dump this wiggling bird into the ring and get it over with. He continued, "All I got is two dollars, Pewter. Wanna see me against that big baby of a rooster you're holding?"

Cesar returned, carrying an old-fashioned kerosene lantern. It was lit, and it cast a pretty, mellow glow in front of the boy as he walked. Luke was nonplussed. "You mean we went to all that trouble to get that door back open so you could get that thing? It's not bright enough to light ab... to light ab..."

Pewter injected smugly, "Yeah, it's way dim. About like Cesar."

Cesar ignored the jibes. "My grandpa fought cocks in Mexico. It's a shitty sport, but I love *mi abuelo*, so I brought this lantern to honor him. It's his. So shut up. It's symbolic, man."

"Help me close this thing," Luke yelled, struggling with the heavy, weather-warped barn door. Ginger sashayed over and they pushed it shut, Ginger grunting prettily, while Cesar carefully positioned his lantern on a hay bale; he smiled. It might not cast much light, but he could see it, and that's what counted. *Abuelo* would be pleased. And he'd never know Cesar took it from his room, anyhow.

Suddenly, without further ado, Pewter threw her game cock into the ring and raised her arm, fist clinched. "Let the battle begin! Bring on your chicken chicken, Larry!"

At last. Larry set his rooster down in the ring and stretched his arms, shaking out the cramped feeling, glad to be rid of the animal. Pewter's rooster had hunkered down on its haunches, seemingly bored and ready to sleep. Larry's wandered about, inspecting the hay bales, giving them an occasional peck, ignoring the other rooster. Luke was disgusted. "Some fighting cocks."

Defensively, Larry said, "It's nighttime. I think they're just sleepy."

"Cock fights are at night. Otherwise, the cops would catch them." Ginger leaned against him. Luke, she thought, was both very wise and also delicious.

Suddenly, Larry had a brainstorm. Pulling on his earring to remove it, he said, "Cesar, help me, buddy. Make your rooster stand up, and put this on his beak." Jumping agilely into the circle of bales, Larry grabbed the other rooster, pinning its wings

Baby Skulls and Fowl Odors

to carry it. Cesar was on deck, holding up the sleepy chicken, but the ring wouldn't stay on its beak, so he dangled it in front of the bird. In the dim light, Pewter was trying to catch Ginger's eye to roll her own eyes in shared disgust. Larry was positioning his bird. "Now, make that ring kind of twinkle in the light," he said.

It was working! Larry's bird had begun to track on the flashing ring, and as it did, Cesar's bird opened its eyes, suddenly aware of the apparent threat moving its head back and forth in front of it. Both boys released their holds, but what happened next had them falling backward, scrambling for the safety of the hay bales. The roosters were fighting! There was a flurry of feathers and a frightening flash of sharp spurs as they shot into the air, wings pounding, kicking and striking. Pewter shouted, "Hurray! They really are soldiers, after all." This irritated Luke, but, caught up in the fight, he kept his mouth shut.

What the teens didn't notice was that the fight was moving inexorably across the arena. Just as Ginger cried out, "But how will we know which one wins?" Larry lost his bet. His brightly colored cock turned tail, flapping mightily, and clawed for the top of the nearest bale. He slipped and fell back into the arena with his foe, still flapping, and the lantern followed him down. There was an instant puff of flame as the dust that the chickens had raised caught fire, then a larger explosion as the kerosene in the lantern caught. Screaming, everyone but Larry surged to the heavy, closed door and began to push and pull on it, wildly at odds with each other. Smoke filled the dark room as the fire licked greedily at the musty bales.

Larry dived into the arena, trying stupidly to clear the smoke with a flailing hand, so that he could see. He was searching for Sienna's singed roosters. While his friends were yelling, "Push on it! No, pull, you idiot!", all coughing and spitting, he felt his way to one of the LED lights. He tried to cast the beam around the ring, but the smoke was thick and curling, blocking the light, choking him. He had to leave.

The door had yielded and amid a rush of people he heard shouts of, "Where's Larry? Where's Larry?" The air from the door had intensified the flames, blocking his vision. He wasn't sure himself where he was. He started to stumble blindly forward, but a shift in flame direction showed him the greater darkness of outside and Luke, silhouetted against that outside space and coming toward him, groping his way toward Larry's LED light. "Get out of here, you damn stupid shit!" Luke had him by the sleeve. "This place is a tinderbox!"

"But the roosters!" Larry was resisting, an addled drowning swimmer fighting his rescuer.

"Forget 'em." Then, in a steady voice, "They're already out, you dope. They're okay, Larry. I saw 'em outside. Now come on."

Larry yielded, stumbling through the flames after his brother, somewhere in the distance hearing Ginger keening dramatically, "Luke, Luke, Luke! Oh, come back, my Lucas!" They reached the door. Timbers fell behind them and ashes flew up, the fire beginning to exude a relentless, fearsome roar. Then something else fell right on Larry from above, screaming like a banshee. Larry knew instantly, and made a grab for it, but it was on the move, headed for open ground. He started to run after it, stumbling and gasping, and as the terrified and confused chicken stopped for an instant, he dived, making another grab. It braced against his bare arm and flew, the spur catching at his flesh, digging in. In its panicked escape, the fighting cock opened a wide swath of muscle and skin down his forearm before disappearing into the night.

Luke, who knew a trick or two from their EMT mother, had stopped the bleeding, applied antiseptic, and bandaged the wound. "Don't tell her," he said. "Don't tell Mom anything. If she turns us in and we're convicted, I can't do the army. You get that? This thing could ruin my whole life. And she'll know that. Mom goes to her morning shift in about an hour, and for all she will know, we are safely asleep here, then in school. So just keep your mouth shut."

He looked at his drained little brother, a child's face pale on the pillow. "Look, I will go to school today, okay? I'll act normal. You don't have to. And I'll tell them again — I'll make sure everybody keeps their lips buttoned, like we all agreed, okay? We'll all just act normal."

That was this morning, and the day drug by, Larry sleeping fitfully and then staring at the wall. Luke didn't get home; he must be staying after school, back in physical training, the shit, trying to act normal, while by now, Larry was rolling back and forth, trying to contain the pain in his arm. Their mom would be home in minutes, and he had to tell her. Even if he didn't need help with this arm, which he did, she would see him in bed and ask what happened. But what could he tell her?

In the end, he covered for them all. He took the blame himself. As she stood, work-depleted and weary, frowning down at her wan youngest son in his messy, blood-stained bed, he knew that it would be him who could get away with it. She would be mad, but she couldn't get too mad at him, not in his condition. "Mom," he said, "I did something really rotten. I got curious about that Sienna, what she had on her place and all, you know? You know how she kept acting funny, like hiding something and stuff? Luke and me asked her if she was going to have a chicken farm, and she told us that she wasn't, 'cause she had something way better in back of the trailer. So Mom, I am sorry, sorry, sorry, but I sneaked in back, just to see. And I don't know what she is talking about, because there are chickens back there. They really do have chickens, and one of the roosters got me with its spurs."

Tiffany's small, strong body had stiffened as he spoke, and her scowl had deepened. Larry decided he hadn't quite made his case; he better keep talking. "Mom, I know I shouldn't have done that, and I'm really, really, really sorry. You know me, I was just curious, you know?" Now came the hard part. It got to the heart of the lie. He had to say it. "I honestly don't think I hurt anything. Just me. Just that rooster hurt me, with its spurs." This last effort brought a lump and tears, and Larry was quiet.

She took a deep breath. How stupid did this kid think she was? Did he think she would believe he flew up to Fowlers'? Who took him up there? And what kind of rooster bloodied somebody up this much? She expelled the breath. She'd get the straight story from him and that other jerk son of hers all in good time. But for now ... she shook her head. The tears, those were real.

"Okay, hold out your arm. Let me see it." Her voice was rough and cranky. Her hands were tender.

22

SHERIFF PAT GARRETT sat alone in a back booth at the restored Cowpath, keeping his own counsel. A young woman he didn't know, whom he simply thought of as a Not-Jenny, brought a menu, but he waved it away. "Burger and coffee," he said, and she folded the menu under her arm as she asked, "Fries? Cheese? Cream?"

"Yes, fries; yes, cheese; black."

"Comin' right up, Sheriff. Jenny's not here. She called in sick, but she said she'd be here for the official opening of this place day after tomorrow."

He knew that; on the way up to Fowlers', she'd said she was going to take a day or two off to hunt for her doll. He'd felt guilty, knowing then that the doll was safe in Riversmet, but he'd thankfully made himself keep his trap shut. Anyhow, why would this unknown little snippet of a waitress assume it mattered to him where Jenny was? People in these small towns guessed far too much about other people's business.

As it was, he had come here for lunch precisely because he knew Jenny would not be here. He had to clear his mind, and that couldn't happen for him around Jenny. The Not-Jenny brought his coffee, saying, "Burger be right up. What do you think of our fixed-up digs, Sheriff?"

Garrett looked around. He hadn't really thought about it when he came in, but he realized now that they'd done some remodeling as they cleaned up. One wall was now devoted to the arrowhead collection that had earlier been in the display case under the cash register. A larger wall had a set of longhorn steer horns surrounded by a collection of old-fashioned farm implements. Most of this had been in the pre-fire Cowpath, but

Baby Skulls and Fowl Odors

it was now lovingly rearranged. The ambience still included a selection of mounted antlers and stuffed animal heads: wildcat, elk, and, in the back, a bear. One thing new was that they had managed to incorporate some excellent twentieth century ranching photographs that were being collected, copied, captioned, and framed by a local historian, Dan Cotten. Garrett also spotted at least three of Carmen Weinant's surprising trout paintings, paintings that somehow submerged you in the water with the fish. He loved those. Every table had new plastic coverings; the tables had lost their dusty plastic flower arrangements, these having been replaced by new, clean plastic flowers. The wood paneled back wall was still covered with local ranchers' cattle brands; these seemed darker and may have been re-stamped. Garrett wasn't sure.

The overall effect of the place was cluttered and claustrophobic. "Well," Garrett said, "You've got lots of interesting stuff in here."

Non-Jenny shrugged. "You could put it that way. Myself, I think it looks pretty junky. Makes me feel boxed in."

The cook's bell signaled the completion of Garrett's burger. A large group of people entered, milled about, exchanged comments, and finally sorted themselves out among the individual booths and tables. Garrett took a big bite of his cheeseburger, one of Cookie's better concoctions, chewing as he narrowed his eyes to assess the various newcomers. "Now, what the devil next," he thought. An interesting odor combination of barbecued meat and caramelized onions drifted toward him from the kitchen, while a group of four at a nearby table received orders of lemonade and iced tea as they engaged in a noisy debate. "KGSP is already on its way from Riversmet; I say we start on up."

"I'm personally all for finding a bush, grabbing some Z's, and waiting for KOPN from Denver."

Garrett was familiar with those television stations. They'd given him trouble in the past. KGSP: "All the things you really need to know about your neighbors," and KOPN: "Everyone has an opinion, so what's yours?" KOPN featured endless commentators and some call-ins, which were usually squelched after a few words, and not much news. What were these people in here up to that was going to get news coverage? He was afraid he knew, and a comment from another person at the table confirmed it. "I do know this; we really should wait until the PETA people get here."

Hmmmm. Garrett wondered who had ordered the barbecued meat; it was unlikely that there were any carnivores in the new arrivals. Looking around, he spotted Clint and Patty Harris by the door, minding their own business as they shared barbecued ribs and cowboy beans with their kid, already a toddler! Man, time did fly. Patty had just been pregnant at the time of the Biedermann case up here, and now the kid was eating ribs. At least that case had been resolved satisfactorily, except maybe for Mac Biedermann, the wife-abusing, drug-dealing son. He disappeared right after it all came down, and as near as Garrett knew, the younger Biedermann was still on the lam. Well, anyhow, this group of people coming in had a mission that was pretty transparent. How the hell did they find out about the chicken farm issue, anyhow? Garrett felt old. News traveled way too fast in this day and age.

One of the women at the table near him had turned her chair out so she could bend, grab her ankles, and stretch the muscles in her legs. She turned her legs this way and that, seemingly to admire them. "Well," she said, "I don't care if we hang out and wait awhile, but not in this crummy place. All those dead animals give me the creeps." Just then, Non-Jenny got tangled in the moving, extended legs as she tried to make her way to Garrett to refresh his coffee. She juggled the hot pot and danced for balance as the leg woman said, "Oh. Sorry," and continued to stretch, moving from the legs to elaborate arm movements that kept her hands swirling in the face of the man at the nearby table.

Watching, Garrett told Non-Jenny, "Thanks, good coffee." This obviously wasn't working, stopping here to find privacy to clear his mind and sort through all the information from the last few days. He'd thought maybe that by sitting in the Cowpath he could get another angle on the fire. No one seemed to think it was any more than it purported to be, an accident, definitely not a crime scene, and yet something about it nagged at him. Maybe he was just procrastinating, gnawing at the fire issue to avoid the real problems. But what about the note? The note was one of the things this morning that seemed to make this whole situation balloon out of proportion. The excess information intake had

Baby Skulls and Fowl Odors

started immediately when he arrived at work. McCracken more or less met him at the door. "Just so you don't think I'm holding out on you, I thought I'd let you know that Tiffany said she is taking a sick day and staying home from work today."

She stopped speaking, and Garrett finally said, "So this is important because ... ?"

Actually, McCracken hadn't been so sure herself if it was important. Maybe not so important as to break her friend's confidence. Still. Jogged from her reflection on this dilemma, she finished.

"Well, Chief, she isn't staying home for herself. Her kid, Larry, got scratched up pretty good last night by a rooster. He's running a little fever, and Tiffany wants to keep tabs on him. Thing is, he got scratched up at Fowlers'. You know, Fowler says he doesn't have chickens. Isn't that what he said? But I guess Larry and Fowler's little girl, that Sienna, they were playing rough with the chickens, so that's how he got scratched. Rooster spurs."

The look Garrett gave McCracken was long and thoughtful. Finally he said, "Thanks for keeping me in the loop, Mac. I'll keep this information in mind."

She had no sooner retreated to her own office than Edith appeared, carrying the big black bag. Garrett, dreading the trip to Alma's, thought, "Already?" but said, "So, what you got there, A-deet?"

"Couple things. I no like workin' around that poor dead baby, but I do the best I can." She pulled the doll from the sack and handed it gently to the sheriff, who turned it carefully over in his hands, then breathed, "Wow. Your mama taught you good."

Edith beamed. "Big dinner for *mi familia*, huh?"

"Big dinner, you bet." Garrett grinned. "Thanks, A-deet. Our baby girl here looks much better. I think she's ready to venture back out into the world. At least as far as Alma's."

"I think so," Edith agreed, her clasped hands those of a concerned mother as she watched Garrett carefully fold the doll back into the box by his desk. "I hope you solve this case, find out who she is."

"Me, too," Garrett said, folding the box top.

"Now," Edith continued, "There is one more thing." Her

voice had a new tone.

Garrett looked up sharply. "Yes?"

"A fellow came by early this morning, a good-looking young Black man. He brought you a note that he found on the steering wheel of his car. He said he has hesitated to stir up any potentially muddy waters, so he didn't come in sooner, but he finally decided that the note is threatening enough that he would be remiss not to report it."

"Well." He was trying to read Edith, whose English flowed like water downhill when the matter was serious, and now, having delivered a masterfully articulate statement, she seemed to be unsure how to proceed. Was the bearer of the note that damned Brady Xyster? "Well," he repeated, "I guess I'd better see the note."

"The young man said the note worries him because he's just taken a teaching position at Peaseford High School for this coming year. He's a science teacher." She handed the tidily folded note to Garrett. Unfolding, he read what appeared to be a quick scrawl:

No one wants your kind in our schools.

"Oh, boy." Garrett pulled at his mustache. "And he was Black?" Edith nodded. "Not too many African Americans in this area. I guess there could be more bigotry than I thought ... " He paused. "Where did he say he found this?"

"Taped to his steering wheel."

"No, I mean, when? Where was the car?"

"Oh. The night of the Cowpath fire. He was having a night out with his buddies, some men and women that all graduated high school together a few years back. Then they got smoked out. Then he found this."

Garrett tried to repress that "gotcha" feeling; too soon for that. Even so. Edith continued, "I think he didn't come by any sooner, not until he had time to think about it, because the group had gotten pretty well oiled, and at the time, the fire and all the excitement kind of turned the evening into even more of a lark. The kind of adventure you tell your grandkids. Before he left here, he gave me a big smile and said, 'Well, at least we didn't have to pay for our dinner that night.' He's a pretty cute guy."

"Mmmmph, young lady. Don't you forget you're a married woman."

Baby Skulls and Fowl Odors

"Why, *Señor*, I never forget *mi esposo*, that lazy slug. *Muy perezoso. Yo trabajo, y trabajo* while he..."

Garrett knew Edith's *esposo*, a hard-working construction boss, and he cleared his throat. Ahem.

"Okay, boss, but speaking of *familia y una comida* ..."

"You never let anything rest, do you? Well, *mi amiga*, you have my calendar. Make reservations. Just give us some time to clear up these Croysant issues first, okay?"

"Restaurant?"

"Your choice. Here in the valley, though — I don't want to see food in San Diego."

She said, "Whoo, baby, lame pun!" and they both chuckled, not sure at what, but maybe just because they were good friends and it felt right. Edith swashed down the hall, whistling and pleased, but before Garrett could reach his desk she had turned on her heel.

"Uh, forgot one thing."

"The menu?"

"No, a news item. Might be relevant. The old Larson barn, by that club house on Oozle Road — it burned to the ground last night."

The sheriff's face fell. "Well, eat my blessed cookies," he swore. "Thanks, A-deet. I guess I'd better get up there right away. Hold the fort."

To which Edith responded, "As usual, Kemo Sabe."

On days like today, the drive from Riversmet to Croysant, almost two hours no matter how you measured it, seemed an eternity. Sometimes he enjoyed watching the sweep of the landscape as it passed, but today his mind was fully focused on trying to piece together the Croysant puzzle. Lots of pieces, but nothing fit. He had no idea what the whole picture was, and he was pretty sure he was missing too many pieces to get there yet. On a hunch, he pulled into the Peaseford Middle School on his way past. When he asked the secretary at the main desk if there was any way he might speak to Sienna Fowler in private for a few minutes, she said, "Of course, Mr. Garrett, I'll have her teacher send her right down." It irritated him that they always knew who he was, but he never had a clue who they were. He envied Hobbs that memory of his.

Kids passing to lunch ogled him and Sienna as the secretary guided them to a small teachers' lounge. Garrett hurried the little girl in and closed the door on the curious faces. He opened with, "Hi, I'm Sheriff Garrett. I just have a couple of questions, nothing scary—I don't want to keep you from your lunch."

The girl's face was surly. "Right, I'll bet that's your primary concern, my lunch. And I know you're the sheriff; I've seen sheriffs before."

Garrett studied her. This wasn't going to be easy. She seemed furious and upset far beyond any of the things that he knew about her situation. He wanted to ask about Larry's scratches and about the mother that supposedly was buried near their trailer, but from the look of this kid, he figured he'd better start by treading lightly. He pulled on his mustache. "Yeah, I was up there when your dad got shot. How's your dad's foot doing by now?"

"Who cares. He's not my father, he's a trafficker. A people trafficker. He prefers trafficking in women and little girls. I've tried to tell people before, but nobody listens to me. They just think I'm blowing a story. That's what you'll think, too."

This stopped Garrett cold. He'd come to find out about a rooster scratch and maybe an illegal burial, and she told him this? It was like stepping off into the deep end of the pool without the gradual incline you expected to lead up to it. Cautiously, he said, "The man who calls himself your father, Chuck Fowler ... are you saying he kidnapped you?"

"I keep telling people, but nobody will listen." It was a cranky statement, spoken without apparent fear or anguish.

"Soooo ... okay then. This is terrible information. I'm going to listen, Sienna. Tell me what's going on, okay? Where are you from? Where is your mother?"

"She's dead." This was stated with such cold finality that Garrett was again taken aback.

Carefully, he said, "Sienna, do you have any family? Has anyone been looking for you since Mr. Fowler ... since he kidnapped you?"

"Nobody now. I had a sister once. Her name was Kay Leigh. It is spelled k-a-y-l-e-i-g-h. That's a pretty name, isn't it?" Briefly, the sour little face grew wistful. "A really pretty American name."

"Where is your sister now?"

The child's voice again turned cold. "Dead."

What was going on here? Garrett took in the angry little face and rigid posture. He supposed circumstances like these might make a child as distant and mean-mouthed as this one. He repeated, "Dead?"

"Yeah, dead a long time now. Personally, I think her father killed her."

Okay, time to gather up the reins. "Look, Sienna, I'm glad you told me all this. I'm going to call my deputy. Her name is Leigh, too, like your sister. Deputy Leigh McCracken. She's a very nice lady. She'll come up and put you into protective custody; she'll make sure you're safe now."

"If you send that McCracken for me, I'll hit her and kick her, and I'll bite if I have to. I'm going back to that trailer tonight. I've got business there that can't wait. You just leave me alone, understand?"

"Sienna, now that I know what you've told me, I can't let you go back to Mr. Fowler."

She shrugged. "So, arrest him. Arrest Chuck. Let's see how *he* likes it."

Again, Garrett frowned, regarding her narrowly. "Perhaps," he said. "Perhaps I will try to pick him up this afternoon. Thank you for answering my questions. And I hope you didn't miss lunch."

She gathered her backpack and left without a word. That, at least, was as he expected.

In the car, Garrett put through a call to McCracken on his private line. "Listen, Mac, I've got somebody I need you to shadow for tonight. It looks to be an all nighter, so you better get a little rest up front today, if you can."

After giving McCracken instructions, he took the drive from the school to the restaurant at a snail's pace, trying to digest the overload of information sitting on his brain like a bad meal on an upset stomach. It didn't work, and his planned quiet time over lunch had clearly been a failure. He hadn't been able to get any insights about Sienna. Or Chuck. Or the burned barn. Or the connections between everything. Or the ugly steering wheel note. When he had finished his burger and fries, he stepped out on the veranda of the Cowpath, stretched, and took a satisfying nip of nicotine-free wintergreen chew. The protesters were still milling about, digging around in their cars and vans, putting on sun screen, talking on phones, fingering keyboards. "Cushy job," he thought, "being a protester." One had pulled a sign from her car and laid it against the fender as she readjusted her gear. The sign said, "No Chickens."

He squinted at the area around the restaurant. There were a couple of bush-covered rises about 50 yards from the parking lot, both with plenty of cover to accommodate a sniper. He told himself he was being paranoid.

A short, wiry man with radical eyes, a grey-haired horse's tail trailing down his back, disembarked from a car that had just pulled up. PETA stickers plastered the windows and bumper. The man looked things over, then popped up in front of the sheriff. "Thank you, Sir. Thank you, Sheriff, for coming up to look out for us. We heard that some of the rednecks in this area are pretty quick with a gun."

Garrett eyed the man thoughtfully, mauled his chew around his lower lip, looked over the veranda railing, and took aim. It was an expert shot, landing two feet in front of two chattering women in North Face outdoor gear. Their eyes shot up to the veranda in horror as Garrett dragged his hand across his skinny little mustache, beginning with the wrist and ending with a smoothing motion with the tips of his index and third fingers. Looking down at the fellow who had accosted him, he said, "You bet. No problem. Any time."

23

ALMA WAS SITTING in her chair when Garrett arrived, carrying the doll. "Oh, bring her here!" she cried. "Just bring her right over here." He handed over the repaired toy and she drew it to her with such a welcoming embrace that Garrett feared, irrationally, that she would crack the little ribs. Alma's personal body awareness had declined in her old age. Her loving grip was twisting one of the doll's legs backward, over the chair arm, and had squashed a tiny raised cloth arm behind her own heavy shoulder. Still, the doll accepted the comfortable lap, smiling, seeming content. "Where did you find her, Lyle?"

She always called him Lyle, which was his older brother's name, and he'd finally decided it was not because she didn't know who he was, but rather, that she simply had the names switched. By now, he resisted the urge to correct her; her fuddled mind would have it mixed up anyhow by the time he saw her again. If not sooner. Instead, he said, "So, Alma, is this your doll? Did you make this doll?"

Tipping her head to the side, as if to get a better look at the little stuffed creation, she said, "Why no, of course not! You know better than that, Lyle. I told you, I didn't make this one."

"Oh." Garrett squatted next to her chair and gently patted the doll's forehead. "She seems like such a fine girl. Do you know who did make her, then?"

"Why of course!" This answer was tinged with an underlying conviction that young people were always a little slow on the uptake. "I thought I told you. Lena. Lena Larson made this doll."

"Lena Larson?" The sheriff was looking into Alma's face, assessing her. "Just how can you tell?"

Releasing the doll from the bear hug, Alma turned her this

way and that. "It's just how Lena did things. See, she's used these large buttons as shanks to hold the stitches in place where she attached the arms. I even remember those buttons — she must have taken them off that old sheepskin coat she used to wear. And see? Look at these stitches, big and bold, but not real picky about matching the thread colors." Alma pinched the doll's cheeks, moved her head to the side, and examined Edith's fine stitches. Garrett tensed, but she said, "See here? Someone has repaired a tear or something by this doll's face. See how these stitches are very even and professional? Not like Lena's — Lena just threw things together. She was real rough. She was an impulsive woman."

Hugging the doll back against her, this time with its face smashed into her old chest, Alma said, "I do miss Lena. Hard to believe she's gone. I didn't like her that much when she was alive, though."

Garrett got off his haunches and pulled up a chair, trying to assimilate these conflicting emotions being expressed by Alma. She continued, relaxed and hugging the toy, "Lena was crazy as a bedbug. Nothing like me. I always stayed home and took good care of Doug. Lena was always out riding and roping, hunting ... she'd hunt alone, or sometimes she met a friend there, and I don't mean an ordinary friend. The guy she met up there in the mountains was a Ute Indian, and sometimes she'd spend half the summer with him. They said she ate stuff even the natives wouldn't eat, bees and nettles and just plain weeds. If she was hungry enough, she'd catch a trout and eat it raw; that Indian man, even he called her a crazy white woman. But he still came to see her. One story was that she fought a bear for a bee hive full of honey, and the fight ended with the bear tearing down the mountain, old Lena yelling and cursing right on its tail. That's just a story, I think. Stories get out of hand, but she really was quite an old girl. Too bad. Now all that is left of her and the rest of that Larson bunch is the old barn over by the clubhouse."

Thinking, 'And not even the barn,' Garrett said, "But she also knew how to sew? Like this doll?"

"Oh, sure. She crocheted doilies and quilted big heavy quilts for winter out of scraps, and she cooked. Sometimes it was good, sometimes crazy. Once when Doug and I dropped by, she served us up a big slice of angel food cake, and Doug took a big bite of that—you know, angel food was always his favorite—but with this bite of cake he got a funny look, and that woman just cackled her head off. 'How do ya' like them apples,' I always remember that is what she said. 'I just stuck the leftover bacon in that cake, right from the pan this mornin'. Mighty tasty, huh?' That's how she said it. We always laughed about it later. Doug and me, we were polite and finished up our piece of cake, but I'm pretty sure Doug didn't like it much." Alma gave a sniff. "Not like he always liked mine." Then her eyes got cloudy, lost in the memory, thinking of her Doug. "Doug was always a good man. He made a point that day to ask for a second piece, just to make Lena feel better."

"So she cooked and sewed, and even made dolls?"

"One kind of doll she made was out of bottles. You could get a doll head and arms from the five and dime, and Lena'd glue 'em on a bottle, then crochet a big, pretty skirt with lots of colors to dress it and cover the bottle bottom. Her favorite colors were to put yellow with a lavender color, and sometimes yellow with orange. Very cheerful. The crocheted skirts made it look like the dolls had legs, just covered by the skirts, kind of old-fashioned, like Scarlett O'Hara in *Gone with the Wind*. You were supposed to use those dolls to decorate your bed." She shook her head, remembering. "I wonder where they all are now?"

"Mmmm," Garrett said. "And this kind of doll, too." He knew he was harping on it, but he wanted to be certain that Alma's faulty memory hadn't played a trick on her.

"Sure," she said. Alma's 'sures' were always drawn out, very affirmative, sounding like 'shoooerr.' "Lena brought this doll by to show me after she made it, since she'd borrowed the pattern from me. I hinted tactfully that I'd love to have it, to put with my other dolls here, but she was a real old fox. She told me it wasn't hers to give because she'd done it for somebody else. Said they'd had her sew a little personal secret inside of it, right in with the cattails, but she wouldn't tell me what it was or who she did it for."

Alma paused to dab at her nose with a tissue, then continued, "I resented that, Lyle. You shouldn't tell somebody about a secret you're holding unless you plan to tell them what it is. I never thought very high of Lena after that. She took her secret to her grave, and she took my low opinion with her, too."

Probably true. Garrett knew that one thing Alma loved was being involved in the information flow of the community. Well, okay, call it gossip; nothing wrong with a little gossip. Garrett also liked being involved. Maybe that was part of why he liked his job as a sheriff most of the time. There was always a lot going on, and he enjoyed being in the center of it.

Well, what else? He recalled something that Alma's girls, Gritty and Carmen, had told him about the dolls. "Alma, did she tell you what the doll's name was?"

"She said she wanted to name it like I named my dolls." Alma's indignant old voice was now heavy with having been personally injured. "So, guess what she said she'd call it? She says to me, 'Alma, I'm going to make this doll a Dell, just like your dolls. And we'll name her after the one who owns her, like you do, so she will be called Ling Ling Dell. Now, that's a right pretty name, ain't it,' Lena says to me, 'Ling Ling Dell.' Well, Lyle, I never heard of such a name in all my life! Makes this beautiful doll sound just like it is a Chinaman."

24

MOST WOMEN OF ALMA'S generation—except maybe for Lena—wouldn't have said 'shit' if they had a mouthful; Garrett knew that. And members of the historically enlightened younger generation would never negatively label a race or ethnic group. Was 'Chinaman' negative? Of course. But Alma didn't know it. She didn't think badly of Chinese people; she'd probably never even talked with an Asian person. The word was just part of her ditty bag of acceptable vocabulary. Still, generation-wise, Garrett was in the middle, not comfortable with either racial epithets or hard-core obscenities. That was why it took him a minute to react to Alma's resentment over the doll's name. Finally, he said, "Alma, I think Ling Ling is probably a little girl's name in Chinese. Myself, I think it is very pretty."

"You do, do you?" She gave Garrett a look that said, "You have your opinion. I have mine."

Garrett fended her with a smile. "I do. And now I need to take little Ling Ling Dell and be on my way." He stood and reached for the doll, and Alma tightened her grip.

"No."

Stopped in mid-reach, Garrett said, "Alma, you told me this isn't really your doll. I need to take her now."

"Is she *your* doll?"

"No, but I ... no, but I ... I just talked to a little girl this morning who said maybe her father killed her sister. And I ... and I thought maybe I could take the doll to her, to comfort her." None of this was true; he was making it up from whole cloth as he talked, but maybe it would work.

"Whose father? The little girl's father, or the sister's father?"

Alma was arguing trivialities like an adolescent, and

Garrett was annoyed. He started to say, "It would be the same father," but just then a big bell clanged in his head, or was it the iconic light bulb blinking? What had Sienna said? She hadn't said, "My dad." When he asked where her sister was, she had said, "Dead. I think her dad killed her." Alma was right. It was not necessarily the same father. He dropped his hands.

"Mrs. Weinant, tell me. Why do you want the doll?"

"Because she should be mine. Lena used my pattern and kept her secret to the grave. Now we'll never know." This was said with infinite regret and no apparent recognition of the fact that what was in the doll was still in the doll. Maybe she thought what was in the doll wouldn't be recognizable as the secret unless Lena was here to explain it. She continued, "And she named her a Dell, one of the Dells, so she belongs with the Dell family here. Lena was stupid and called her Ling Ling Dell. She looks more like Pocahontas Dell to me. So that's why she'll remind me of Lena, somebody trashy enough she couldn't even name a doll right."

"But if you didn't even like Lena, why would you want to be reminded of her?"

"Why, Lena was my friend! People don't have to be perfect to be your friend. Even Hallie wasn't perfect, especially when she got to talking stupid, claiming she shot that guy, and also she got so darned hard of hearing you couldn't get her to listen so you could talk sense into her, but I loved Hallie. And I didn't like Lena much, how she acted and all, but I loved her, too. They're both gone now. Both my friends."

Garrett just stood, staring down at a very emotional, very old, very wise lady. Now she added, "And I love this doll, too."

Checkmate.

He drove to the Larson barn and parked, but he wasn't very interested in looking it over for right now. It was just a big pile of ash, and he had other things on his mind. Pulling out his private phone, he dialed Edith. Hobbs was there, and he had her put him through.

"Asa, I need some detection. Got time? There's a newcomer up here, calls himself Chuck Fowler. The one Barnswallowper shot in the foot. I need you to see what you can find out about him. Things have come up—I'll fill you in more later."

"Sounds intriguing. I'll see what I can do."

"Also, see what you can learn about Fowler's deceased wife. I don't even have a name for you on that one."

"You don't mind givin' an old fat guy a challenge, do you?"

Garrett smiled. "Not even a little bit. And while you're at it ..." He hesitated. Should he? He knew that he surely did not have pure motives, but ... what was it his mama used to tell him? Faint heart never won fair lady. All right, then. Plunging in, he finished, "While you're at it, I need you to also check on this other newcomer up here, Brady Xyster."

"That guy with Jenny? That should be easy—I'll just ask her."

Fortunately, Hobbs couldn't see Garrett's apoplectic reaction to the teasing words. All he got from the phone was Garrett's growled, "Background check, you idiot. No asking Jenny. Not anything."

On his end of the line, Hobbs smiled and said, "Gotcha. I'll get back. Got a little paperwork here before I can start."

"Thanks." The word a grumble, then Garrett was off the line. He gazed reflectively at the heap of ashes that had been a barn. In two or three places weak tendrils of smoke rose hopelessly, having been deprived of the last of any fuel to feed on. Finally, he got out his phone and accessed Gritty's number. He got her answering device and recorded a heads up, that the doll was back at Alma's and would be safe for now. Then he pushed 'end' and tossed the phone back and forth between his hands. Finally, he said out loud, "Oh, hell, just do it."

Jenny picked up on the third ring, and when he started to talk, his voice took a brief vacation. He cleared his throat and said, "Hi. Sorry. Frog. Anyhow, this is Garrett. I've been thinking. I couldn't offer you much of a meal yesterday at Sonic, big hurry and all. Would you let me make it up to you with a more leisurely dinner this evening, maybe at The Harvest Apple?"

"Why, Patrick, how nice! Is this business or pleasure?"

"I'm hoping mostly for pleasure." Ling Ling Dell crossed his mind, and he sent her packing.

"That's great—what time?"

"I'd like to pick you up about 7:30. I've got a little work to do first." He thought, "I'll need to get back to Riversmet to shower and shave, and I'll need to drive back. Four hours." He contemplated what he should do if it was Xyster who opened her door when he knocked. But she had said, "How nice." And now she said, "Perfect." He felt like a smitten teenager. Downright foolish.

He left the Larson barn and turned pensively up Oozle Road. Looking ahead, he saw it: a dense cloud of dark gray smoke boiling up at the foot of Fourier Ridge. Now what? He stepped on the accelerator and forgot Jenny. As he came out of the gully and crested the little rise where Fourier Lane took off from the main road, he saw a mess of activity. One fire truck had started up the lane toward the smoke, and the firemen from the other seemed to be trying to deal with a swirl of people. Protesters. He pulled up behind the parked fire truck and took in the scene.

Tommy Nikolich, a senior member of the fire squad, walked over to greet him. "Howdy, Sheriff. Glad you're here."

"What's up, Tommy?"

"Oh, crap." Tommy shot a bolus of chew over the road edge, this one nicotine. "It wouldn't be anything if it weren't for that bunch of pests from the big shitty." Shitty. Right. Think city. Garrett eyed the group of at least two dozen people, several recognizable from his Cowpath encounter. They were pacing, consulting papers and maps, staring up the lane toward the area where the smoke could be seen, thicker now, boiling forth in black clouds. "Maybe you can do something with them."

"Phmmph. Maybe. Maybe need another fact or two. What's going on with the fire?"

"Oh, that. It's a half-ass controlled burn. Garfield Fourier called in and told us he'd found a bunch of shit up along the back road to his ridge, and he was going to get rid of it. He said that if anybody reported a fire, he wanted us to know that it was just him burning trash."

"Pretty good size trash fire." Garrett dipped into his own chew, and both men mauled the stuff in their mouths and contemplated the smoke. Now flames could be seen, shooting sparks high into the air.

"Yeah. And we've gotten more than enough calls, mostly from this ignorant bunch of crack heads. What are they doing here, anyhow?"

"Well, it does look like it's burnin' pretty good. Probably

good thing you're here. These people seem to be protesters, kind of unhappy about a chicken farm."

"Unh." Tommy grunted, watching what was now a visible blaze. "I'm glad I sent the boys on up. I guess if you got this under control, I better gather the rest of my troops and take this other truck in." He turned to go, then turned back. "Chicken farm, huh? Who wants to put a chicken farm up here?"

"Damned if I know," Garrett said, thinking to himself that the last thing he wanted was to "have this under control." He had other plans for this afternoon. Tommy was saying, "And why can't they have it? It's a free country—no law against chickens that I know of."

Garrett grinned and nodded. As the fire truck pulled into Fourier Lane, he got in his own vehicle and radioed in. "Edith, I'm up on Oozle Road above Croysant. Who you got today in this neck of the woods?"

"Red's in Peaseford, and you know where Mac is."

"Right. Well, send Red up to do some crowd control. Get Louie out, too, wherever she is. Just in case. For back up."

A woman was knocking vigorously on his window, so he got out and unfolded to half again her size. "Yes, ma'am?"

Undaunted, she tipped her head back, her lips grim. "Where is the chicken farm?"

"Ma'am, as near as I know, there is not now and never was any chicken farm."

Half a dozen people had drifted in to join her, listening inquisitively for what might be said. "Don't be coy with me, Mr. Fuzz. Are they burning it down over there to destroy the evidence?"

Garrett's normally gentle eyes had gone icy. "Evidence of what, ma'am?"

Another bystander had pushed forward. "Look, we know there's a factory farm somewhere around here, but we just don't know where. The tip we got from here in your community said it was at 2432 Oozle Road, and that's what it says in the county records, but we got into the Tinker Chicken files and the location number they have on their application is 2423. That's two different places."

"Well, yes, indeed it is." Garrett was suddenly thoughtful, his eyes going back to the cloud of smoke, which was now diminishing somewhat. "Yes, 2423 and 2432 are definitely two different places. Numbers look a little the same, but different. Where are you people camped?"

"Croysant Reservoir campground. Not much water in the rez. Some of us wanted to boat."

"Well, I'll tell you what. I've been watching you, walking all over this guy's land. You haven't been keeping to the public roadway. You're trespassing up here, and you've been computer hacking to get into Tinker corporate files, and I have lots of grounds for arrest. Being picked up by a country sheriff can be a lot different from being picked up in the city, so I recommend you head back to your campsite and leave these people up here alone until you can get your facts straight."

One man walked quickly from the grass back into the road as Garrett spoke, but a tall, muscular woman standing to his left said belligerently, "Arrested by you and what army, Fuzz Man? We all have phones with cameras, and we can document whatever abusive crap you try to dish out."

Glancing up, Garrett saw with an inward sigh of relief that Red was approaching in a cloud of dust. Better yet, his half-brother, Eric, was with him. Eric wasn't with the sheriff's office, but he was a big bruiser and always managed to be around when he thought his little brother might be in trouble.

"I guess we have a few people who can help out if we need to do an arrest." As he said it, he realized that Duz Weinant, Clint and Lew Harris, and little Pete Johnson had come up the road and were standing behind him. Lucky was on a leash, and Lew was murmuring, "Take it easy, Lucky. Don't you go for 'em unless I say the word 'attack.'"

Several of the protesters were already drifting back to their cars. The ones nearest Garrett were staring in baffled confusion at the empty leash dangling from Lew's hand. Sheriff Garrett rubbed at his mouth to help hold in the smile. "Don't unleash her, Lew. These people are getting ready to depart peacefully."

And they did, some more sullenly and reluctantly than others, and all frowning back repeatedly at where Lucky wasn't, but finally, the area was cleared. It took longer to disburse the triumphant neighbors. They seriously needed to hash it over.

"Just a trash fire," Garrett told them. "Garfield was just burnin' trash, big pile, cleanin' up his new place. He called

Baby Skulls and Fowl Odors

Tommy first to let 'im know, so they're helpin' out."

"So what are those outliers doin' here?"

"They're all F'ed up, got their facts all wrong. They think someone up here is tryin' to raise factory chickens."

"Well, are they?"

"Not that I know of."

"I don't like that factory chicken meat myself. Frieda gets our chicken from Jilly Brown. Been raised right."

"Me, neither, but those outliers got no business here."

"Can't tell the difference in chicken if you get enough spice on it."

"Just salt and pepper. Dip your chicken in flour, fry 'er in plenty of grease, and tastes like chicken. Heh heh heh." This advice and delighted cackle coming from Lew, pleased at his own joke. "As for Lucky, she gets the skin. Can't have chicken bones; Doc told me bones would kill her."

While Garrett tried to imagine what it would be like to be Lucky's veterinarian, the men finished what they needed to say and headed for their cars, giving Lucky a friendly pat on the head, telling her she'd done a good job. Garrett thanked everybody, then asked Red to keep an eye out around the area, just in case. He wondered if Mac had texted Red about where she was. He hoped not—Red would be drawn like a summer-hatched fly to roasting meat, and it would blow her cover.

Or maybe not. Garrett pulled on up K-4 Road to find a handful of bedraggled protesters pacing listlessly up and down the road, carrying "No Chickens" signs and looking uncertain. It wasn't until Garrett was parked and out of his car that he did a double take. One of these protesters had a hoodie pulled snugly over her head, flashy leopard leotards, flip-flops over feet that had multi-colored bright toenails, and a face coated in rouge, heavy mascara and eyeliner at the eyes, and lips that had grown to twice their real size as they dripped with bright raspberry lip gloss. He had to yank his eyes away and stare at his goal, the trailer door, to avoid eye contact.

As he started to knock on the door, the hoodied apparition came up the steps behind him and said rather loudly, in a squeaking voice, "He's not in there, Mister. We've been trying to talk to him, but all we saw so far was his kid getting off the bus, and she is in there, but he isn't. It would help if we could talk to him, but I guarantee you, he's not here. I guess we'll just have to hang out here and hope he shows up so we can tell him what we think of his chicken farm."

A couple of the people on the road had stopped, listening and nodding. Garrett, in a frantic battle with his mouth and eyebrows, all twitching and bobbing every time he looked at this woman, said over a poorly suppressed snort, "Well, all right then. Thank you for the information, ma'am." He retreated rapidly back up the hill, nodding pleasantly at the limp sign holders, and gained the safety of his car. It wasn't until he had turned and driven back past them that he allowed himself a more satisfying, much louder, snort. Then he glanced at his watch. All right! Still time to get to his date with Jenny. Date. Yes, he supposed so. It was probably a date.

It was just as he turned back onto Oozle Road that he happened to glance over into the thick sage and rabbitbrush covering a nearby knoll. A movement caught his eye, and he realized that someone was hobbling through the brush. He slowed to watch; the man was turning his head, searching, shading his eyes from the sun, poking at bushes, stopping repeatedly to look around. Garrett pulled to the verge and stopped the car, and as he did, the man looked up sharply, then dropped, disappearing behind a bush.

Wasting no time, Garrett jumped out of his car and pushed briskly through the undergrowth until he reached the place where the man had disappeared. A hunch. It was him, all right. Chuck Fowler looked up from where he had crouched, pretending surprise. "Oh, hi, Sheriff. I didn't see you there. I ... I'm looking for something. I lost something. My hat. Yes, my hat, and I thought—the wind blew my hat. I thought I could find it here."

Pat Garrett had never seen a guy look any shiftier.

25

GARRETT LOOKED AT HIS WATCH and tried to recalibrate how much time he had left before he was supposed to pick up Jenny, and his heart sank. He didn't have a goat's chance in hell. Then he looked at the man hunkered miserably in the brush at his feet, hands pushing ineffectively on the ground beside himself, foot outstretched, and crutch dropped hurriedly just out of reach. Garrett sighed. When duty calls ... He retrieved the crutch and said, "Here, let me give you a hand."

Leaning on his crutch, Chuck Fowler brushed at his jeans and said lamely, "I really don't see my hat anywhere around here."

Garrett's response was a dry, "I don't either, Mr. Fowler. You are Chuck Fowler, aren't you?"

He nodded dejectedly. "That's me."

"So, Mr. Fowler. I've been looking for you. Some things have come up, and we need to talk."

Fowler's eyes became shifty again, shooting everywhere over the sage and rabbitbrush, avoiding the sheriff's steady gaze. He was holding his injured foot up, leaning heavily on his crutch. Garrett pulled at his mustache, scowling. This was a conundrum. If this guy was on the run because he was a human trafficker and was afraid they had found him out, then what was he doing down here in the sagebrush, hobbling around, looking for all the world as if he really had lost something? Eyeing the miserable human wreck in front of him, Garrett thought, "If he runs, he can't run far, but I can't just leave this wretch wandering around out here in the sagebrush, either." Maybe the poor, distracted guy was demented. Early Alzheimer's or something. He looked to be mostly skin and bones.

"I'd like you to come with me to The Lucky Lantern, and

let's get a cup of coffee. You look beat, and like I say, you and I need a little chat."

"Okay." Fowler looked at the sheriff's car as if it were an alien space ship to which he had been commanded, impossibly, to fly.

Garrett said, "Okay. It's okay. Just take your time." And it did take time. Garrett, maneuvering behind him, could see that the man was about to cave in with exhaustion. How in hell had he even made it this far down the mountain from his trailer? It must have taken all day. And why? What was he thinking? Was he really on the run?

Once the sheriff's vehicle had been attained, Fowler sank silently and gratefully into the seat and leaned his head against the window, eyes closed. Garrett hated to stop at the Lantern and make him get out to hobble around again. He should just run him on into Riversmet and book him. Make life simple. The guy could sleep on the way down, and Garrett wouldn't have to worry about questioning him until morning. But what about Jenny? He couldn't do all that and still make it to their date. Grimly, he pulled into the Lucky Lantern—back to the original plan.

As he brought the car to a halt, Chuck Fowler raised his head. "Sheriff, I know you won't believe me, but they're just pets. She's so proud of them, but those chickens, they really are just pets."

The look Garrett shot him was astonished. This guy was maybe running from a kidnapping charge or worse, and he was worried about chickens? What's with the chickens, already?

Fowler was struggling out the car door with his crutch and sore foot, so Garrett didn't say anything. They'd talk inside. Instead, he followed him as he made his way haltingly up the ramp and through the restaurant door. The Lantern was primarily a bar, with a cavernous, pointless restaurant attached that had descended from the busier days of yore. Garrett didn't frequent the place, so he trusted, correctly, that they could have privacy here. He was right. The place was empty. He took a corner booth at the front in order to bring the hobble to a halt as soon as possible. The waitress's tag said, "Luetta."

"Luetta, just coffee for me, but I don't think Mr. Fowler has had anything to eat for a while, so he's gonna need a sandwich

Baby Skulls and Fowl Odors

or something." To Fowler he added, "Chuck, I'm buying, but you need something fairly fast. I've got another appointment."

Fowler nodded obediently. "Hot wings and coffee, thanks. Cream for the coffee." Back in the bar they could hear shouts of laughter and the clatter of pool balls. There was loud western music, but fortunately not so loud as to drown out conversation here in the restaurant section.

Garrett waited until the waitress was done bustling in and out with the order. She gave the coffee creamer to Garrett, and brought nachos instead of hot wings. She also brought a compensatory basket of dried-out dinner rolls, reheated, with flat pats of margarine melting on the side. "Sorry. All out of wings, so since you're in a hurry I just brought nachos instead. That's what we have. This one is hungry—she tipped her head to indicate Fowler—so I brought rolls, too. Thought it might help out." While she talked, Fowler put three packets each of sugar and cream in his coffee and downed it in one gulp. His hands were shaking.

"Thank you, miss. Could you please bring more coffee?" Then he looked gratefully and trustingly at Garrett. "You know, I'm not diabetic or anything, but I have always had a tendency to get hypoglycemic on an empty stomach, and I haven't eaten all day. Thank you, Sheriff. I appreciate this." He then proceeded to eat, demolishing everything on the table, the nachos with their scanty squirt of canned cheese, two more cups of coffee with cream and sugar, even the stale rolls with margarine, as Garrett watched in wonder. This wasn't going to be easy.

When the man finally came up for air, Garrett began. "You know, Mr. Fowler, I don't think you need to worry about chicken farm issues. Those protesters can be annoying, but they'd have to make something up to accuse you of doing anything illegal. Everyone in this area farms chickens. What you need to worry about is a far more serious accusation someone made against you today."

Looking less weak and more alert, Fowler wiped his mouth with a napkin. He leaned in. "A more serious accusation?" His eyes were no longer shifty; they were puzzled and watchful.

"Yes, Mr. Fowler. I stopped at the school earlier today to ask your daughter about a school friend she has, Larry Gallenas, and instead of answering my question, she told me you are not really her father. She said you have kidnapped her, and that you traffic in women and little girls. She wants to see you arrested."

Fowler's reaction was astounding. Garrett wasn't sure what he had expected, but not this. Briefly, Fowler's eyes got large and his mouth dropped open, then he burst into uncontrollable laughter. Gasping for breath, he said, "That would be my Sienna, all right. I need to let you know ... I need to let you know what's going on with Sienna."

Finally containing himself, he looked serious again, and perhaps sad, but also, for whatever reason, he looked relieved. He said, "Sheriff, let me reassure you, Sienna is my daughter. I'm more than willing to have DNA tests or whatever it takes to guarantee that fact either to you or to a court of law. Where the problem is coming from is that Sienna has always been a little girl with a huge imagination. She's had imaginary friends and whole game scenarios from the time she could barely talk, which was early, and it didn't take her long to figure out the Internet. She's all over it, gobbling up facts and ideas. Movies, games, everything. She's really bright, and she puts everything together, sometimes not accurately, as you might expect with a twelve-year-old, but always creatively.

"I think you realize that I lost my wife, Sienna's mother, just a few months ago. Sienna is furious with me. She blames me for the loss."

Listening carefully, Garrett said, "Why would she blame you?'

"I've read about it. Read a lot about grief. Sometimes when we are so hurt, we feel the need to blame someone, even if it's wrong. Those last weeks, before we lost Sienna's mother, those were hard weeks, and Sienna didn't feel that I did what should have been done to take care of her mom. Also, I am grieving, too, of course, and this doesn't always make me the best father. Honestly, I am depressed. One sad dad. I keep trying to pull it together, but I'm not often successful."

Garrett didn't know what to say. A recent church sign board was crossing his mind: "You have a friend request, from Jesus." Well, this guy sure wasn't Jesus, but if what he said was true, he did need somebody to cut him some slack.

Fowler was stirring a fourth cup of coffee. Telling his story seemed to have allayed his anxiety. He had color in his face, and his slumped and sagging shoulders had straightened. "You know, Sheriff, my plan was to come here, get away from it all, and get Sienna a fresh start, but it isn't working. The kids at school seem to bully her all the time, and she fights back just like she always did, by bragging and yelling and making up stories. And obviously, she's still mad at me, since she told you I kidnapped her. At this point, that's probably how she sees it. I don't think she sees ... " he hesitated, "... sees all that I have risked to try to make her feel better," he finished.

"Mmmmph." Garrett's eyes were sympathetic. "Look, I'm real sorry about all you've been going through. But with an accusation as serious as Sienna has made, we still have to take you in until we can get things cleared up. I'm real sorry."

"And Sienna? She must be home from school by now — yes, of course. Hours ago. I don't want her alone up there at night."

"I've got a deputy on it, real nice lady — she'll look out for your daughter while we get things worked out."

"I hope she doesn't hurt her."

Garrett was appalled. "Our people don't hurt children!"

For the second time since he'd met him, Garrett got to see Chuck Fowler smile. "I was just kidding. What I meant was, I hope Sienna doesn't hurt your deputy."

The sheriff called Louie and Red down from Fouriers', where there were no longer any crowds to control, and sent them to Riversmet with Chuck Fowler, telling them to keep him in protective custody; as they pulled away, he looked at his watch. He needed to pick up Jenny for dinner in less than an hour.

"Shut up them wind pipes, Lucky. It's just the sheriff." Lew squinted up at Garrett, making out his face in the gathering darkness of evening. "Damn dog sets up an awful racket. Keeps me apprised a' them intruders, though. And I do get 'em more frequent these days. Old-timers. Like ghosts, they come, wanderin' in. Some good 'uns, some bad 'uns. Now, what was it you be wantin', Sheriff?"

"Uh ... " Garrett felt a little foolish, but he hadn't had any other ideas as to what to do. "Lew, I need to clean up; I been busy with the protesters, and now I ain't got time to make it home and get back up here. Would you let me borrow your bathroom?" Garrett, always oddly vain about his carefully shaved, large bald head, kept a bag of toiletries in his police car. Just in case. At least tonight he could wash up; he'd have to give up on any ideas he might have had about that good-looking civilian shirt hanging in his closet at home, though.

"Why, you betcha. No problem." Lew was clearly thrilled to be helping the sheriff. "You got a date up here with that pretty little Indian gal?"

What was it with people? The whole community always seemed to be three jumps ahead of him with respect to his own life. Was nothing ever private? To Lew, he said, "Just dinner, Lew. I kinda owed her a dinner."

"Well, come on in, and never you mind them raised hackles on Lucky. Just a bad habit of hers. She ain't mean or nothin'; just give her your hand and let her smell it."

Garrett dangled his hand into the air in the living room, then a shiver ran up his spine. He would never admit that perhaps he had felt the warm, wet air released by a dog's interested, exploratory nose moving across his fingers, followed by firm, muscular moisture coming from something like a tongue stroking his dangling wrist. No, he certainly did not feel anything like that. But at least this was true: Lucky left him alone after that, and he was able to clean up in peace.

26

MCCRACKEN HAD PLANTED herself beside a large, sweet-smelling sage on a knoll near the trailer. In less than an hour, Sienna appeared on the rickety wooden porch.

Having given the protesters the slip as they passed the first turn in the road heading to their camp, McCracken had used a penlight to keep from stumbling in the encroaching dark while making her way back up here. This was a good spot. She rummaged in her backpack, bringing out sneakers to replace the flip-flops, facial cream and kleenex to remove the make-up, jeans to cover the leopard-skin leotards — in short, the things she needed to restore the real McCracken. She pushed her hood back and shook loose her wild red hair, then, because the Colorado spring evening chill was setting in, she zipped up her hoodie. Everything in place, she swigged water, nibbled a granola bar, and pulled out her phone to look at her texts, her phone having snorted repeatedly as she supposedly protested the Fowler chicken farm. The most recent gave her infinite satisfaction. Garrett didn't like to text, but he would if necessary, and he had broken his self-imposed texting taboo to get through to her. The message was, "Have Chuck. Watch Sienna."

She thumbed back, "You betcha — will do. Nice use of modern technology in the real world, Chief. LOL." Grinning, she shoved her phone in the hoodie pocket, let her eyes roam across the beautiful sky, now thick with stars, and continued to watch the silent trailer. A light glowed feebly in the back; it might be a bedroom; it might be a television set. Or not. Would they even have television? Could they get it, or wi-fi, or anything, up here with the bulky shoulders of the mountains all around them? Maybe Garrett's message had come earlier while she'd been out on the road, and this one wouldn't go until later. Phooey. She looked over the area around the trailer, trying to see a satellite dish or some such, but saw nothing. The moon was clawing its way up behind the pinnacles topping the eastern mountains, and she watched it idly for a while, noticing how it brought the light and shadow in the trailer area into sharp relief. She started to play a game with herself: look at the area, memorize it, close your eyes and try to recall what you saw. If she were like Hobbs, she'd recall everything, first try, but she wasn't Hobbs, and it was fun to open her eyes and look for what she'd missed.

She closed her eyes a third time. They shot back open immediately at a scratching sound being made by a door opening across wood flooring that had been set just a little too closely under it. Sure enough. There was Sienna, flashlight in hand, standing on the trailer porch. She swept the beam around, searching the area, and McCracken froze, curled into her clothes. The light moved past without picking up the deputy in its beam, and as she peered cautiously from her hood, she thanked the deep sage shadow. Sienna now moved quickly down the steps and reached for something next to the trailer. Leaning forward, McCracken made it out in the moonlight. A shovel.

Sienna headed straight for McCracken's spot, but stopped about halfway up the incline. Propping the light as well as she could, she started to dig. And dig. And dig. Occasionally she'd stop, lean on her shovel, and talk to herself. McCracken could hear her. She was saying, "Where the hell did he go now? He's always right here, in my face, but now that I need him ..." She sniffled. "I can't get this out by myself. Doesn't he realize that things are getting too hot to handle around here? What is he thinking?" She would continue in that vein for several moments, apparently needing to cope with the solitary night, then she would go back to digging.

She moved an impressive pile of dirt and rock, mounding it up beside the increasingly gaping hole, occasionally crawling into the hole itself to grunt and struggle to remove a larger rock by hand. From her vantage point, McCracken estimated that the hole was perhaps reaching a foot and a half deep, maybe two by three feet along its rectangular sides. She got the impression that the hole was going down so rapidly in this hard soil because it had been dug before, fairly recently. She could hear small vocal

Baby Skulls and Fowl Odors

sounds among the grunts and whoofs coming from the shoveling twelve-year old, and she decided that the little girl might be crying. Should she intervene, making her presence known? She was weighing the pros and cons of this possibility when she heard the purring sound of a newer model car coming up the hill toward them. Sienna melted into the shadows so rapidly that, for a second, McCracken's eyes lost her, then the little girl readjusted herself, which briefly revealed her, plastered tightly against a nearby juniper.

The headlight beams picked out the big rise east of the trailer, then the trailer, then the road again as the car achieved the turn. It pulled into the much-used wide spot in the road and stopped. Even knowing where she was, McCracken could barely make Sienna out, now melded with the juniper. The headlights went off and someone emerged from the car.

In the moonlight, McCracken couldn't tell much about the person. He or she seemed relatively short, wore slacks and a jacket, and had very short hair. He or she didn't seem too smart because she — Was it a she? It seemed to move like a little she, but McCracken cautioned herself to keep her observations objective — but she maybe wasn't so smart because she was attempting to navigate the slope down toward the trailer without a flashlight. In the dark, the endeavor was precarious. Moonlight was little help, barely illuminating the sharp incline littered with rocks, bushes, and branches, not to mention the "No Chickens" signs which were now mostly lying down, having had a rough week. Picking her way, the person tried to keep to the path that was beginning to be worn by human activity, but the path wasn't sure, and she slid and stumbled, and yes, it was a she. One particularly intimidating slip brought out a clearly female squeak of "Oh! Oh, damn! Ouch!" Next, she lurched toward the hole Sienna had been digging. McCracken held her breath, fighting her urge to spring to the rescue, but a fall into the hole was successfully averted.

Finally, the woman made it to the trailer, mounted the rickety porch steps, and began to knock vigorously on the trailer door. As she knocked, she called into the dark: "Mr, Fowler! Mr. Fowler! I really need to talk to you. I know it's late, but I might know something that will help with your chicken farm troubles." Knock, knock, knock, and again: "Sienna? Are you there? Please, somebody, answer the door."

The next three events happened simultaneously. First, the woman turned dejectedly, moaning to herself, "Oh, this is just such a mess. I feel awful. I just don't know what I should do." At the same time, Sienna released her tree and headed straight for the road. McCracken, on a hunch, was already running toward her; now, she cut her off and tackled her. The commotion erupting in the brush on the hill above the distraught woman by the trailer caused her to hurry frantically down the steps and rush toward her car, her eyes focused upward, trying to see what was causing the snuffling, brush-cracking, thumping sounds above her. "A bear!" she said. "Oh, no, I must have awakened a bear!" And with that, she fell full force into Sienna's hole.

Now, McCracken took her role as Garrett's sidekick very seriously. She was tough as nails. She worked out. She trained her responses. She developed fierce muscles and powerful running abilities. This was one squirmy kid, but McCracken handcuffed her, then took a good grip on an arm. Sienna squawked, "Ow! You're hurting me!" She could tell that the deputy had her unless she could soften the grip by an appeal to mercy, but the deputy, who had sisters, didn't release her.

"Not near as bad as I'm gonna hurt you if you don't settle down. Just where do you think you're going, anyhow?" This gritted between clenched teeth while McCracken unsnapped her good LED police light and shot the beam in the direction from which she had heard a thump and painful cry.

Sure enough. The woman was struggling to get up, out of the hole. She turned her face toward the beam and blinded, covered her eyes with her hand. McCracken, needing to see her own footing, moved the beam away and started down the hill, pushing Sienna along in front of her.

When they reached the hole, the deputy snapped, "Now, you, missy. I'm gonna let loose of you for a minute and help this lady out of this big hole you been digging, but don't you even think of running, you hear me?"

Trying to utilize the deputy's proffered hand, the woman said, "I can't stand up. I think I sprained my ankle."

Behind them, Sienna shuffled her feet and without looking, McCracken said, "Sienna, settle down. I mean it—no monkey business."

Baby Skulls and Fowl Odors

"Sure, just great, arrest me on my own property," Sienna burst out. "But what's she doing here? Aren't you Garfield Fourier's wife? You got your hair cut, but I'm sure that's who you are. What do you want here, anyhow?"

"No, no — you're right. I'm Honey Fourier. And I'm sorry, Deputy, but I can't put weight on this ankle."

McCracken took in the dressy little shoes the woman was wearing, shoes no doubt slick as glass on the bottom, and figured Honey was lucky not to have sprained her ankle sooner. What was she doing here, anyhow? She didn't comment, however. Instead, she maneuvered Honey into a seated position on the bank of the hole, and said, "Look, Sienna, I don't suppose you have an ice pack or some frozen vegetables in the trailer, do you?"

"Not really." Sienna was looking crankily down at the seated Honey, who was rubbing her ankle. "Besides, I still don't know what she's doing here. It's late. Where's Garfield, anyhow?"

Honey looked up. "I know it's late. Where's your father? I came to apologize to him. He doesn't have chickens; there aren't chickens here. What I mean to say is, I know he isn't trying to start a chicken factory farm here. But I know who is, and I should have said something sooner. I thought your father might help me. I ... I'm having trouble with Garfield over all these issues, and I'm so sorry." Still rubbing her ankle, she shook her head ruefully. "But it's okay. Don't worry about the ice pack. I can't seem to do much of anything right around here, and I may as well give up and just call Garfield. He can come get me. He'll be patient with me, like he always is."

She was patting at her jacket pockets. "Now I don't have my phone. What next?"

"Well, I sure can't look for your stupid phone for you," Sienna snapped. "Deputy Dawg here has me all cuffed up."

Holding her tongue with difficulty, McCracken flashed her light into the hole and caught a gleam. Stepping down, she retrieved the phone and handed it to Honey, but her foot had hit on something hard. A button in her brain clicked. That wasn't a rock. She'd bumped against metal. Moving the light toward her foot, she found herself looking at what appeared to be a partially buried, very large microwave oven. Or ... or ... she used her foot to push away more dirt. Or a safe. She continued to push at the dirt. A small safe. She could tell. She had uncovered the lock.

Honey had reached Garfield and was saying, "It's me, Gar. I need some help; I'm over at Fowlers'. Can you come get me? I know. I'll explain when you get here. I'm so sorry, sweetheart. I am so sorry!"

Sienna had also sat, her feet in the hole, her cuffed hands on her lap, her eyes watching McCracken. "Seriously, Deputy. I think you must know where my father is. You know, I really, really need him right now. Could you tell him that? Could you just tell him that much? Maybe he would hear *you*."

Lifting the light toward Sienna, McCracken softened. Tears were running down the little girl's face. She looked defeated. Then McCracken stiffened. Directly behind Sienna, about twenty feet down the hill and near the trailer, her light had caught on a hefty-sized juniper, and now lingered on a branch about halfway up. What the hell! Sienna, seeing McCracken's face, started to turn, but McCracken shifted the light. Through her tears, the little girl asked, "What are you looking at?"

"Nothing, Sienna. Just checking your trailer. Nothing, really." But it was. It was something. She wasn't sure what it meant, but she was sure she had seen it. Contrary to what Honey had said, there was a chicken here. There was at least one chicken here at Fowlers', sleeping contentedly on a branch above the trailer.

27

SO, WHAT DID JENNY and her sheriff, Patrick Garrett, talk about once they had been seated in that fine and fragrant restaurant, The Harvest Apple? Well, first, of course, like any normal country people, they discussed the weather. "Wonderful rain." "Sure greened up the dobies." "Good for the ranches — hope we get a lot more this year."

Now, Garrett and Jenny were not so young any more, so the weather comments naturally led to a short discussion of health issues. "Any more, when it rains like that, though, to be honest, my muscles and bones really start aching." "You, too? Sometimes it takes me ten minutes to get out of bed in the morning." "I know, I know." This conversational tack suddenly felt a little too intimate to both of them, so their eyes veered around the room, and they settled on restaurant decor as a safe haven.

"They've done a good job keeping this restaurant up, haven't they?" "I never know if the lighting is special for keeping the ferns alive, but they do look healthy." And then drinks arrived, a Margarita for her, a double shot of Jim Beam for him, Garrett feeling somewhat guilty because he was still in uniform, but he told himself that, after all, he wasn't really on duty, and would have changed had he made it home. The order went in, and Jenny recalled that they had gone to the same high school. She tossed out a "remember when," they reminisced, and things began to go more and more smoothly. "Remember when, well, you know, our mascot was the bulldog, and remember that we got a real dog, somebody's family would loan him to parade at games? That one time some of the kids got hold of him and dyed him the school colors, bright red and white?"

Laughter. "How did the family react—did they get in trouble?" "Don't remember. Probably. He was sure cute, though."

The food arrived. Much to Garrett's satisfaction, Jenny was an uninhibited eater. While he dug into grilled sirloin and Texas fries, she ate French onion soup and road kill, a restaurant specialty that featured chopped sirloin covered with large, fresh mushrooms. She had ordered sweet potato fries, and when Garrett said he'd never eaten one, she insisted he taste one. This wouldn't have been so bad, but she held the large, lacy-patterned thing up to his lips and he had to take the bite from her fingers. She didn't seem to notice the blush creeping from his collar bone to the top of his large, bald pate. She merely asked if he'd seen any good movies lately, and when he named a DVD he'd borrowed, she cried out, "Oh, I love that one! I just love Harrison Ford—the excitement! I also love comedies, though. Those are what I like. And some historical films." They agreed on this, on musical tastes, and much more, and perhaps because the sweet potato fry had gotten them started, they agreed to share dessert. Cherry pie was amenable to both, and ice cream should be added. It was just as Garrett, contented, had pushed a last bit across the plate into Jenny's territory that she said, in a change of mood voice that stopped him cold, "Patrick, we need to talk."

He looked up stupidly, coming to the surface from his other, happier world. "Talk?"

"Yes, Talk." She was nervous. She meant business. What was this about? "Patrick, I know you're shy, but surely you must ... you must realize that you mean more to me than any other person in the world? Don't you? And I would really, really like to ... to ... have a relationship with you."

The sheriff had gone very still. His mouth worked a wad of chew that wasn't there, and his big ears went bright red. No woman had ever talked to him like this before, and the woman who was talking now was, well, it was Jenny! The object of his apparently poorly hidden desires. He swallowed, his Adam's apple bobbing visibly and noisily.

Jenny wasn't done. She continued, "The problem is, we have both lied to each other. We can't have a relationship built on these lies."

"Lies?" Garrett repeated after her, floundering.

"Yes, my sweet, dear Patrick. I know that you have my doll, and haven't told me. I know this from just watching you, because I'm beginning to know you so well. And I know you know that I haven't told you the truth about the doll. I'm sure you know what is really in her stuffing. I need ... " At this point, she took his hand in both hers and cradled it, looking earnestly into face. "Patrick, I need you to take me home now, and come into the house with me where we can have privacy, and spend time to get this all sorted out. It's important, Patrick. I kind of feel like both our lives depend on it. Our futures, maybe together."

Garrett allowed her his one hand, but the other flew to his drooping mustache. He still felt stupid, like they'd been walking along and she had suddenly sprinted away, leaving him staring, addled, after her. And then a terrible thought finally pushed its way into his conscious mind, his main worry for all these recent days. He had certainly been repressing it, but now, there it was. Finding his reluctant voice, he let it out. "But Jenny, what about Xyster?"

She half laughed. "Oh, good old cousin Brady? He won't be there. I think he somehow managed to mess up pretty bad on his job; I'm pretty sure he got fired. He never really tells me what he's up to, but he's always broke, and when I told him I needed some privacy in the house, at least for tonight, he whined that he didn't have any place to go, so I gave him money and sent him to that nice little bed and breakfast in Croysant. So don't worry about B. He won't be back tonight, and I'll see what I can do later to help him out. Okay? Patrick, will you please do this for me?"

In his job, Garrett had once taken a bullet in the thigh, and another time received a numbing thump to his head, but never had he been rendered more stunned and speechless than he was right now. Jenny had overwhelmed him. He could do nothing but surrender.

He paid the ticket—sixty dollars or six thousand, he didn't look; it was irrelevant—and followed that woman to the car. The fresh air helped, and the quiet drive up to the mesa, neither of them speaking, allowed him to unravel his twisted brain. Jenny made coffee and parked him in a Hobbs-style overstuffed chair, squashy and very comfy. She pushed a stack of bedding to the end of the couch so she could sit, and Garrett realized that was where Xyster had been sleeping. Oh. He took a careful sip from the steaming cup, then let Jenny lead, but now he was ready. She said, "Patrick, where is my doll?"

He countered with, "What makes you think I have it?"

"Don't be tiresome. I've meticulously followed every lead to find her, but more importantly, I've thought back to your own words and actions when we talked, and I just know. I don't have proof, but Patrick, some part of me seeks you out, and so, I just know."

He couldn't help but smile. "You've got me, then. For now, your doll is back at Alma's, for safekeeping. That's where she turned up, and I took her back. Alma seems very fond of her. But Jenny, you have put me in a hellishing position. You know very well that the doll you keep claiming as yours has a skeleton in it. I have to explain that. It is my job. Is it your little daughter? Can it be possible that the woman I'm starting to realize that I may love is actually a madwoman?"

It was Jenny's turn to blush. "Oh, Patrick," she murmured. "Oh, Patrick." She put her head forward, into her hands, and breathed deeply, then raised her face. "Patrick, it is not my little Maggie in that doll; it's my niece. I never knew her, just that the name given her was Xi Kai Li. It's such a long story, and it will sound far-fetched, but it is a true story, Patrick. I never want to lie to you again."

Garrett said nothing, but he was a man with long limbs. His arm now navigated past the obstructing end table between chair and couch, allowing a large hand to rest reassuringly on her shoulder. She said, "I have to give you a lot of ... a lot of family detail and early history.

"You see, when I came back from my San Francisco hippy days, I studied to be a paralegal at the University of Colorado. That's where I met Mike Jones. He was just finishing up his legal studies, but he had a consuming interest in Native American affairs. Shortly after I met him he changed his name to Threewinds, and he received his Juris Doctor under that name. I, too, was interested in Native American problems—you know me, Patrick. Indian Wannabe. Anyhow, I packed up and went with him to Sicangu, the Rosebud Reservation. Sicangu. That means 'Burnt Thighs.' At any rate, we married in 1985, and little Maggie was born right after, 1986. You kind of know the rest of that part, about she and Mike being killed in the car wreck and all.

Baby Skulls and Fowl Odors

"What I need to tell you about, though, is Mike's family." Jenny got up and refilled their coffee. "You see, he never talked about his family if he could avoid it, because apparently he actively disliked them. That whole part of his life was obscured by a dark cloud of anger, and I didn't probe much. It was painful to him. Here is what I do know. His mother was Chinese, and his father was kind of a Heinz 57 lineage. Mike loved his father very much, but he died before Mike and I met. Mike was sixteen, and vulnerable, I think. Also, he was at a teen-brain rebellious stage. When his mom remarried, Mike was eighteen and he just left home and made his own way after that. I think he loved his mother, but he was very angry with her for the remarriage. Apparently the stepfather was a shady character, blocky built, strong, and quick with a knife. Mike said he was a mean bastard. He was Chinese, too, like Mike's mother.

"The story could end there, except that a couple years after Mike left, his mother, Liu Yang, had a baby girl, a little stepsister for Mike. Her name was Feng Ling. The family surname was Xi, so Mike referred to her as Zee.

"Patrick, the problem was that Mike believed the old man abused the little girl, and he didn't know what to do about it. It is my one great regret, Patrick, about those years with Mike. He was so alienated from Liu Yang, his mother, and he could tell that something bad might be going on, but he had no leverage to deal with it. He was at a loss, and he died believing himself to be a coward for not intervening somehow and rescuing his little sister. I regret that so much; I'm so sorry about the burden of guilt that he had that he didn't deserve to bear. Zee was seventeen when he died, and after his funeral I tried several times to contact her, to reach out to her, but she was unresponsive until ..."

In unspoken agreement, Garrett and Jenny both stood up, stretched, poured themselves the last of the coffee, and sat at the counter. The movement helped the tension, and facing her at the counter, Garrett was able to take possession of her hand. "She wouldn't answer you?"

"Not until about five years after Maggie and Mike died. I was living right here by then, and she pulled into my driveway at two o'clock one morning. It startled me. She pounded on my door, and when I opened for her, she said, 'Just a minute, Jenny.' I was still struggling to recognize who she was!

"She ran to her beat-up old van that she had left running and pulled a bundle from the front seat; it looked like a wad of blankets. She ran back and shoved it at me, and I took it, saying 'What is this?' but she didn't answer me directly. She was just wild, and talking very rapidly; I thought she might be on drugs.

"'I've been driving over twenty hours, Jenny,' she said, 'And I gotta keep going. Who will find me? He will. Lord knows — maybe he won't even try. But he has people. But I am so afraid. But you must bury her.' That is how she talked, her words boiling out and tripping over themselves, and I got it through my head that I was holding a dead child. I tried to get her to calm down. I laid the little bundle on the porch swing and said she needed to come in the house, but she refused. She wouldn't let me touch her. I started to turn on the yard light and that made her more crazy. She said, 'Turn it off! Turn it off! They will see me here!'

"She said, 'Just take her, Jenny, and give her a beautiful burial, like you did your own baby. Make it traditional Lakota. Put her high, high, high on a scaffold, where nothing can touch her, and let the wind claim her.' At that point, I started to shout, telling her that wasn't what we did with Maggie, that hardly anyone does the scaffold now, that we must call the sheriff and report what happened.

"She got glassy-eyed and sing-songy then, and sort of danced backward. She half-sang, 'Nothing happened, nothing happened, nothing happened. She died in her crib. Crib death. The police will end me. He will end me. I am in trouble trouble trouble. Only Mike loved me! You loved Mike, no police, don't call don't call don't call. Just put her high high high in the sky, and let the wind free her, my little Kai Li.' She went on in that vein, saying, 'She is dead dead dead and she didn't deserve it and I didn't deserve it. Never never never deserved it.' Then she said, in a voice so piteous I can't even repeat it, but I still hear it echo in my head, she said, 'Please, Jenny, please help me.' I was just horrified. 'You couldn't help me before, but you can now — raise my baby up. Put her where he can't reach her. Please.' That is what she said.

"I remember that I started down the steps toward her. I wanted to hold her and comfort her. She was pale, thin as a rake. But I underestimated how far she had backed away, and

Baby Skulls and Fowl Odors

suddenly she was in the old van, it still running, and she shot back out of the driveway and down the road. I made a feeble attempt to run after her, but I knew it was hopeless. Instead, I climbed heavily back up the steps and, shaking all over, I opened that dreadful bundle."

Garrett growled, "I knew you then, even that long ago. I wish you had called me."

"I know. Now, I wish I had, too. But then ... well, that was then. She had really unnerved me—legal issues and Lakota issues and issues of Mike and how he had yearned to help her. She must have come immediately at the baby's death, because the child was merely ... was merely pale, not ... Well, she looked like a sleeping child. No mark on her. What would happen, and to whom, if I called in the law? I had zero evidence that the man, the father, had done anything, and Zee had made it clear she wouldn't back me. For all I knew, she would accuse *me* of something. I didn't really know Zee, and the talk of addiction forestalled me, too. Yes, Patrick, now ... now I would give anything if I had called you, back then. Now I know you. But it has been years, maybe twenty, and even though I can still vividly feel my terror and confusion, just as I felt it at that time, I can no longer fix it. I can't fix what I did."

Softly, Garrett asked, "What did you do, Jenny?"

"I did what Zee asked me to do. I looked down at the little body, and I saw that she had been carefully bundled into the quilt my mother had made for Maggie's funeral, for the giveaway at the Lakota funeral, and I wrapped her back, and I put her on the scaffold, and I let the wind free her.

"There used to be an old woman in this community who was a distant relative of mine, some kind of great-aunt of my father, by marriage, that kind of thing. Anyhow, she had quite a reputation, a reputation for being a little wacky, but also capable. She spent a lot of time in the mountains and survived on the land. She had a Native American friend; well, he was Ute, but I guess they used to do platform burials, too, sometimes, like the Lakota. So I called her."

Garrett already knew, but he must ask. "What was her name?"

"Lena. Lena Larson. I doubt you knew her—she passed away a while ago. But the project was just up her alley. She and the Ute guy—she called him Colly. He was named for that famous Ute chief, Colorow, who used to bum biscuits and syrup off the white women; remember him?" Garrett shook his head, not sure, and she continued. "They built a nice little box, pretty much like a coffin, only a lot of it was good, strong wire, like chicken wire, to let the wind blow through. We three roamed around down here in these little canyons until we found a good, secluded place. That wasn't so hard; these canyons running off this mesa are plenty rocky and brushy. What we did, too, is after we'd whacked and climbed and sawed and nailed and fitted until we had something that suited us, hopefully secure from cougars and coyotes and other scavengers, we tried to put some limbs and brush back in, to sort of camouflage her. Honestly, Patrick, it was the most gruesome, weird thing I ever did, and yet, working with Lena and Colly, the shock began to wear off a little, and when we raised Kai Li in her little box, Colly talked about sending her so high that she could reach the spirits and live with them in heaven.

"We had kind of a little ceremony, and Colly rapped on a small drum he had brought and did Ute songs, and Lena seemed to know how to join in ... well, in the end, I didn't feel so bad about it all. I visited sometimes, over the years, and took her flowers."

"But you told me it is Kai Li's skeleton in the doll."

"Yes. Zee came back. You won't believe this—she had decided she had to see her child, or at least the scaffold. She was calmer than she had been that first time; she came in, had coffee and all. She said she had finally escaped her father for good because he'd been killed in a knife fight in Puerto Rico. I thought everything was okay. I led her down into that little canyon, and she just stood staring up at the box on the platform. You couldn't see inside it from the ground, but she stared and stared and stared, and something slipped inside her. She cried out, 'No! No, Jenny! This isn't right. We can't just leave her out here. She's all alone. We can't leave her out here, blowing in the wind. Get her down, Jenny! You have to get her down! She is so alone—she must be crying!'

"I guess I was still trying to be rational, and I said, 'But Zee, she's been out here for three years, and the Indians never take down a corpse from a scaffold' and that did it. She started trying to claw her way up the tree, and I thought—oh, lord, Patrick, what I thought was, 'wacky woman calls for wacky woman.' I told her I'd go get help, then left her there and ran up to the canyon rim to get phone reception so I could call Lena.

"Leave it to Lena. When she showed up, she had a hammer, a sack, and a rope. Patrick, she was in her eighties at the time, but she shinnied up that tree like a monkey. She pried the coffin open, stuffed the bones in her sack and tied the sack to the rope, and lowered it down. She said, 'There you go, sugar. There's your sweet little kid.'

"I think her matter-of-fact approach acted like a tonic to Zee. I'm not sure anyone had treated her like that before and she settled down, thanked Lena, and didn't act up again for the rest of the time she stayed with me. What she did do, though, was go through a whole grieving process. She carried the sack to the house, held it to her chest, and sobbed. She talked about demons and dreams, the demons who hurt innocence, and the dreams she had had for her little girl. She talked that she herself had never had classy clothes or toys or even a doll, and how she had wanted to give those things to her little girl and so-on. She even let me put my arm around her and she sobbed into my shoulder, as if she were releasing a whole lifetime of pain for herself as much as grief for her child. She kept saying, 'And now look where she is. What can I do to love her now?'

"That's when Lena, looking very sympathetic, burst in with, 'Oh, you poor sweetheart. Let's fix this. Let's make your own baby into a doll. That way she can be your doll and your baby, nearby to love forever.' Patrick, I can still hear myself gasp. I abruptly wanted that old woman out of my life. I was saying, 'Oh, no, Lena. What do you think you are doing!' I even said, 'Lena, I think she meant like a Barbie doll,' but Lena ignored me. She was on a roll. Zee had kind of wilted against me, and Lena took the sack of bones, all business-like, told us she'd be back when the doll was done, and left.'"

Jenny sighed, depleted. "That's kind of the whole story. Maybe one strange little twist—it only took Mrs. Efficiency a little more than a day to make that doll, but for that day Zee and I actually talked, visiting like the sisters we should have been. We talked about our little girls, and about Mike. Zee told me that Kai Li was, in fact, the child of her own incestuous father; he had abused her since she was twelve. Her mother knew, but did nothing—then I loathed the mother even more than the hideous father. During that precious day, we watched television, made sandwiches, and even, believe it or not, discussed celebrities and hair styles. I saw some of Mike in her, Patrick, and in that short time I came to love her. Then, that very evening, Lena showed up with that doll, the one you have been carrying around and leaving at Alma's. Lena called her Ling Ling Dell, don't ask me why, and said she'd worked on her steadily, without sleep, since she left thirty hours before. Even Lena looked beat, and I couldn't believe she could finish that fast, but then, she was Lena, always amazing.

"She described in great detail what she'd done, all very pleased with herself, like she had done taxidermy on a fawn she had found dead in the forest. The skull is perfectly placed, her little arms both have the tibia and fibula, and so-on, that kind of talk. She said the dear baby was resting in a sweet bed of cattail down, and that the moccasins had been the most difficult to do because the beadwork hurt her arthritic hands.

"After she'd gone on and on, with Zee nodding, apparently appreciatively, the strange twist happened. Zee suddenly stood up, thanked Lena, handed the doll to me, and said, 'I have to go now.' Once more I was left speechless—well, kind of. I started babbling, asking where she thought she was going, trying to give the doll back, trying to get her stopped, all the while her going toward the door. Finally, she did stop. She said, 'Jenny, I have the same addiction my father had. That's where I'm going now, to feed it. I can't be trusted with anything, especially not my baby. I would lose her. You're going to have to care for her until I can get my head on straight, then I'll come back for her. Please, Jenny, I have to go, and you are the only person in this world I would trust with that precious baby. I'll come back for her as soon as I can.' And then she left, and I haven't seen her since.

"Patrick, I am done, and I need a drink."

Sheriff Pat Garrett left Jenny's just before daylight. He was ashamed of himself—he knew that he now had most of the pieces to the Croysant puzzle, and that he should be thinking about how to put it all together, or at least he should be contemplating Jenny's story about how the doll came into being, but he wasn't. He couldn't concentrate. Instead, he rolled happily out across the dobies toward Riversmet, and as he drove, elbow out open window, breeze across his head, a smile on his face, he hummed a little ditty his daddy used to sing to his mama:

Well, I jumped in bed and covered up my head
And said she'd never find me,
But I knew damn well I lied like hell
'Cause she jumped right in behind me!

He hadn't been gone from Jenny's even a half hour—the sun had just begun to cut across the mountains—when Jenny heard a sharp knock on her door. She had been dreamily collecting coffee cups and tidying the couch, contemplating a return to the warm bed, and she was jolted when she opened the door. She gasped, "Zee! What are you doing here? You are Zee, aren't you?"

"I'm Zee. You probably don't recognize me after all these years. I didn't intend it should be so long, and I swear, what I need is your help again—I need your help so bad. It seems like that's all I ever do, doesn't it—just ask you for help."

28

TWENTY SECONDS BACK in his office totally dissipated Sheriff Garrett's blissful virtual reality. His desk was piled high with paperwork that had accumulated in just one day. A folder had been placed in the front and center position that Edith used to signal, "This is important." Edith, in fact, followed him into his office, with McCracken directly behind, the tail on the puppy. Ensconcing himself behind his desk and riffling at the waiting paperwork, Garrett said, "Okay, ladies, what have you got?"

"You first, Edith. Mine might take a little longer," at which the sheriff sighed, folding his hands on the desk and rolling a pencil with his thumbs. His eyelids drooped.

Edith grinned. "*Sí, Señorita*. Mine's easy. Two things. First, Sheriff, the locksmith will be in the lab at eleven to open the safe, and second, that folder under your pencil-twisters there contains the report from the coroner about the Croysant skeleton."

Finally, the adrenalin arrived. Garrett's eyes opened and he looked at Edith. "Croysant skeleton?" he repeated. Momentarily, he thought she was referring to the child in the doll, but as she said, "Yes. The one Jenny found at Fowlers'," his brain kicked in. Oh, that skeleton. Now he was impatient. He thumbed the report, wanting to get at it. But safe? What safe? He frowned at Edith, "What safe?"

Edith started to say, "Oh, the one Deputy McCracken dug up last night," but McCracken interrupted. "A-deet, I haven't had a chance to report yet. The sheriff doesn't know anything about the safe."

"*Oy, caramba!* My work here is therefore complete." She proceeded to take her light step and upbeat mood out of the room, but as she left she called over her shoulder, "Don't forget:

locksmith, lab, eleven of the clock."

Finally fully awake, Garrett called after her, "Thanks, A-deet," then said, "All right, Mac. Pull up a chair and tell me what's on your mind."

McCracken did just that, recounting how Sienna had come out of the trailer to dig the large hole in the dark, how Honey Fourier had driven up and fallen into the hole, and how, in trying to retrieve Honey's phone, she had bumped her foot on a metallic object that turned out to be the door of the safe Edith had mentioned. "I called Louie to take over the procedure with the safe, because I was still worried about losing Sienna."

"Good idea. So where is Sienna now?"

"Maybe wrong, Chief, but I took her home with me and texted Red to come up and help. I just didn't want to further traumatize that kid with Social Services. Or to get wound up in irrelevant red tape. We've been watching her in shifts all night, taking turns at catching a few Z's, but actually, all that fuss may have been unnecessary. Up at her place, she tried to run, at first, but once Honey and I showed up and the object in the hole turned out to be a safe, the fight sort of drained out of her. She just drug into my place and I tucked her into my own bed, and when I left this morning, Red was drinking coffee and playing Flappy Bird, and Sienna was sleeping like a log. I feel like the kid is just depleted."

"Flappy Bird?" Garrett thought, but what he said was, "You did good. I'm glad she's safe. So, why did Honey Fourier come pounding on the door at that time of night?"

"Chief, she wouldn't say. Just what I told you, that Chuck Fowler didn't have a chicken farm, but she knew who did. She said she'd come to apologize, because Mr. Fowler was having problems with the protesters, and she should have said something sooner. By the time I got all my business taken care of, her husband was there, helping her struggle up the hill on her sprained ankle. He was way sweet and solicitous to her. Boy, Chief, if I was superstitious I'd watch my feet around that place. First Fowler gets his peg shot out from under him, then Honey turns that ankle—the place seems to have the curse of the wounded mummy feet on it or something."

"Hmmmm," Garrett pondered, but McCracken continued. "The other thing, no matter what Honey says, Fowler does have chickens. I saw a rooster in a tree over by their trailer, looked big in the dark. Long, shiny black tail feathers. He seemed to be just sleepin' on a juniper branch."

"Mmmmm," Garrett repeated. "Guess there's no law against chickens. Or chicken farms, for that matter."

McCracken was standing up. "I know you got stuff to do, so I'll see you in the lab at eleven." She eyed the folder still unopened under his hands, and added hopefully, "It'll sure be interesting to see what the coroner says about that skeleton."

Not without sympathy, Garrett said, "I'll be sure to let you know, Mac. Maybe at eleven."

"Right. Oh, and one last thing, no doubt not important, but I thought it was interesting that Honey Fourier got herself a nice new do. Maybe trying to look more relaxed to fit into the community. Her hair was about shoulder length and straight, remember? Very urban and classy. Now it's real short, in a tight little Afro. It brings out the African-American in her and she really looks good, but in all that turmoil last night it took me a few beats to place who she was."

"I'll be damned," Garrett said noncommittally, and pulled at his mustache. An elusive, odd connection was trying to work its way through the heavy rush hour traffic in his brain. Ruminating, he opened the folder from the coroner as McCracken opened the door to go.

Abruptly, he slapped his desk and said, "Mac, wait. Close the door, and you'd better sit for this one." She sat, and he ruffled through the report pages, quickly scanning each one, and finally looked up. "Mac, Doc Thomson didn't have much trouble with this one. There was tissue from which to extract DNA, and the mouth was intact for dental examination, and the guy had a rap sheet a mile long, so when Doc sent his samples on in to CBI, it took them zero time to identify the corpse. You won't believe who it was." Garrett stopped there just to watch the agony of unsatisfied curiosity play across McCracken's face.

"Come on, Chief!"

Not really being a big fan of torture, he told her. "Mac Biedermann."

McCracken's eyes widened. "*That* Mac Biedermann? The S.O.B. drug smuggler and wife beater that disappeared after we found out who'd killed his abominable father, Reider? The guy

Baby Skulls and Fowl Odors

who lived in the tepee where the Fowler trailer is now?"

"One and the same. I always just thought he went on the lam after we exposed how he treated Alice, and after we found out about the cute little cocaine drop he'd set up down by the Cowpath. I figured his past would catch up with him sooner or later. But it looks like it caught up with him sooner. Somebody put a rifle bullet through his heart."

They both sat staring, dumbfounded, at the report. Finally, McCracken said, "But who?"

Garrett said, "Man, I don't know; this info bit doesn't fit anywhere."

The alarm on McCracken's phone emitted a witch's cackle. "Oh, crap, Chief. It's eleven o'clock."

The safe wasn't all that large, and it had been dusted off and set on the lab table for easy access. Garrett scrawled his name on some legal papers, and now he, McCracken, Hobbs, and Louie leaned forward, watching the locksmith work with the expertise of a burglar in a hurry. As the lock gave way and the door opened, everyone leaned forward to peer in, Louie on her toes, wielding a flashlight to better illuminate the safe's contents, but immediately they all fell back, covering their noses and gagging. The locksmith slammed the door and as they came up for air, Louie said, "My lord! That thing really packs a whang for somethin' so small."

29

WHEN EDITH TAPPED DISCREETLY on Garrett's open door, McCracken's gagging sounds could still be heard from down the hall and Garrett was trying to clear the odor by blowing his nose into the big red bandana he used for a handkerchief. "Sheriff, there are some people here who want to see you, but they don't want to spoil your lunch hour." The timing of her statement tickled her and she giggled.

Looking up at Edith with cough-reddened eyes, Garrett wheezed, "No problem, A-deet. Right now, lunch is not a problem. Send 'em on in."

The trio was led by Luke. He held himself military-erect, his jaw set and his stance determined. His mother looked grim, and Larry, trailing behind, held his bandaged arm, his face achingly sober. Luke said, "Mr. Garrett, I need to talk to you about that Larson barn that burned down. There's a lot of confusion up our way right now, chicken farm stuff and all, and before you go adding that barn to your investigations, you need to know that me and Larry did it. We burned that barn down." Larry was taking in every word his brother said, his head bobbling up and down like a dashboard doggie. Tiffany's mouth had drawn down even further, and the sheriff, trying to read them, thought he noted a tear edging down her cheek.

He asked, "Why would you do that?"

Larry burst out, "We didn't mean to do it," and Luke cut in, "We are stupid shits, Sir. My brother and Sienna Fowler are friends, and she kept bragging to him that she had fighting cocks. I got tired of hearing Larry talk about it, so I bet him that they were just chickens and wouldn't even fight." Luke's cheek had begun to twitch uncontrollably, a tick that happened to him when he was stressed. Or worse. He was having trouble continuing.

Larry mumbled, "So we decided to get the chickens ..."

This freed Luke to butt in. "We didn't want to bother Sienna." He felt he must put their case in the best light. "So we went in at night and got 'em. Two roosters. We had no intention of stealing them, Sir."

"That Larson barn is ... was ... Mom's," Larry added, helpfully.

"But, the problem was, when we set 'em down to fight, we ... we knocked over a coal-oil lantern and the straw in the barn caught fire."

Larry was caught up in the story. "We barely escaped with our lives! And the roosters ..."

"... We can't return the chickens, Sir. They either escaped, or they got fried. We can't find 'em."

"But we didn't mean to do it," Larry stressed. "We didn't mean to steal Sienna's ..."

This time Tiffany cut in. "Sheriff Garrett, I don't know what charges you will have to bring on this. I actually begged Luke not to come down, but he insisted. You see, I don't want him in the army, at least not yet, but it means ..." She looked up at her tall son and blinked. She was a strong woman, and didn't appreciate people with leaky eyes, especially herself. It took a visible gritting of teeth to go on. "Sheriff, getting into the army has come to mean an awful lot to Luke. But if he gets into trouble with the law, they won't let him in."

The sheriff felt a shiver of irritation run down his spine. He had enough on his plate without having to sort out the implications of these kids' confessions of delinquency. "So, Luke, why did you insist on tellin' me this?"

"It didn't seem right not to. I was afraid somebody else might get in trouble for what we did. Fowlers'll be lookin' for their chickens and everything, and you might go after those protesters for burnin' the barn or something."

Larry looked down, unable to say anything. He knew Luke wasn't worried about him or Cesar or even Pewter, much less Sienna or the protesters. He was covering for the beauteous Ginger, and she'd probably blab, anyhow, and tell who really was there and what really had happened. He was disgusted, but he clamped his mouth shut to keep from being the squealer.

Garrett scowled at his desk, rubbed at his chin, then said, "So, Ms. Gallenas, you owned the barn?"

"Lena Larson left it to Hallie, you know, my aunt? Hallie Flute? And Hallie left everything to me. So I guess it's probably okay, isn't it, if my boys burned it? You know, just getting rid of trash on the place?"

"You don't plan to bring charges?"

For a terrifying moment, Tiffany was silent, and both boys' heads swiveled to stare at their mother. She met their eyes and said steadily, "No, not this time. This time I won't bring charges."

"Good," the sheriff said, "And now ..." His eyes turned to the paper stack on his desk.

Larry whispered, "What about the roosters?"

Garrett had re-opened the coroner's folder. He wanted to double check what he had read. Mac Biedermann, of all people! Disinterested, he looked up. "Why don't you just go have a reasonable talk with your neighbors, tell them what happened, apologize, then apologize a lot more, and offer to buy roosters to replace the ones you borrowed? See if that works."

Larry said shakily, "We can't afford to do that, Mr. Garrett. Sienna told me those roosters are worth thousands of dollars."

Click. Garrett stared at Larry. Of course! Contrary to what he had been saying to everyone, it could be illegal to have chickens. Now things were coming together! Chuck Fowler wasn't setting up a chicken factory farm. He was engaged in something far, far more criminal. Carefully, he said, "You are right, Larry. Now I see that the chickens could be a problem, at least for someone. So let's do this. You go on home now and let me work on the chicken problem. Wait and see; there should be a solution to this."

The three stood uncertainly. Things hadn't been resolved, but now Garrett really wanted them out of here, so he gave them a dismissive nod. As they left, though, Tiffany hesitated. She seemed to come to a decision. "Boys, go on down. I'll meet you at the car. I need a private moment with the sheriff."

Approaching his desk, she said, "Look, Mr. Garrett, I don't want to hold you up, but this is about something completely different, okay? I know you guys dug up a corpse up by Fowlers', and I just want to say, because Nancy Jane is such a

Baby Skulls and Fowl Odors

rabble-rouser and all, and shot Fowler in the foot and all—well, I can just see that she might be a suspect. Or you might bring her in for questioning. If you do—and believe me, I'm not saying you should, because it wasn't her who shot that guy. She wouldn't think of doing that—but if you question her, I'd like to be there. She's my cousin, you know. I know how she is. She gets so excitable, and she might say goofy stuff that isn't true. You know, like she kept saying it was her land. I'm not saying you should bring her in, understand? Just that I need to ... that I could help if you let me be here if you should do that."

"Well." Garrett studied Tiffany. "Ms. Gallenas, so far we haven't any suspects with respect to the corpse in Croysant. There are no plans at this time to question Nancy Jane Barnswallowper."

"Okay," Tiffany nodded. She'd had enough training in professional protocol to know he wouldn't say any more. He wouldn't promise to let her know if he was going to question Nancy Jane, but she hoped she had at least put a bug in his ear.

She had. "Shot?" Garrett thought. "How did she know that?" He looked at the report on his desk, the one only he, McCracken, and the coroner's people knew anything about. Still studying her, Garrett said abruptly, "Tiffany, are you racist?"

Totally taken aback, she said, "What? Racist? Of course not! Why would you ask that?"

"That day McCracken was texting you to ask if Jenny Threewinds was there at the time of the Cowpath fire, and you texted back something about her being out with the handsome Black guy, LOL. Doesn't LOL mean 'laughing out loud'? Why were you laughing at the Black guy?"

Tiffany was terribly amused. "I wasn't laughing at the Black guy! At the time, I thought Jenny had taken up with him as a main squeeze, although later I found out he is just her cousin and was crashing on her couch." As she continued, Garrett wondered why it was always him to be the last to learn these things. "So, everyone knows you're sweet on Jenny, and I was LOL'ing the contrast. That guy is a hyperactive, talkative, good-looking little twerp. Not a bad guy, you understand, but a big contrast for Jenny to choose over you. You are big and quiet and competent and ... " She stopped abruptly.

He couldn't help but smile. "And ugly. Okay, I get it." He

was quiet, then said, "Tiffany, who started the fire at the Cowpath?"

If the woman had been taken aback by his first question, this time she literally flinched. Garrett's eyes narrowed. Carefully, she said, "They said that fire was an accident—I heard it was a grease fire started by some rags that accidentally got shoved against a burner."

"But Ms. Gallenas, if it was an accident, why was there a note? A group of former classmates—they'd graduated high school together—came in from out of town and were eating there at the time of the fire. A couple of them were Black, and one of the Black guys has been hired to teach in Peaseford this coming year. Also, someone coming out from the fire thought they heard shots. The note said, 'No one wants your kind in our schools.' Ms. Gallenas, you showed up almost immediately when Lew fell, as if you were nearby. Did you hear the shots? Do you have any idea as to whom might be so full of racial prejudice as to leave an ugly note like that?"

Tiffany had gasped, "Oh, no! I didn't know," but as he stopped speaking she gathered herself and said, "Honestly, Sheriff, I don't know. I have no problem whatsoever with anyone from any other race. Not Black people, not Asians, not any other race. And I don't know of anyone in Croysant or this area who does."

"All right, Ms. Gallenas. I appreciate all the information."

"Yeah, well. Guess the boys are waiting. Better go. So ... thanks, Sheriff."

She didn't move. The sheriff raised his brows, questioning. "There are some people, though," she said slowly, "that shouldn't be in our schools, and maybe somebody could get angry enough to fire a warning shot at them. Or to leave a note." Now the sheriff's eyebrows were becoming increasingly elevated, and Tiffany, once decided, kept talking rapidly. "You know, I personally don't hold much truck with all the military recruiters in our high schools. It's just wrong. It violates our constitutional guarantees of privacy or something. Anyhow, I know it isn't right. The army needs to back off our kids, quit buzzing around them like buzzards after road kill, and picking them off while they are so young and impressionable. I don't know who it would be, but *if* I knew, and I say *if*, I might admire somebody

Baby Skulls and Fowl Odors

who'd get mad enough about that shit to take out a few frustrations. Smoke out recruiters. Scare 'em a little. Even if it didn't do any good in the long run." She shrugged, adding, "And didn't hurt anybody, really, you know," then turned on her heel and slipped out the door.

Garrett let out a whoosh of air. "Right," he said to himself. "Right." He remembered that Jenny had told him some of the group was in uniform, but he had been so focused on the imaginary racial issue that he just scooted right past everything else. Still talking to himself, he said, "Jesus, I don't want somebody up here shooting at our troops. But that wasn't a confession. That couldn't be construed as a confession." He was talking out loud. It took a chuckle from the open doorway to reveal McCracken, Hobbs, and Louie listening just inside. Hobbs gave him a stadium-sized grin.

"Ya talkin' to yourself again, Pat? That ain't a real good sign of a sound mind."

McCracken joined in. "Didn't mean to bother you, Chief, in the midst of your private conversation with good company and all. We just thought you might like to run out with us to grab a burger."

Garrett, recovered, growled, "How about Louie goes out to get us a bucket of chicken so that the rest of you slackers can keep workin'?"

"Bleeah!" Louie said, a sharp gagging sound, as Hobbs said, "Maybe you're plannin' to eat chicken a little too soon after our safe-cracking episode."

McCracken grinned. "Nothin' gag you quicker than suckin' in a big whiff of rotten chicken. We shoulda worn gas masks—hazardous duty."

Garrett was suddenly serious. "I'm not sure just why yet, but I think we better keep this dead-rooster-in-the-safe information in the department for a while. Kind of our own departmental HIPAA privacy thing." Garrett was reaching for his hat. "I'll ask A-deet to tell the locksmith. I been gettin' a awful mess of information to piece together, and it might be to our benefit not to have the word about this stinkin' dead chicken spread all over the community."

As they started out the door, somebody chortled, and

Garrett said, "Yeah, I know. I said, 'Spread the stinking dead chicken around in the community.' Every day, I have to work with adolescents."

After they ate lunch at the diner (everyone having burgers except McCracken, who demonstrated her iron stomach with a chicken salad), Hobbs meandered back into Garrett's office and settled into his big, brown easy chair. "Well, Pat, I dug up a little info for you to add to your information mess. You want me to hit you with it now?"

"You bet. Why not?" Garrett yawned, rubbed the back of his neck, then grinned. "I may have to sleep on it, though."

Hobbs grinned back, one of those annoying, knowing grins. "Busy night?"

"Oh, certainly, Mr. Hobbs. And if you're like everyone else in this valley, you probably know more about it than I do. Now fire away, because I'm gonna run up to the house for the shower and clean clothes I missed out on yesterday. It looks like it could be another long afternoon."

"Gotcha. Okay, let's start with the one that interests you most, Mr. Brady Xyster, the guy that lives with Jenny."

"He's her cousin," Garrett interjected defensively. "She's just givin' him a place to crash—seems to be broke."

"Right." Now it was Hobbs' turn to rub his chin. "Makes sense. See, Xyster is, well, was, a front man for Tinker Poultry. You know them? That big meat outfit that advertises, 'We tinker with your turkey till it titillates your tummy,' and so-on?"

"Yeah, I know the outfit. 'Who'd want to cuddle it when you can cook it' in big letters beside a poster of a cute chicken. That outfit."

"That's the one. 'Our chubby chicks are just for chewing.' Anyhow, Xyster was supposed to be in this area finding a farmer he could get under contract to grow chickens for Tinker. It has to be done underhanded, because if most real farmers knew what they were getting into, they wouldn't do it. I didn't learn much more, you know, corporate secrecy, just like their recipes, but apparently he failed and got fired."

"So," Garrett said, "That explains his no funds, and maybe a lot of other stuff."

"It does indeedy. Now, the other guy you were interested in, Chuck Fowler. He's as clean as a fresh-washed sheet. Even

Baby Skulls and Fowl Odors

seems like a real nice guy; I talked to a couple of his former friends and neighbors, and they said they hated to see him move away. His boss said he hated to lose him, but family should always come first. The boss helped him transfer out here, and he should be running a truck out of Riversmet in a couple weeks."

"Boss?"

"Yeah, he works, that is worked, for Fed Ex in Carlsbad, California. Real efficient driver, good customer relations — everything was all good for him, except for his wife."

"Wife?"

"Yup. Seems he was just crazy for his wife, but she got arrested a few months back. Fowler told his friends that he was frantic, didn't know what to do. He felt like scum to desert her, but he'd tried for years to help her and he felt like he should think of his kid now. He finally made this very painful decision to just pick up the kid and move away. He thought he should get the kid completely out of there. Apparently the addiction that got the woman arrested kind of runs in the family."

Garrett, working his mustache, said, "Is that right? Well, I'm afraid I know what the lady was hooked on. It followed her kid to Colorado."

"Yeah, I figured you had it. Cock fights. Gambling on cock fights."

"So, both Sienna and Chuck say the mother is dead. What happened? Did she get some disease in prison, or did somebody kill her in there?"

"No, Pat, that one you got wrong. She was a good girl in prison, and got released on parole about a week ago."

30

"I DROVE ALL NIGHT, Jenny."

Jenny smiled. "It seems you have a habit of doing that." She contemplated the pretty little Chinese woman who had just settled onto her couch. Mike's little sister. Why, she must be in her forties by now, and Mike would have been in his sixties if he had lived. How time flew!

Both women were drinking coffee. Each had had a sleepless night. Jenny thought, "Mine was better," but she said, "Zee, I know you've come for your baby, little Kai Li. I know where she is, and she is safe, but I don't have her right now."

Zee's tired face looked haunted. "Don't worry about the doll. Not important, not right now. My troubles now are so much worse. I can barely speak them."

On impulse, Jenny leaned forward and took her hands. "Zee, I always wished I could be a true sister to you. You have to tell me what has happened. You came all this way for help, but I can't try to help you if I don't know what it is."

"I just got out of jail."

Taken aback, Jenny cried, "You have escaped from jail! What in the world ...! What could you have possibly done that put you in jail? Are you wanting me to hide you?"

"No, no, no ... Don't misunderstand. I'm out on parole. I'm here legally, with the full blessings of the parole board. You see, I have been married to the kindest man in the world for fourteen years, and I'm sure he helped my case. He always stuck up for me, even when I was arrested. He left town, to protect our daughter, but before he left, he wrote a glowing letter to the parole board extolling my virtues. As if I had any." She had dropped Jenny's hands and was hunkered miserably over her coffee cup.

Gently, Jenny probed. "But what were you doing, Zee? What got you into so much trouble?"

"You remember my father, Xi Wang Li, how awful he was? Both he and my mother were so addicted, and I was raised there. I got the same addiction—I couldn't beat it."

"Oh, honey!" Jenny exclaimed. "Drugs! You were on drugs."

Zee's head jerked up sharply. "Oh, no! I must have misled you! I have never done drugs—never in my life! My father was addicted to gambling!"

"Gambling!"

"That man bet on every cock fight he could get to until he was killed in a knife fight over a disputed outcome in Puerto Rico. I learned from him to love those fights, Jenny. He took me to the ring from the time I was tiny, a baby. I helped raise the cocks, too. Oh, Jenny, they are beautiful things. Legs of amber and pearl, and feathers of ebony, silver, and gold. There are gorgeous ones with mahogany feathers and black tails so thick and long that they sweep the ground as they strut through. I loved them so much."

"But, Zee, don't they die in the fights?"

"Some die. I wanted to think of it as being like a bullfight. The bull dies, but in great splendor. Bull fights are respected, powerful rituals all over Spain, all over the Latin American world. I convinced myself that cock fighting was a ritual like that. In Kaifeng, where my mother's cocks came from, they only fight at certain times of the year, on certain days of the lunar month. They fight in a specific place, called the fighting hollow. Some of the fighting hollows in Kaifeng are the Iron Pagoda Park and the Grand Xiangguo Temple. I dreamed of going there, just to see them.

"Cocks are trained, like any sports figure. For example, I used to walk our cocks at certain times—the walks are called 'driving the cock.' He runs ahead and the trainer runs after him. We'd do this for increasingly long times until the cock was strong and brave, fit as a fiddle. At the fights, they balance the cocks for matches. Only the cocks that are the same size, weight, and age are allowed to fight each other. The guy in charge is called a cock head, and he works with the owners to be sure the fight is a fair match, and is stopped at the right time. All that is in China; I used to want terribly to go participate there."

All Jenny could say was, "Oh, Zee."

"People are crazy about their fighting cocks. When the bird gets hurt in the ring, they will call for a time out and suck on the bleeding bird's wounds with their very own mouths, trying to ease them."

Again, "Oh, Zee."

Zee sighed. "So, I guess it might not be so bad, but the people like my father, and eventually me, who gamble a lot on the fights, they contaminate it. It gets to be all about the money. It spoils any good aspect, the spectacle, the ritual, the beauty of the roosters. Once people start gambling, they get crazy. Fights get fixed, high stakes get wagered." She shrugged. "Lots of people worldwide are cock-fighting enthusiasts; some are straightforward, but so many are crooked. One of my goals, before jail, was to make it to the World Cock-fighting Championship Fights in Cali, Colombia. That's how much I was into it. That's why I did so wrong by my family."

"But cock fighting is illegal in America, isn't it? At least some of America?"

"Oh, you better believe it! I'll say! It is illegal in all fifty states. There are fines of $100,000 and more, and sometimes jail terms of as long as twenty years. Even watching a cock fight can get you arrested. And transporting fighting cocks across state lines? Man, that is deep federal doo doo.

"Some states resisted. They tried to keep what they called a 'game fowl industry.' One senator in Oklahoma had a plan to get it so cocks were fitted with little boxing gloves instead of razor spurs. They were going to have electronic sensors to record the number of hits by each rooster to see which one won." The image of the boxing-gloved birds made both women smile. Zee continued, "I don't know how that all came out, but I do know that not too long before they broke up my own cock-fighting ring, some Romanian princess and her husband were arrested in Oregon for holding cock-fighting derbies on their ranch. You see, it still goes on all over. And it's still very, very illegal."

Zee fell silent, and Jenny, fumbling for words, finally came out with, "It does sound like an exciting world."

Raising her eyes sadly, Zee replied, "Maybe. Like drinking.

Baby Skulls and Fowl Odors

Like drugs. It's an addiction — you come to need it, and it messes with your brain. The gambling and competition catch you worse than the roosters, and, Jenny, it has cost me my family. I had a new start in life, and could have put all the horror of my early years behind me. Kai Li had been begun in hell and lost in hell, too, but then I was given a living child and a wonderful husband, and I let cock fighting and gambling tear them away from me."

"I am so sorry."

"I was in a good prison. If there is such a thing. At any rate, they put a lot of effort into my rehabilitation. God, you won't believe, but not only did I mourn the life I had thrown away, my own life, but they also had me grieving for the roosters I had thrown into the ring, especially the ones who lost and died. For the first time, it actually dawned on me that my beautiful roosters, too, had been slashed to death in the name of my addiction. The heat of the fights and the intensity of the sport blinded me, and the therapists made me see again. There was one woman there — well, I think she really liked chickens. She'd been raised on a farm, and she would cry, real tears rolling down her cheeks, when I told about my lost roosters. It was weird, but it worked. I think I am over it. At least I hope. I hope and pray that I am done with it."

"Oh, Zee! I hope so, too." They were quiet. Jenny sipped her coffee, but was no longer tired. She felt a need to get to the root of this. "But you said ... you told me you came here for help. I don't understand what you need me to do. Do you need a safe place to stay for a while, until you can get on your feet?"

"Jenny, you are so kind, but no, that isn't it. I have come here to try to reconcile with my family. I have little hope of it, but at least I need to apologize to them, even if they reject me. I need you to speak for me."

"What!"

"I'm afraid to face them, but I am so sorry — so sorry for what I have done to them. I need to at least tell them that. And I just can't get my courage up. Could you please come with me? Please, stand beside me? I feel so small."

Jenny's mouth opened, then closed. How could she do something like this? But how could she turn her down? "Zee, I feel like I'm missing something. Who are these people? Where are they—must I go to California with you?"

"No, no, they're right here—you can see the mountainside where they live right over there, out your picture window." She stood and pointed. "Maybe you already met them; they've been here a few months. Did you meet Chuck Fowler? And our daughter, we named her Sienna." Zee lowered her eyes and swallowed. "Sienna. Like the beautiful, red-brown of a rooster." She wheeled back and knelt by Jenny, grabbing for Jenny's hands, squeezing them bloodless. "Oh, my god, I never thought I would let Sienna be hurt like this. I couldn't help about Kai Li, but what have I done? This is my fault, the danger Sienna is in. I have thrown her in the ring. She is no rooster! I must try to fix this. Oh, I must fix this!"

"Well, okay," Jenny yielded. "Okay, I ..."

"The thing is, Jenny, this isn't really altogether about apologies. Chuck and Sienna may have four of my prize birds; they may have brought them here, across state lines, and kept them. They will be in horrible trouble with the law, if they get caught, all because of me. You see, when the police came, in the confusion, I was able to get our four best birds into Sienna's room. I told her to hide them. I told her to take care of them, that they were my legacy to her, all that she would ever have that had been part of her mother. Oh, Jenny! Do you see what an idiot I was! I actually told her she should think of me as dead, and just be responsible for those birds. What was I thinking! I wasn't. I am ashamed! So ashamed. You must help me! We must get this stopped."

31

GARRETT SPRANG CHUCK FOWLER. He arranged for Red to get him out of jail and take him and Sienna home. Pushing his paper stack aside, he then hurried out his office door before something else caught him. Instead, the something else caught him at home. His land line started ringing just as he opened his door. "No rest for the wicked," he growled.

It was Jenny, causing his annoyance to evaporate. "Patrick, Mike's little sister showed up here this morning. Can you believe it? After all these years! She drove an all-nighter from California, and I talked her into a nap, but I need to hurry. Before she wakes up, I want to tell you what she told me. Do you have a minute?"

Of course. Pat Garrett would always have a minute for Jenny. She gave him the full story, stressing her own anxiety about Chuck and Sienna's possession of the illicit roosters. Garrett, listening carefully, said, "Jenny, try to keep a lid on her till evening, at least. I need to think about this."

"Got it. Knock on wood, maybe she'll sleep another couple hours. Poor little thing is exhausted, a real wreck."

Garrett started his coffee pot. He measured it thick as tar, and while it made he ducked into the shower, one of his favorite places to think. As the water doused him, he mentally listed all the stuff that had been going on at Croysant, and tried to pull out the events that he needed to actually deal with. Well, not the three fires. One, the Fourier fire, was legal and unrelated. Two were explained—he could let the Larson barn rest, and he supposed he may as well let the Cowpath fire rest, too. Everyone else seemed content to call it an accident. There was the doll skeleton. What in the world was he going to do about that? Then there was all the chicken stuff: the protesters; Xyster's chicken farm, which wasn't illegal no matter how much he might prefer that it was; the fighting cocks and the rooster-in-the-safe, all of which were going to cause trouble for the wrong people (and yet, could Zee's intention to reform be trusted?); and finally, Mac Biedermann, turning up in a hole in Fowlers' (or was it Nancy Jane Barnswallowper's?) yard. Only the Biedermann thing was a case where he now had to sort out who did it, and he was pretty sure he knew the answer to that one, too. Reluctantly, he stepped out of the shower and treated himself to a quick glance in the mirror at the surprising body that had been admired so thoroughly last night. He had never realized what a fine body it really was!

A quick glance, that was all he allowed. Then he toweled himself off fiercely, getting the blood flowing, dressed, and headed for the coffee pot and phone. He may as well start with the one case that actually still felt like a case. The doll and chickens, with their tough ethical dilemmas, could wait.

Carmen Weinant put him through to her husband, Duz; Garrett explained what he needed, and Duz said, sure, that he figured he could try to help. He'd meet Garrett at his mom's in a couple hours if the sheriff could let him finish moving a little irrigation water first. Garrett asked if he should call Alma ahead, and Duz said, "Nah, she wouldn't remember. She'll be there."

Back out through the dobies Garrett went, headed once more for Croysant, but finally he was fully awake. He got into thinking mode by naming plants and land formations as he drove: rabbitbrush, sage, tumbleweed, and those interlopers, Russian olive and tamarisk. Then there were mesas, with flat tops and steep sides, and hills, that went up round. Gulches, gullies, and the occasional knob. And in the distance, canyons and gorges. Once he had wondered about how to distinguish buttes and mesas, so he had googled it up. Mesas, he learned, were big enough to graze cattle on. The smaller, flat-topped, steep-sided formations were buttes. Not as many buttes in this area, he thought. More of them in Utah.

The naming worked every time. His thinking shifted from the landscape he was driving past to the landscape in his mind. More difficult, this. Proper procedure said that doll must go into the lab, but if he were to believe Jenny, and God help him, he did, then what would be the point? The child had been killed

Baby Skulls and Fowl Odors

years ago, and the person who had killed her was long dead. What good would an investigation serve — it could only cause pain. Ethics and duty. He emitted a sound like a groan, and moved on to the roosters. He liked Chuck Fowler, and apparently the wife was trying to reform. There was duty, and Sheriff Pat Garrett was a dutiful public servant, but he also had a deeply rooted community conscience. He was a kind man. This was tearing him apart. He could no longer tell mountains from molehills, buttes from mesas.

He was already in Peaseford, meaning he was early. Duz wouldn't be at Alma's for another forty-five minutes. He slowed way down, irritating the driver behind him, and cast about for something interesting to see along the quiet small town streets. There was a sign for the annual library book sale. He pulled in, to the other driver's relief. He may as well kill time at a book sale as anywhere else.

Standing in the hallway and peering into the main room of the building, he saw table after table, all loaded down with stacks of books. Library volunteers, some in trim slacks, shirts, and blouses, others in jeans and T-shirts printed with the logo, "One World, Many Stories," were pulling donated books from large boxes, taking them to the community room, and attempting to sort them onto the tables: fiction or non-fiction? Sports and travel, tools and health ... westerns, romance, sci-fi, the classics ...

Mingling among the volunteers and doing the same carrying and sorting, and yet clearly a different breed of fish, was a hodge-podge of men of various ages and types, young, old, bearded, shaven, white, brown, tall, short — all somehow belonging together and not really fitting in here. Garrett was, in truth, dazzled by the scene. Suddenly, he spotted Red walking officiously around, apparently doing not much. Red spotted him at the same time and blushed, making the red hair itself glow.

"Well, hi, Boss! I was just here, supervising this work crew." Red was talking fast, trying to cover his tracks. "They're here on work release from the jail, right? You know, when I picked Chuck up, I got talking to Tom. He was supposed to be doing this, but he wanted real bad to go with his wife and kids to meet his daughter's plane. Real bad. So I said I could do it for him. Didn't seem too busy at the office, everyone getting by while I babysat the kid, so I didn't figure you'd mind."

Garrett didn't reply, just looked in amazement at his delinquent employee, then at the squirming mass of people lugging and sorting books. A wiry little white-haired chap, carrying what looked like a half set of encyclopedias, was pushed against him by the crowd. He looked up, laughed, and said, "Why, howdy, Sheriff. You a customer? These books are the best bargain around today—everything here goes for a donation. Or even for free. Go on in and look around."

"Well, I think I will." Garrett eyed Red, standing anxiously and guiltily by the door. "So, Deputy, looks like you better get busy, do your job here. Keep an eye on these offenders. But I wanta talk to you before you leave."

A trim, dressy woman in front of him with a library volunteer tag that read, 'Laurene Hossenfoos,' had cornered one of the work crew and was thanking him effusively for coming in to help. Garrett thought that the man would surely prefer to be out in the fresh air, carrying and sorting books, than sitting in his jail cell, marking time, so why the big deal of thanking him? Why did she do that? Why were all the free people walking around here making such a point to show such welcoming, you-are-just-like-us faces to the men who would soon be going back with Red to continue their terms of incarceration? Did the volunteers feel guilty, somehow, for the men's plight? Did they hope to elevate them, show them that whatever they had done against society, all was forgiven and they could soon come back out of jail and fit, without opposition, into a world where people followed the rules? It was the same condescending attitude with which you reacted to the handicapped guy blocking the aisle in the wheelchair in Walmart, smiling at him all kind and normal, letting him know that you can see he is a mess, but you are willing to allow for it, and hope for the best for him, anyhow.

Or was there something darker in the volunteers' reaction? Were they secretly afraid of these men, unable to grasp the inner workings of a person who could go so far against social norms as to be locked away from other people? Were they overly polite because deep down, they sensed that something writhing inside these men might be very different, and it might surface to hurt the decent people? The kind-hearted, law-abiding, library-volunteer social order might be susceptible to chaotic forces that didn't, after all, appreciate it. For some reason Tiffany Gallenas

Baby Skulls and Fowl Odors

crossed his mind. Law-abiding Tiffany, who had done nothing except hurry to help Lew Harris when he fell. Perhaps.

He studied the group as the work crew and earnest volunteers and book customers interacted, and he thought, "It kind of boils down to the individual. You don't really know other people, do you, just the story you tell yourself about them." This led him to ponder further. "But then, people act on the stories they tell themselves about other people, and pretty soon, you are part of everyone's story about you, and that is who you are, who you become, a whole person formed from a community of stories, some right, some wrong." He decided this was either a profound insight, or useless garbage, and drifted with the crowd into the community room.

Looking around, he could see why the sorters were having difficulties. Talk about stories! Not only might a book fit either on the gardening table or the medicinal herbs table—where to place it?—but even the huge, over-reaching categories of fiction and nonfiction had slippery boundaries. Fiction often showed the truth of real life, while non-fiction seldom fully hit the mark in portraying that piece of reality it had chosen to bring into language. Interesting. He looked at his watch. Duz should be winding up the irrigation project he'd described to the sheriff, and ready to head to Alma's. Hurriedly, Garrett picked out two biographies of famous classical musicians, bravely placed in nonfiction, and a crime novel, which surely must have caused uncertainty when it was placed on a fiction table. He stuffed a twenty in the donations jar, was thanked by the volunteer and thanked him in turn, then hurried into the hallway to find Red.

"You have to go all the way into Riversmet to get these boys home?" At Red's affirmative nod, Garrett said, "All righty, then. See you back at work tomorrow. And by the way, I need you to text McCracken and have her meet me at Fowlers' at about six." Red nodded again, chagrined. He knew this was his penalty for trading out his work day without checking in at the office first. While he was driving offenders back to jail, he would miss seeing McCracken, and maybe not be in on whatever was going down up by the burial site of the corpse. He nodded again, obediently, but Garrett was already headed down the hall, hoping to himself that he was presenting the same friendly, professional, and slightly neutral face to inmates, used book shoppers, and volunteers alike. It wasn't that easy to do, because he knew that, unlike everyone else here, the men on the crew couldn't take books back home, that is, to the jail, with them. Used books brought into a jail were a no-no—they might contain contraband: drugs, perhaps, or a razor blade, a weapon. Actually, that is what all books are, Garrett thought, containers for weapons. All books are armed and dangerous.

Garrett plopped his own books in the back seat and drove. Passing the church billboard, he read, "God wants to reap spiritual fruit, not religious nuts." Good one. Whoever picked out those messages sometimes came up with some real doozies. Garrett loved this one. It empowered him to temper the performance of the duties of his office with what he knew in his conscience to be right. By the time he pulled into Alma's drive, his heart felt lighter and his mind was purposeful. He entered, as tradition required, without knocking.

Alma was there, feet up, in her chair. That felt right. Surprisingly, what also felt right was Ling Ling Dell, also feet up, nestled comfortable on Alma's lap. When Garrett appeared in range of her fading vision, Alma's hold on Ling Ling Dell tightened, and she said, "Why, hello, Lyle. You didn't come to take this doll away from me, did you?"

"Oh, no. No, Mrs. Weinant, she's fine right where she is, for now."

Duz arrived, and Alma, seeing her son, said, sharply, "Douglas Ulysses Zane Weinant, you're late again. Did you clean your shoes before you came in? Or maybe you should take them off."

Garrett said, "Late?" and Duz grinned.

"I cleaned my feet, Mom. And Sheriff, I been late since the day I was born. You know, I was quite a clunker of a baby, and it took her quite a while to squeeze me out. I think, in Mom's opinion, I started my career of draggin' my feet right then, and I been late ever since."

Alma's risky hearing had only caught part of this. "Duz, I didn't say you were a bad baby with chunky feet. You were a wonderful baby; I've always told you that."

Duz pulled a chair up beside her and said, "I know, Mom. Almost as good as the woman that bore me." He patted her arm.

Baby Skulls and Fowl Odors

"Have a chair, Sheriff," then, "Look, Mom, the sheriff is not just doin' a friendly visit today. You have some important information he needs, because he's out solving a murder today."

"Oh, what happened?" Alma was excited. She loved being in the middle of the action, and she loved being the one to know things. Duz looked at Garrett and nodded.

"Well, Mrs. Weinant. One day you told me that Hallie shot some bad man, and another day you told Jenny Threewinds that somebody buried something up at Nancy Jane Barnswallowper's place. I didn't really get what actually happened. Do you think you could tell me again?"

Alma pinched her lips, then said, "No, I don't think so. It sounds like you plan to get Hallie in trouble, and I don't want to see her hang for doing what was the right thing."

Before Garrett could respond, Duz again patted his mother's arm and said, "Oh, Mom, you know better than that. They never charge old women with murder." As Garrett looked up, dumbstruck, Duz continued, "Remember, Mom? It's like a statute of limitations. Once a woman reaches ninety, she's considered to be too old to arrest. What would they do with some old lady in jail? And you know, Hallie is well past ninety." He didn't add that not only was Hallie well past ninety, she was also dead. Instead, he continued, "So, I think you should tell the sheriff what Hallie told you about what happened, so that he can close up the case and get on with his paperwork about it."

Looking skeptical, Alma said, "Well, okay, Duz, if you think it's the right thing to do. But it would be better if he just talked to Hallie."

"Oh, he will, but that's how policemen work. They get all the information they can from everyone so they can tie the loose ends. So you should go ahead and tell him what you heard, okay, Mom?"

Reluctantly, she turned to Garrett and said, "Well, Hallie didn't tell me all that much. She said it was toward evening, and Tiffany had come by to hear some old-timey stories Hallie might know. Tiffany wanted to hear old stories to share with her kids. I think that's right—is that little Tiffany already old enough to have kids? Hard to believe." The narrative stopped, and Alma's eyes began to drift shut.

Before Garrett could intercede, Duz said sharply, "Mom,

wake up, damn it. What did Hallie say happened?"

"Oh. Oh, well. Where was I? Oh, that's right. Tiffany wanted to hear Hallie's old stories. Duz, why don't you and Gritty ever come by here to hear my stories? I know some pretty good ones, too, if you'd ask."

Under his breath, Duz muttered, "Because you never get 'em told," but Alma had continued. "So, anyhow, Nancy Jane had told them she'd just whip up some supper for them. You know, Nancy Jane and Tiffany are both Hallie's nieces, but Nancy is a lot older because ... well, I can't remember why, but anyhow, Nancy had probably heard all the stories before. Hallie repeats herself a lot. So Nancy Jane cooked. And Tiffany ... Oh, I remember why! Hallie's older brother, Jim Flute, he was a lot older than her, then her little sister Lizzie married that Gallenas. He was a Mexican, but they said he was okay, anyhow." Again Alma stopped, mulling it all over and feeling satisfied to have explained the nieces' ages. Then she said, "Oh, and Nancy Jane was Jim Flute's girl. I didn't make that clear."

After a long, weighted silence, Garrett decided it might be okay if he nudged Alma along. "What happened then, while Nancy Jane was cooking?"

"Oh, not much. That disgusting young man that used to live up in the tepee on K-4 Road came up to the door. He beat his wife, you know. He was trash. I guess he was going to rob them. He probably thought Hallie was alone there and had money, since she was old. They say she is over ninety now! Can you believe it? But he didn't count on Nancy Jane. She's a tough one, that girl—never could run right over her. So when that man popped up at that back kitchen door, Nancy Jane told him he couldn't come in. According to Hallie, he said something like, 'Who's gonna stop me? You and the army?' and started to push in, anyhow." At last, Alma was on a roll.

"So Nancy Jane grabbed a frying pan, big heavy iron one, and started over to fight him, but Hallie always kept a rifle by her chair. She had grabbed it—well, I don't know where Tiffany was, but Hallie knew where her rifle was, and when she looked in there and saw Nancy waving that pan and starting across the floor, she also saw that little skunk pull a gun out of his shirt, so she just raised her rifle and let him have it."

Duz and Garrett exchanged shaken looks, but Alma

nodded to herself, satisfied. "Hallie put a stop to him, all right. Some people just shouldn't be allowed to hurt honest folks. After she shot him, I guess there was a big argument as to what to do with the body. Little Tiffany wanted to call up the sheriff—I guess that would be you, now, Lyle. My, how you've grown since I saw you last! But anyhow, Hallie told Tiffany in no uncertain terms, 'Young lady, you don't cackle if you ain't laid, and we ain't done no wrong thing here.'

"Nancy Jane, of course, she comes in on the side of her aunt. Very respectful, that young lady. She told Tiffany nobody even knew or ever wondered where that guy was. Nobody liked him; nobody'd hunt for him, anyway. He was just a chicken-thievin' weasel, so less said, the better.

"So instead of botherin' you with all of that, Lyle, they just loaded him up in Nancy Jane's truck and took him up and buried him by where his tepee used to be. Hallie told me she didn't figure that was too unkindly of a resting place."

Alma resettled herself in her chair and readjusted Ling Ling Dell to conform. "So that's all Hallie told me. Does that help you any, Sheriff? Oh, and by the way, Duz, there's some cookies in the kitchen. I would think you would offer Mr. Garrett a cookie."

32

THE LAND DISPUTE was going to be settled. Of course, Chuck and Sienna were there, it being their home, and Chuck looked even sadder and more worried than usual. After calling Jenny and making plans with her, Garrett met McCracken and sent her to get Nancy Jane and Tiffany. He drove to Billy and Jilly Brown's for a brief chat. He needed them there, he told them, because Jilly was club president and would need to help get this thing resolved, chickens and all. After the Browns', he headed to Harrises' and picked up Lew. He and Lew found a blanket to protect the back seat of the sheriff's car, and Lucky rode the full way up to Fowler's with his ghostly head hanging out the back window, his tongue lolling saliva into the breeze.

That was all the sheriff needed for his purposes, but other people were there, too, having made a point to casually drift by, crane their necks to look, then find a wide place to park up or down the steep, crooked road. In case they "might be needed." Of course. This was Croysant, and word had gotten out. Garrett didn't care—the more the merrier—but Tiffany was not all that happy to see Luke and Larry arrive in Luke's truck, then hoof it to the center of the developing flash mob, all ears.

Garrett began speaking in a normal tone of voice, causing the buzz around the police tape to quiet as people leaned forward to hear. He said, "Lew, you're an old-timer in these parts, and ..." Someone inadvertently stepped on the invisible Lucky's tail, the dog yelped, and Lew cut in, "Shut 'er, pooch. You'll be okay."

Sienna said, "I didn't hear anything," and Chuck placed a fatherly, silencing hand on her shoulder, whispering, "It's okay. You know. Grown-ups."

Baby Skulls and Fowl Odors

The disturbance settled, Garrett continued. "Anyhow, Lew, I know in the old days, you used to hire out to help surveyors around here, and I think you know where this property line is between Chuck Fowler and Nancy Jane Barnswallowper. Do you?"

Lew, pleased to have his knowledge recognized, said, "Oh, you bet. You bet."

"And whose property are we standing on right now?"

"This here's Nancy Jane's. Always has been. Come down with her father Jim's place to her. Don't amount to much, just scrub brush and cactus, and now it's got that darned hole in it, but what's hers is hers."

"Okay, thanks, Lew. That's good. But whose land is that trailer on?"

"Oh, it used to belong to the tepee guy, or his drug pushin' father, I guess. I think some newcomer bought it ..." Lew narrowed his eyes, peering around the circle of people to see if he could identify a newcomer.

"You're probably referring to Mr. Fowler over there. He purchased a few acres of this land from the Biedermann estate." Garrett gestured at Chuck and Sienna, and Lew, squinting in their direction, said, "Could be. Could surely be."

"So, Lew," Garrett continued, "You know there has been some dispute over who owns what here. In fact, you were up here earlier when Ms. Barnswallowper shot Mr. Fowler in the foot, and as I recall, you got pretty worked up. What I want to ask you now is, why do you suppose there was so much confusion about who owned what?"

"Well, Sheriff, it's obvious. You see that loop in the road there? Newcomers, they always get confused out here in the hills. They get to thinking that property lines follow fence lines and roads, but that ain't true. The property lines are straight; they come from old surveys. Unless an owner specifically arranges for it, they make a square. The roads, though, they follow terrain, and cut back and forth, in and out of that square. Now, the fences, they got put wherever it worked to build 'em and fix 'em. First settlers, neighbors, well, things had to go where they were practical."

"This would mean that the property line between Barnswallowper and Fowler is ... ?"

"Goes straight across. The section probably begins up north of here—the plat in the records office will say something like Section 6, Township 37 North, Range 8 West, N.M.P.A. I don't mean that's what it really says; I'm just giving you an example. N.M.P.A. means New Mexico Principle Meridian. So you can see, these are all historical boundaries, important to the Bureau of Land Management and so-on, but the words don't mean much to the general public. What you need to see, Sheriff, is that the road loops into Fowler's place, just above and to the north of here, then loops back into Barnswallowper's. You can kind of get the idea of the property line if you look at where the road loops start and end."

There was a brief "amen" moment as the Johnsons and other local landowners murmured, "That's right, Lew." Looking around the group, Garrett's eyes found Luke and Larry. "I think everyone sees what he's saying, but Larry and Luke, do you think you could walk that line for us, just to make it clear?"

Luke looked at the terrain, and Larry looked at Luke. Luke said cautiously, "I could try," and Larry followed with, "You bet, Sheriff. We could try." The boys went up the road to the first bend, then gamely made their way down through the brush and rocks, working to set a straight course. Watching, everyone could see that the large hole (Mac Biedermann's erstwhile grave) was to the west of the property line, and that the small hole (which had contained the odiferous rooster) was to the east of the line.

"Okay, boys, thanks. That looks to be pretty close to right." Garrett's eyes moved to where Nancy Jane was looking on, and he gave her a strong, uncompromising stare. "Now, Ms. Barnswallowper, you just heard Mr. Harris describe this loop of land that is yours as being worthless, as being just scrub brush and cactus. In fact, I think landowners up here generally just let the land caught one way or the other by these twisting road loops go wherever it goes, since it balances out. And yet, this little piece of land here meant so much to you that you were willing to shoot somebody for it."

"I just shot him a little bit, Sheriff."

McCracken burst out, "Oh, for god's sake, Nancy," but Garrett said, "Look, Ms. Barnswallowper. I think this piece of land was so important to you because you were the one who

Baby Skulls and Fowl Odors

buried the corpse we found in the grave right there, and you didn't want Mr. Fowler digging it up once he got started on his building project."

"I don't rightly know if this is any of your business, Sheriff. You just proved that this is my land, and in the way I see it, what I bury on my land is my business. I got a constitutional right to privacy or something like that. Probably all I should say right now. I'm gonna get me a lawyer."

Tiffany, rolling her eyes, said, "Oh, puh-lease, Nancy. Give it up, already. You got caught with egg on your face, but the sheriff ain't gonna do anything to you, because he don't go after people who didn't really do anything wrong. Right, Sheriff? I think when he needs it, we should give him the straight story."

The words were fraught with meaning. Tiffany met Garrett's eyes, a trace of a grin with 'Cowpath fire' written all over it. He grudgingly admitted to himself that he might like this spunky woman, but all he said was, "Right, Ms. Gallenas. So what happened here?"

"Well, to make a long story short, Mac Biedermann was breaking into my Aunt Hallie's house last year. He was going to rob us, or worse, and Aunt Hallie shot him in self-defense. Then we brought him up here and buried him."

"Ms. Gallenas! Why in the world didn't you contact the authorities?"

"Frankly, I don't know. Not calling was Nancy and Hallie's idea."

"I see. You must realize that this could make your story hard to prove, with only you and Nancy as witnesses. It might not have been Ms. Flute, and it might not have been self defense. Do you still have Hallie's gun, for example?"

Luke and Larry were stunned. Their mother? How had she got up to all this without them knowing? They needed to defend her. "You bet she has Hallie's gun ... " Larry started, and Luke finished, "It's right there at the house. Mom, why didn't you tell us? You need to trust us to ... "

"Later, Luke. We'll talk later," she said firmly. "The thing is, Sheriff, I have something better. It's a mess because of the circumstances, and Aunt Hallie and Nancy pooh-poohed me, but you know, the reason I was at Aunt Hallie's that night was to record some old stories. I was talking with her, getting a video of her telling them on my iPhone, and when that bastard broke in, I did this weird thing that modern people are always doing—I ran behind Aunt Hallie to the kitchen and turned my camera on him. I guess it felt like a weapon."

McCracken was agog. "Holy Smoking Gun, Batman! You got a recording of the whole thing?"

"I did. Like I say, it's a mess in a way—the picture goes from his face to the ceiling and jerks over to Hallie's back and so-on, but it's all there, and the sound is pretty clear. I should know; I've played it more than once, agonizing over whether to just let things stand, or come in and turn it in, after all."

"You still have it?'

"I still have it."

"Okay. That's good. Look, Ms. Gallenas, you bring that recording into my office tomorrow morning at ten. Ms. Barnswallowper, you be there, too. That will be soon enough to sort this all out. It won't hurt to have a little privacy."

This was true. The gathering neighbors had become a crowd, and they were thrilled. This was exciting stuff. Certainly they knew that Hallie always had it in her, and this only went to prove it. They leaned forward to hear better. What else did the sheriff have up his sleeve?

"You want me to confiscate that recording, Chief?"

"No, Deputy McCracken, I think it will be okay. Ms. Gallenas, here, is a responsible citizen and she has cared for the recording this long. I'm sure she can be trusted to get it down to us tomorrow. After all, that will be in everyone's best interest." He shot Tiffany a look which she met without flinching, and thus the Cowpath incident was dismissed.

"By the way, though, Deputy, it's probably time to tend to that other business we talked about."

"You bet, Chief. I get your point." McCracken stepped away from the crowd, pulled out her phone, and began to text furiously, as the sheriff, mauling his nicotine-free wintergreen chew, walked down the hill, crossed the invisible property line, and stood by the other hole. He spat to the side of it, rubbing the back of his neck, seeming to weigh options. He was disingenuous. He said, "So, Mr. Fowler, because of that property line confusion, and the corpse and all, our department got a little jumpy when we discovered that another hole was being dug right here. We

Baby Skulls and Fowl Odors

took the liberty of finishing the excavation, and I guess you know that what we found was a safe."

McCracken's phone snorted. For once, Garrett was pleased. It meant she'd succeeded in reaching Jenny.

"Yes, sir, that is our safe."

"Well, the issue is, what should we do with it now? Probably just return it. I take it that it must contain important papers, perhaps plans to work with Tinker Chicken to have a franchise here, something like that?"

The neighbors all went, "Ooooohhh!" and Jilly Brown stiffened, prepared for action. Before Chuck could respond, however, his daughter exploded. "What is the matter with you people? The people in this place are the meanest, craziest people I ever met. My father and I would never have a Tinker Farm!" Her fists were clenched; she was facing off with the lot of them, a tiny fireball of fury. "We don't do ordinary chickens. My rooster was a real rooster. He died, and that's what is in the safe."

The approaching car was just another engine to everyone but Garrett. He recognized Jenny's engine. He pulled at his mustache, thinking, "Now I gotta do this right." Looking down at the frantic child, he said, "Why did you bury your rooster in a safe, Sienna?" He hoped she'd say something simple, like worry about coyotes digging up the rooster or something, but she didn't.

"You better not open that safe. That rooster is a fighting cock straight from China — it'll give you bird flu. That's why we buried it in a safe, so it wouldn't spread it around. It died from H5N1, the very worst kind. You better watch out. Now you are all going to get it. And you are all probably going to die."

Garrett's lips went grim. Damn kid. Trying not to panic, people began to mince away from the tight cluster that had formed around the hole, but Chuck Fowler, gathering strength from somewhere, was shouting, "No no no no no! No bird flu! No! Everyone needs to hear me!"

The desperation in his normally limp voice halted the general panicked flight. Curiosity trumped fear, as it will, and Chuck Fowler, still shouting, said, "There is absolutely no bird flu here, just an unhappy little girl who misses her mother and spends a lot of time on the Internet. Sienna's mother is ... well, gone, and when she left, she entrusted her favorite roosters to Sienna. None of them came from China. There is no way to import live birds like that from China — the one that died was part of a line of prize chickens that came from Sienna's great-grandfather. Here, in America! He was an American chicken!"

Now the crowd was hushed, moving closer again, partly because no one had heard Chuck Fowler speak this much before, and it surprised them. He continued, his voice calmer, "The rooster died from old age, but Sienna just couldn't accept the fact that she'd lost one of the roosters her mother had entrusted to her. She insisted it had to have died of bird flu. Making up that story seemed to comfort her. And Sienna, she's had such a hard time without her mother. I just kept trying to go along with her imaginative stories, hoping she could eventually work through her loss. She insisted we bury the rooster in a safe, so we bought the safe at Walmart, and that's what we did."

Jilly Brown was crying. What a wonderful little girl, to love chickens so much! Sienna, though, was falling apart. "It did not, Dad. It did not die of old age! It didn't. And mother didn't die, either. You know that. It's a lie. Everything is a lie. We can't keep saying that any more."

It was then that Xi Feng Ling spoke. They hadn't noticed her moving through the crowd in the gathering dusk, but suddenly there she was, in front of them, kneeling and holding her arms out to Sienna. "No, honey, no. I didn't die. And I am so sorry — I'm so sorry I told you that you must believe that. I was such a stupid, stupid woman." She looked up at her husband. "I am so sorry, Charles. I'm so sorry for what I did, and all the pain I have caused you."

The wash of emotions crossing Chuck Fowler's face cannot be described. Some in the crowd later said it was relief, others mentioned amazement, or even puzzlement, but most agreed on joy. It surely was joy. He stepped forward to touch his wife's hair, as if to be sure she were real, but she was still talking to Sienna, who had gone rigid in the face of the proffered hug. "Birds do die of old age, my dear sweet love. The most that roosters ever live is twenty years, and Da Xi Gong Ji was at least sixteen, maybe more. We can look. I have American papers on him — there is no flu. But he was very, very old. Your Great Western Rooster didn't die because of anything you did. It wasn't your fault. Probably Little Western Rooster will die pretty soon, too. He's not much younger than Old Da."

Sienna responded with, "What are you *doing* here?"

"I guess that needs explaining, doesn't it?" Zee stood and walked into the welcoming arms of her husband. The embrace took some time, but at last she turned to her daughter, as well as the enthralled neighbors. "I'm out on parole. I had a terrible addiction. I was addicted to gambling and cock fighting, and that is very illegal." (Later, many of those present would argue that Zee Fowler had been addicted to cocaine, which caused her to gamble to buy it, and so-on, but those misconceived stories need not concern us here. In the end, everyone did agree that she'd succeeded in kicking the habit, whatever it was.)

"The law caught up with me, and I had to serve time. My poor husband has been trying to protect Sienna from what I did. Oh, Charles, I am so sorry." No more could be heard, as Chuck had again pulled his wife to him, muffling her voice against his chest, and Sienna had sidled in for a place under the wing of her arm.

Garrett thought, "There. We've almost got it made." He gave the little family time to gather itself, then in a voice heavy with significance, he said, "Well, Mr. Fowler. So all you have here is just some pet chickens, right? Some birds your wife and Sienna treasured, as pets?" He stressed the "as pets," and Chuck Fowler, still shaken to his roots, and unable to return to the immediate illegal fighting cock problem, said in befuddlement, "Pets. As pets?"

A small voice from the group of gathered people spoke. It was Larry. "Mr. Fowler, all Sienna ever showed us was pet chickens, remember? Luke held one. A nice, pretty, old black and white rooster. Really gentle."

For once, Luke didn't finish for Larry. He had had no clue as to where his brother was going with this. But Chuck Fowler, thus nudged, caught on at last. That's right! There were no fighting cocks on his place except for old Xi Gong Ji, who was too far gone to look like a fighter. Otherwise, they were all gone. He hadn't been able to find them. Oh, thank god, the damn roosters were no longer putting him in terrible jeopardy from the law!

Visibly relieved, he looked at the sheriff with grateful eyes. "You're right, Sheriff. No chicken farm. Just pets." His voice was shaky.

Garrett, also, sighed inwardly with relief. He was home

free; the whole Fowler family was off the hook. Just as he was congratulating himself for having the courage to do the right thing, Lew said, "Why, looka there! Lucky's got him a bird. Look at that puppy point—never a day of training in his life, but he's got great form. And them's real pretty birds he's pointin' at. At least two of 'em. Wonder what kind they are? Don't look to be native to here, do they?"

No one could see Lucky's wonderful pose, but most of the crowd could see the roosters. Jilly Brown, ever the soap opera fan, her face still wet with tears from the romantic scene that had just played out before her, spotted the roosters and cried out, "Oh, my god! Those are roosters! I have never, ever seen such beautiful roosters in my whole life. Oh, Billy, I love them!"

The best laid plans of mice and men. Garrett, defeated on the brink of success, said weakly, "Looks like roosters, all right. Maybe escaped from someone's hen house. I suppose whoever catches 'em could have 'em, if nobody claims them."

What was he saying? He wasn't sure.

33

NOT QUITE IN THE COMMUNITY loop yet, Garfield and Honey Fourier and Brady Xyster had not realized what a commotion was taking place just over the hill from them. Their long talk had been on a different topic, involving paper, pens, calculators, and pauses while Xyster used his apps to access the endless cloud of information floating about the world. Once they had agreed, though, they decided no time was too soon to go see Chuck Fowler, who, they felt, was such a nice man, and needed cheering.

They arrived to find a mob of human beings running wildly about in the Fowler yard, shouting things like, "I think I see one," and "There he is," and "I got 'im! I got 'im! Oh, damn." All this was taking place amid occasionally alarmed squawks, some of which were emanating from the hen houses behind the trailer, as the hens became increasingly concerned about the welfare of their escaped leaders.

Garfield, not yet in complete control of local etiquette, didn't search out a wide place, but stopped in the middle of the road, edging over just far enough to let a skinny car with a master driver squeeze past, if necessary. He got out, his open face aglow with happiness and good will, then he helped Honey out past the steering wheel, as the passenger side had been wedged so tightly against the bluff that bordered the roadbed that it was impossible to open her own door. He then went to see what wonderful things his fine neighbors might be up to now, with Xyster bouncing closely down the road behind, stopping twice to silence his bossy and musical phone.

The Fowler family, McCracken, Jenny, and the sheriff had formed an awkward cluster, watching everyone else dive into bushes and stretch up to branches as they tried to bring the elusive roosters under control. Lew stood by, too, cautioning his dog to be still, occasionally wishing he'd brought along his damn shotgun. That'd get 'em.

Garfield, taking in the scene, brought his curious eyes to rest on Zee, but Chuck Fowler was equally curious. Who were these people with Garfield Fourier? After everyone had stood a few more minutes, watching the scene, Chuck said, "Mr. Fourier, this is my wife, Zee. She just rejoined Sienna and me here tonight, but I think she'll be staying awhile."

"Just call me Garfield. Call me Garfield." He enthusiastically pumped Zee's hand, then said, "Well, you may not know my brother-in-law, Brady Xyster? I think he'll be around awhile, too. That's what we came to talk to you about."

Honey stepped from behind her husband. "Just a minute, sweetheart. You get so excited. Before you gush all over the Fowlers with yours and Brady's grand scheme, I want to welcome Mrs. Fowler to our community, too." She gave Zee a warm hug. This not being the kind of thing Zee was accustomed to, she returned the hug clumsily, peering past Honey's shoulder to shoot her husband a trapped look.

Honey, however, was taking in the looks on several of the faces that were returning from the hunt, and she burst out with a belly full of laughter. "You all don't recognize me, do you? I really am Garfield's wife, no new mistress or something. He no doubt thinks, if only. Instead, I'm the root of his problems." She beamed around at the crowd.

"You see, I had a weave. You know what that is? It's how beauticians can fix African American hair so it doesn't look and act all kinky and curly. Once they weave in a bunch of other hair, it doesn't look at all like African American hair."

The chicken hunt had not been successful, so almost everyone was drifting back to see what was happening in the vicinity of the sheriff. Honey took it in, and raised her voice so they could hear. "You see, everybody, I didn't trust all of you. I had stereotypes. I thought the people in this backwash, redneck place would surely be really prejudiced. Racial bigots. So I decided I'd just pass as white, so you'd accept me. For Gar's sake. I really wanted to be accepted into this community." She pinched the skin on her arm. "Looks pretty white, don't you think?"

Baby Skulls and Fowl Odors

From her mother's armpit, Sienna said, "Not really." Zee said, "Hush, Sienna," but Honey laughed again.

"Maybe not so much, but I had most of you fooled for a while. My weave was great. I felt like I looked like an Arabian princess or something. Weaves cost a bundle, by the way, and you have to be damn careful not to bump them. Nobody can touch them, not even your husband. So you see, I was really willing to go a long way to fit in."

Frieda Johnson yelled from the back, "You didn't have to do that! We would have accepted you for who you are—we always do, out here in the sticks." ("Well," thought Garrett, "That might be stretching it," but at least a chorus of voices agreed with the sentiment.) Nancy Jane, however, still out of sorts about the whole situation, said grumpily and loudly, "Honestly, woman, I knew you was Black from the first. Never thought nothin' was wrong with you, either."

"Well, all that makes me feel better. Now, at least. You see, all that concern about my being an African American is what got my twin brother, Xyster, up to his chicken farm shenanigans, and got me in trouble with Garfield." There was a murmur from the crowd as their eyes went to the tall, good-looking African American man standing over a foot taller than Honey. He had been seen around the community, but lord! Was this where he fit in? They thought he somehow went with Jenny.

Honey continued. "Right, Brady Xyster is my twin brother. Just believe it. And it was the fire he brought on that woke me up. I couldn't believe I had been so blind! Once I saw what happened, I just went to Riversmet and found somebody that could strip that weave out of my life. Finally, I feel free."

Garfield, unable to be quiet any longer, reached over and gave Xyster's head a good, friendly, brotherly roughing. "This little old son-of-a-gun decided he'd start a Tinker Chicken Farm up on our place, of all things. Of course, Honey is partners with me, so he blackmailed her. He told her if she didn't give him access to our place to raise chickens, he'd expose her to the community as an African American. Poor wife! To think that worried her so!"

Honey took it up. "B got supplies through Tinker and started looking for someone to run the farm. He even had those construction materials that caused all the trouble hauled right onto our place, without even asking me." Honey's eyes had narrowed at Xyster, but Garfield chuckled.

"That's when the manure hit the rotating device, all right."

Xyster, still twitchy, poked at his phone and at the same time said, "Yeah, boy, that's when Gar blew his stack and stoked the fire."

Honey clarified. "That's right. When Garfield came home and saw those construction materials on our place and found out from me what they were for, he was furious. I've never seen him angry like that before. I had to tell him about my role in all of it, and he just went white. Well, whiter. He didn't say a word, just went and got gasoline, poured it over all those chicken farm supplies, and hollered, "Burn, baby, burn."

"Well, later I calmed down." Garfield did not look repentant.

"They got the numbers mixed up on Brady's chicken application down at town hall. Our road number is 2423, and you, Mr. Fowler, are 2432. Either the clerk or B got the two and three switched, so everyone thought it was here at your place that the chicken farm was going to be.

"Sienna, that's what I came to apologize for the other night, when I fell into that hole. All that chicken farm fuss, it should have been at our place, not here."

Honey ran her hand over her now nappy head, and Sienna said, "Well, thanks. Just so you know, Mrs. Fourier, you are beautiful. They didn't accept me in this community either."

Garfield, dismayed, said, "Oh, young lady! You are beautiful, too. Just hang in there—I think they will. I think they will."

Xyster, shifting about, hyperactive and ready, said, "So, are you going to tell them?"

"Oh, you bet, bro—you bet! Listen up, everybody; can I get your attention? You all that are here need to be the first to know. Honey and Xyster and I have exciting news. We've got a plan for a new enterprise, and we came over to see if Chuck would be interested in joining us. Now it would involve Zee, too, of course, and, well, yes, all of you. We are hoping for the support of all of you, the whole, well, the whole damn community!" He was beaming.

"See, I think you are starting to realize just what an eco-nut I am. I love this country, and I want to preserve the environmental heritage on our place. I also have a soft spot for animals.

Baby Skulls and Fowl Odors

I sure don't like to see animal abuse, and I think that's what factory farms are. That's why I got so mad at Brady and all the no good he got up to. But we're okay with each other now, aren't we, bro?" —here he gave Xyster's head another good pawing— "And we have all come together on a great idea. We want to bring all our resources to bear, and make the best, most eco-friendly, most community-friendly, cage-free, organic-fed chicken farm we can come up with. We're already studying on the details, how to do it. Tell them our slogan, Brady."

"No, it's okay. Go ahead, Garfield."

"No, it was your idea. Go ahead."

"Come on—tell them, Gar."

"Oh, for heaven's sake," Honey cut them off. "I'll tell everybody. The slogan for our new enterprise will be:

"From Shangrila for Poultry to Paradise on your Plate."

Jilly Brown began to clap enthusiastically, and after a short, uncertain pause, one, then two, then a dozen, and finally, all, clapped along with her.

34

"I DIDN'T SEND THE DOLL to the lab."

Garrett and Jenny were at Carmen Weinant's. They had left McCracken in charge of crowd control, knowing that once the sheriff left, things would gradually settle down anyhow. He had to go—he had made this appointment with Duz to meet with them, and it was time. Gritty was there, too.

"You see, Mr. and Mrs. Weinant, and Mrs. Anderson, you are the only people outside of a few select employees down in the sheriff's department who know about the doll. We need to talk about what to do with her, but first, I want Jenny to tell you the story of the doll. Jenny, can you begin at the beginning?"

Her face was so sweet. Garrett treasured it and the warm voice as she complied, beginning at the beginning. "You see, it all started when I married a man I loved very much named Mike Threewinds, who was worried about the problems the Native Americans were having on their reservations ..."

She told the story, and when it was over, everyone sat in awed silence, letting it sink in. Finally, Garrett spoke. "Your mother has the doll now; Alma has it, and she doesn't want to give it up. I think she should keep it."

Gritty cleared her throat. "But what about Zee? Her child ..."

Jenny spoke softly. "Many Native Americans allow the grandmother the primary role in caring for their first child. Xi Feng Ling has a living child to concern her now. I think when I explain to my sister what has happened, this arrangement will make her happy. Alma loves the doll."

Duz scratched at his unshaven cheek, thoughtful. "Sheriff, that doll has bones in it."

"I know." Garrett reached for Jenny's hand. "All of us have

Baby Skulls and Fowl Odors

bones inside us: secret vices, handsome brothers, lost children, ancient yearnings and sorrows. You never really know who other people are, because you only rarely see their bones. All you know is the story you tell yourself about them. And people don't know you—you are part of everyone's story, and they act on those stories, forming you, until at last you are fully formed from a community of stories. We all have bones inside us, but we flesh them out—we bury them, control them, cherish them—with the stories that surround us.

"It is a rare thing to see the bones of another, but we in this room have been privileged to see inside Ling Ling Dell. Ling Ling Dell is also formed by the stories we tell about her. Now, your mother loves that doll. For her, the doll's story is about friendship and excitement, triumph, secrecy, and beauty, and it is about her own children, long since lost to adulthood, but who come to her as children still, through the doorways of memory. That doll—she is just such a doorway."

There was a chill rain again that night, and Jenny held him warm and close. He slept, but she contemplated the little empty chair by her bed. At last, the doll was gone. At last, the doll was home.

Acknowledgements

First, I want to sincerely thank Margaret Bad Warrior, who teaches at the Oglala Lakota College in South Dakota. She took time to write me a wonderful, informative letter about Lakota burial practices, among other things, and I took her words to heart. This is a light, fictional novel, but I hope I have held true to the spirit of all she told me.

Second, I want to thank Bettina Helm, DVM, MPH, who is an Avian Import Specialist at the National Center for Import and Export with the USDA/APHIS. I e-mailed her with an absolute explosion of questions just as political hassle withdrew funding and shut down our government in October of 2013. Her department was also shut down, but Dr. Helm answered me anyhow. Her first sentence was, "I have started this e-mail multiple times trying to answer your questions, and it is a little difficult, without creating a story!" She went on to give me the information I needed, including a firm warning to stay away from bird flu as a central plot element. I think with her help I have my facts straight. Dr. Helm, as you said, I did have to work a little to adjust my scenarios, but I think you will appreciate that it only added to the fun, and I appreciate you!

Next, I want to wholeheartedly thank Delta County Undersheriff Mark Taylor. I called him more than once to ask about labs and fingerprints, skeletons and locks, work crews, DNA, dental evidence, and so-on. He was always helpful and patient, giving me the facts I needed no matter how trivial my questions.

Thanks also must go to my competent and efficient editor and publisher, Earth Star's Anne Miller. She is just such a joy to work with.

My granddaughter, Roxanne Carpenter, deserves super-thanks: she juggled the demands of a first pregnancy and a full time job to find time to update the map of the Croysant area.

Baby Skulls and Fowl Odors

~~Without these and the following people there would be no fowl odors~~. Hey! Wait! Who would scratch out such a fine sentence? Well, my [chicken] hawk-eyed copy readers, that's who. They have saved me from many a similar *faux pas*. My first readers were Sara Ferguson, Erin Gallob, Tanya Gallob, Diana Matus, Rita Claggett and Pam Hassinger. These are the kind of chicks that gobble misplaced commas as if they were wayward June bugs.

First readers have been followed by a supporting cast of thousands, well, hyperbole, but anyhow, I will name a few: Doug and Judy Gallob; Cheyenne Gallob; Davy Gallob; Amanda Pipher; and all the others of like ilk who have been subjected to early Fowl Odors and cheered me on, even so.

Finally, thanks to the inimitable David G. Gallob, the guy who rules where I roost, and who lets me mercilessly plagiarize his sayings without putting up a squawk. I love you, honey!

About the Author

Karen Weinant Gallob is a Colorado rancher and an anthropologist who taught for several years at Metropolitan State College in Denver. She is interested in the relationships among language, culture, and human perceptions of reality.

She has published articles, reviews, stories, poetry, and a four-volume science fiction novel, *After the End: The Sumbally Fallacy*. *Baby Skulls and Fowl Odors* is a sequel to her cozy mystery, *All the Bad Stuff Comes in Threes*. She is a member of the American Anthropological Society, the Colorado Author's League, and two local book clubs, the fun one and the classy one—it's never easy to tell which is which :)

Here are Karen's instructions for how to hypnotize a chicken:

1. Obtain a chicken and a short stick.
2. Lay the chicken gently on her side, pinning the lower wing between the bird and the ground and holding the upper wing still, folded against her body. Her head may come up trying to look around, or else it will lie expectantly on the ground. No problem.
3. Now move the stick very slowly, rhythmically, even rather musically, in an arc from below her beak to the top of her head. The stick will be almost vertical, one end drawing the arc on the ground in front of her, the other held by your gently moving hand.
4. Before long, you will be able to release your grip on the chicken, lay down the stick, and walk away. The hypnotized chicken will continue to lie where you put her, still staring at the stick. Some chickens will lie like that for several minutes. It all depends on the chicken.

Baby Skulls and Fowl Odors

A Pat Garrett, Leigh McCracken Mystery

by Karen Weinant Gallob

Not your copy?

If you'd like to order your own copy of this book,
or get a gift for a friend,
please use the order form below.

ORDER FORM

Please send me _____ copies of **Baby Skulls and Fowl Odors** by Karen Weinant Gallob.

Enclosed is my check or money order for $11.95 for each copy plus $5.00 shipping and handling (total $16.95 per book) *(Colorado residents please add* **82¢ state sales tax** *for each book ordered.)*

Name _____

Address _____

City, State, Zip _____

Send a photocopy (or clip out) of this order form to:
KAREN WEINANT GALLOB
2240 Clear Fork Road
Crawford, CO 81415

Also available as an eBook from Amazon.com and Nook

To find out where to order *All the Bad Stuff Comes in Threes*, visit **www.earthstarpublications.com/BadStuff.html**

www.ingramcontent.com/pod-product-compliance
Lightning Source LLC
Chambersburg PA
CBHW022356040426
42450CB00005B/205